FRENCH ENTRÉE 5

The **P&O European Ferries Guide** to Brittany

Patricia Fenn

Quiller Press

ACKNOWLEDGMENTS

To Michel Renouard, for sharing his profound knowledge of Brittany and the Bretons. I commend his book *A New Guide to Brittany* published by Ouest France to anyone who wishes to know more about the province.

To M. Dumur of the Finistère Chambre de Commerce, for advice and help far beyond the call of duty.

To Hervé and Anna Coatalan and Beatrice Racinet for local guidance and generous hospitality.

To Pauline Hallam of the French Government Tourist Bureau for London back-up.

First published 1986 by Quiller Press Ltd
46 Lillie Road, London SW6 1TN
Updated and reprinted 1987, 1989

Line drawings: Ken Howard
Area and port maps: Paul Emra
Cover design: Alex Charles
Design and production in association with
Book Production Consultants, Cambridge

ISBN 0 907621 54 6

Printed in Great Britain by
Richard Clay Ltd, Bungay, Suffolk

Contents

Notes on using the book – and an appeal

1 The area maps are to help the reader to find the place he wishes to visit on his own map. Each place is given a reference on the relevant area map, but they are not designed to replace a good touring map.

2 A number in brackets at the beginning of a telephone number is the area dialling code, used when making calls from outside the area.

3 o.o.s. stands for 'out of season', Other abbreviations such as f for francs, are standard.

4 L, M or S in the margin stand for 'L' = Luxury, 'S' = Simple and 'M' for those in between.

5 H stands for Hotel and R for Restaurant in combination with 4 above, ie (H)S, (R)L etc.

6 stc means service and taxes are included (*service et taxes compris*).

7 The ➤ symbol means the establishment fulfils exceptionally well at least one of the author's criteria of comfort, welcome and cuisine – see also pages 25–6.

8 P stands for parking.

9 Credit cards: 'A' = Access, 'AE' = American Express, 'V' = Visa, 'DC' = Diners Club, and 'EC' is Eurocard.

10 ▌❪H❫▐ means Hotel of the Year.

11 Prices, correct at time of going to press, represent a room for two people, except for demi-pension, which is per head.

12 ▲ and ▼ stand for readers' reactions, for and against.

Author's appeal

In order to keep 'French Entrée' up to date I need all the latest information I can get on establishments listed in the guide. If you have any comments on these or any other details that might supplement my own researching I should be most grateful if you would pass them on.

Please include the name and address of establishment, date and duration of visit. Also please state if you will allow your name to be used.

Patricia Fenn,
c/o P&O European Ferries Group P.R. Dept.
Channel House, Channel View Road, Dover, Kent

Author's Foreword to Third Edition, 1989

The first edition of any *French Entrée* is the result of a year's single-handed research. Every entry has been personally vetted.

However, the day of the visit might have been depressingly grey or encouragingly bright, I might have just got up or be longing to go to bed, the chef might have been on top form or just walked out, and I readily admit that these are unavoidable limitations on my judgment.

But now the immeasurable benefit of another two years' assessment by an army of volunteers, in all kinds of weather, in all manner of moods, can be added to the original text and second edition. Brittany has inspired an even larger number than usual of kind readers to share their experiences.

In this edition, I have been able to indicate reaction to my suggestions by the thumbs-up or down symbols. Up means that the majority is decidedly in favour, down means a boo-boo. Where opinion is split down the middle, both signs indicate the indecision; where there is no sign, there has been no feedback.

In addition, here are lists of new recommendations – hotels and restaurants (page 188), uninspected by me, which have impressed readers during 1987–8. When the time comes to re-write *F.E.5*, they will be top of my list to visit. (Where there is no acknowledgment, it is because the authors requested anonymity or because the signature is illegible.)

There have been some entries that provoked a torrent of praise or disapproval. Only one of the three Hotels of the Year has received 100% thumbs-up and that is the luxury Ti al-Lannec at Trebeurden. I am able to endorse everything I wrote about it, except of course the prices. Rooms are now 295–540f and a meal costs from 155–285f. Still superb value; if you can afford it, don't miss this treat.

Alas, the (S) hotel choice, the Auberge St. Thégonnec has changed its image completely and can no longer be ranked in the Simple category. Readers have been justifiably disappointed to find it is now not what they expected, and I am sorry that this should be so. However, one accepts that the chef, Alain Le Coz, has grabbed the chance to show off his considerable talents to a wider audience (mea culpa) and the prices do not seem unreasonable. During the week there is still an excellent 70f menu; otherwise its 120f or 160f. And the rooms are still a modest 100–250f.

The M choice, the Hotel de Bretagne at Pont l'Abbé has been a headache, since reports swing alternately from 'superb' to 'disastrous'. I now regretfully have to face the fact that the superb cooking I enjoyed, the pleasant rooms I was shown, the warm hospitality I met, has not been the lot of some of my readers. Its a case of when the Bretagne is good, its very good and when it is bad it is truly horrid. Which is not good enough.

More indignation over the Ferme du Letty at Benodet, which duly achieved the Michelin star I forecast, but has subsequently upped its prices to prohibitive levels. The erstwhile crêperie now charges around 350f for a meal.

Hotels and restaurants that have received consistent praise ever since the first edition, include Les Voyageurs at Berven, the Armorique at Fouesnant and the Hotel de France at St. Pol-de-Léon. Without any doubt the Restaurant of the Year would be Le Bricourt at Cancale, which I consider to be not only the best of FE5 but of any of the other Entrées, and that includes the recently published FE8 which covers the rosette-studded Loire region. Olivier Roellinger achieved his second star, as I hoped. His 100f mid-week menu merits a special journey to Brittany.

I hope that from these new ideas more and more successful holidays will result and am most grateful to all my intrepid and eloquent aides.

N.B. Prices are *not* up-dated.

Patricia Fenn

Introduction

Here then is No. 5. Like its predecessors, 'French Entrée 3' on Normandy and 'F.E.4' on the North, it aims to cover one area of a vast and diverse country in the kind of depth that should leave the reader in no doubt what he's in for. Michelin, the eatin' sleepin' man's bible, uses symbols between which the tourist must search for a hint that the hotel is next to an early morning market or the church clock, or that the chef has just run away with the patronne; I hope to paint the picture more vividly so that the reader can decide for himself if its right for him.

The arrows (see p. 23 for a list) are the ideals, worth arranging a holiday around, tested and verified. But it's no use suggesting only these paragons; they may be too far, too full, too expensive for the occasion and this is when second-best is far far better than none at all. So other ideas, with suitable reservations, have been included to offer a range of choice. Where there is an outstanding restaurant or hotel, hard to miss, but not to be recommended, I have described it too, in order to warn away as well as towards.

However I make no claims that this is a dispassionate book. As it is the work of a committee of one, it is unashamedly subjective and often prejudiced. As long as you know what those prejudices are, I believe you can choose wisely and go prepared.

For instance you will find few large chain hotels included, not necessarily because they are not worthwhile, but because it is not difficult for any fool to locate one without my help and they are so predictable that they need no description. My preference is for smaller hotels, preferably family-run to ensure continuity of interest, with lots of 'character'. This gets me into no end of trouble of course. The play-safe plastic cube would be an option I sometimes sigh for when a reader complains 'my wife found some fluff under the bed in a hotel you recommended'. (What was she *doing* under the bed?)

But generally readers have agreed, and have shared their own discoveries of the kind of hotel and restaurant that rarely gets into the smarter guides or package tours. Their help continues to be invaluable for updating purposes, whether written in approval or more in sorrow than in anger. By answering every letter personally I hope to show my gratitude.

Hotels are still much cheaper in France than they are at home because the French sell rooms not beds. Two can sleep as cheaply as one, but for a third occupant you will probably have to pay a small supplement. Family rooms represent excellent value for a cheap one night stand. Children are usually welcomed and treated like adults so long as they behave like adults. Sunday lunch sees them clamped to their dining chairs for several hours with scarcely a wriggle or a whine.

Children's menus are sometimes on offer but never hesitate to ask for an extra plate so that they can share yours. Ask for an extra plate for adults too if you wish. A *menu gastronomique* between two is not at all a bad idea, as is a *menu dégustation* –

small portions of many courses – giving the opportunity to sample new dishes.

Insistence on eating one meal in the hotel is a problem. Make quite sure when you book what the form is, to avoid inevitable ensuing unpleasantness (and only the French can be quite so tight-lipped). I was told that compulsion was illegal but came across it so often that I checked again with a senior tourist official. 'Madame,' he said, 'in France we have good laws and bad laws. We obey the first and ignore the second.'

Eating must come top of many reasons for going to France. Sadly I would claim that more guidance is necessary nowadays, since not every restaurant serves the kind of French meal we dream of. The deep freeze has arrived and been welcomed, and with the blocking of menu prices, short cuts are not uncommon. The course I mourn most is the vegetable. Time was when it was invariably served as a treat in its own right – a little entrée, perhaps a gratin or soufflé, would precede the meat, accompanying veg were as much evidence of a chef's judgment and skill as the main course. But now all too often its flaccid tinned beans and indiscriminate *frites*.

That said, the value is indoubtedly there *if you know where to look*. At all levels it is possible to eat better for less than at home. At the top, this is the time, if ever there were, to splurge on a gastonomic adventure. Save up for at least one meal at a starred restaurant if you care at all about good cooking.

La Nouvelle Cuisine:

Which brings me to the nouvelle cuisine. Can any vogue have had so much rubbish written about it? To my mind Brittany happens to be an example of what hazards the fashion for 'new cooking' can bring. Here is an area rich in the natural resources of fish and vegetables, hitherto prepared simply and generously by cooks who knew nothing of gastronomic chic but succeeded by buying the freshest and best and dishing it up with as little fuss as possible. Exquisite. Nowadays many of these poor chastened patron-chefs feel obliged to have a go at preparing dishes that look deceptively simple but in fact require endless time, expertise and finance to get them deliciously right. When they are good they are very very good but when they are bad they are *affreux*. The horridness extends to the size of the portion as well as the quality and the customer is rightly indignant at being required to pay so much for so little. Bear in mind that it is no accident that the most popular dish in Brittany is a *plâteau de fruits de mer*, the ingredients requiring only to be plonked on a platter, and save the (genuine) thrill of sophisticated noove cuise for a trained chef. Olivier Roellinger at the Restaurant de Bricourt at Cancale would be an ideal choice.

Markets

We Brits go to France to sleep cheaply, eat well and to shop. The markets are more than just a utility – they are part and parcel of the French scene and everyone loves them. Take your time strolling round the colour and hubbub, and experience the pleasure of buying from someone who knows and cares about his wares. The man selling you a kitchen knife will be an expert on knives and will want to know what you need it for; the cheesemonger will choose for you a cheese ready for eating today or in a couple of days' time, back home. Trust them.

Choose for yourself the ripest peach, the perfect tomato, and buy as little as you need and no more, so that you can buy fresh again tomorrow. Stock up on herbs and spices, pulses and dried fruits, soap scented with natural oils, honey from local bees, slices of farmers' wives' terrines – every village a veritable Fortnums on market day.

Closing Times

The markets, like the rest of the town, snap shut abruptly for lunch. I regularly get caught out by not shopping early enough; if its going to be a picnic lunch, the decision has to be made in good time. From 12 p.m. to 2.30, and sometimes 3, not a cat stirs. At the other end of the day its a joy to find shops open until 7 p.m. Mondays tend to be almost as dead as Sundays and its likely to prove a grave disappointment to allocate that as a shopping day.

It does not pay to be casual about the weekly closure (*fermeture hebdomodaire*) of the restaurants. It is an excellent idea to ensure that not every restaurant in the same town is closed at the same time, but do check before you venture. Thwarted tastebuds are guaranteed if you make a special journey only to find the smug little notice on the door. 'Sun. p.m. and Mon' are the most common and often it will take a good deal of perseverance to find a possibility open then.

Booking

Sunday lunch is the Meal of the Week, when several generations settle down together to enjoy an orgy of eating, drinking, conversation and baby-worship that can well last till teatime. You should certainly book then and on fête days (list on pp. 16–17). Make tactical plans and lie low, or it could be a crêpe and a bed in the car.

As Brittany, especially in the coastal areas, has so short a season, it is particularly important to book ahead if you have a special choice in mind. If you do not speak French, try and find someone who does to make a preliminary telephone call. If necessary, write in English and let them sort it out but make sure when you get the confirmatory letter that you understand what you've booked. Many hotels nowadays will ask for a deposit. My method is to send them an English cheque; they then either subtract the equivalent from the bill or return the cheque.

Make good use of the local tourist bureaux, where you will find English spoken. Let them do the booking for you if you have problems. This is the place to pick up maps and brochures.

Maps and Guides

Good maps are essential and I must stress that those in the front of this book are intended only as an indication of where to find the entries. Michelin 230 covers the whole of Brittany, but if this is a bit cumbersome, best buy 58, 59 and 63. I recommend the purchase of the Green Michelin guide to Brittany too. It is published in English and will fill in all the cultural gaps.

The red Michelin, apart from all its other virtues, has useful town maps. Its a bit slow to spot a newcomer though, unlike its rival Gault-Millau, also now in English, though I prefer the French version. This gives more specific detail but has less comprehensive coverage and is strongly biased in favour of *la nouvelle cuisine* (its authors did invent the label in the first place); it is useless for the really basic hotels and restaurants.

Logis de France do a good guide to their hotels, obtainable at the French Government Tourist Bureau at 178 Piccadilly. This is the place to go for general advice, free maps and brochures and details of the admirable gîtes system, which provides simple self-catering accommodation in farmhouses and cottages. We have stayed in gîtes all over France and found them invariably reliable and cheap, and often more comfortable and interesting than hotels, but you have to be quick off the mark to book the best in peak season.

Hotel chains issue their own guides; that of the Châteaux Hotels Indépendants is well worth following up. These are hotels converted from châteaux, mills, manorhouses, often with owners newly converted themselves to hotelkeeping, and trying hard. I looked at all those in Brittany and several are recommended highly.

The Relais et Châteaux chain is decidedly upmarket and getting more so by the minute. At best, they are sublime – superbly luxurious, with wonderful food, ideal for a special occasion, and by English standards not expensive for the standard they offer. At worst, they are over-priced, pretentious and full of Americans. The Breton bunch are generally a disappointment and I have said so and why.

The Relais de Silence badge is worth looking out for, since it guarantees a quiet night – very high on my priorities.

Categories

I think I must be the only guide-writer who claims to visit every entry personally. Another difference is that French Entrées are not designed for one income group. My theory is that we all have need of different kinds of bed and board on different occasions (even the poor have birthdays, even the rich lose their credit cards). So the categories: 'L' for Luxury, 'M' for Medium and 'S' for Simple, are designed to suit some of the people some of the time.

'L' will meet only exacting standards. Not only must the hotel be comfortable, it must be special in some way – its building, its service, its furnishing, its site, its food. For my 'L' Hotel of the Year, the Ti al Lannec at Trébeurden, everyone of these desirables is fulfilled.

Anything above 300f a night for a double room would come into the 'L' category, and quite a few below. When you consider this is equivalent to £14 a head, you can realise that luxury hotels will be available in France to readers who could never consider their equal at home.

I would expect recommended 'L' restaurants to cook exceptional food and serve it in elegant surroundings. The chef should be able to add a touch of genius to mere professional competence. Here are the places to judge the *nouvelle cuisine*. If the limited choice on the lowest menu happens to appeal, you'll get a bargain, often cheaper than at humbler establishments, and cooked with the same flair as the à la carte extravagances. These menus are often only for lunch and rarely at weekends. Otherwise expect to pay upwards of 120f in this category.

The best 'M' hotels are comfortable and pleasant, well equipped and, by virtue of being mainly family-run, assuring a warm welcome. My 'M' Hotel of the Year, La Bretagne at Pont l'Abbé, has bedrooms as comfortable as any in the book, but it would not pretend to be a luxury hotel. Essentially bourgeois and proud of it.

The food in this category should be good enough for *demi-pension* to be acceptable. This is where the modest stars can be found – the *chef-patrons* who lack only the long professional training to equal the big names. Their ingredients, though more modest, should be just as fresh and preferably local; their dishes, though less elaborate, should show some individuality and no short cuts. Marcel Cossec of La Bretagne is a shining example. The price range is roughly from 150–250f for a double room with bath, or around 100f without, and from 65–120f for a meal.

When judging the 'S' group, bear in mind that there is nothing quite like them at home. At under £4 a head for a bed, and £3 for three courses, certain allowances should be made. It is still perfectly possible to get a double room for 75f and a meal for 35f. (Look at l'Abri des Flots at Mordreuc as an example of sheer, honest, no-frills value.) For this you should expect undoubted cleanliness, hot water in bedroom washbasin and shared bathroom, but not powerful lightbulbs, thick piled carpet, fleecy towels and free packets of bath oil, nor even soap. Above all, the welcome is important in these modest, invariably family-run establishments. Here is where you are most likely to get to know the *patron* and/or the locals. You'll get atmosphere even if you have to forget your back-home standards.

I get more excited letters about 'S' establishments than for any other. And I can understand the thrill of the chase for a bargain. However a bad meal is never a bargain and it is all too easy to end up with a waste. Don't even think of asking the *patron-chef* to come up with something too *recherché* for his limited talents. Stick to the simplest dishes on the menu and if he buys honestly and freezes nothing, you're on to a winner.

In the Auberge St. Thégonnec at St. Thégonnec you will find a very superior 'S' hotel indeed. I have picked it as my Hotel of the Year in this category because it embodies all the qualities of unpretentious values that one dreams of finding at bargain prices but so rarely does. At the same time Marie Thérèse and Alain Le Coz offer the kind of comfort that comes from personal concern – the best. I am sure readers will be as happy about this discovery as they have been for the Auberge de l'Abbaye, the FE3 Normandy choice in this Simple category, and I look forward to their letters.

Wine

Restaurant wine is a common hiccup in more ways than one. The prices are meant to be controlled like those of the menus but somehow they creep up to ridiculous mark-ups. It is not uncommon to find the bottle of plonk that costs 6f in the supermarket on the menu for six times that amount. The *patron's* local reputation stands or falls by his house wine, so at least try the 'Réserve de la Maison', 'Choix du Patron', though these are more likely to be red than white. Travelling alone, I often want just a glass of wine, and this is maddeningly difficult to achieve. Wine bars may have arrived in Paris but certainly not in Brittany. See also the Jancis Robinson article on p. 174.

Breakfasts

A sore point. The best will serve buttery croissants, hot fresh bread, home-made preserves, a slab of the slightly salted butter favoured in Brittany, lots of strong coffee and fresh hot milk, with fresh orange juice if you're lucky. The worst – and at a price of between 150 and 400f this is an outrage – will be stale bread, a foil-wrapped butter pat, plastic jam, a cup of weak coffee and cold sterilized milk. Synthetic orange juice can add another 100f to the bill. If you land in a hotel like this, get out of bed and go to the café next door.

Bread

Everyone loves French bread but debutantes to France may not realise how much it varies. Look for the boulangerie with the longest queue and buy your *baguette* or *pain* there. Ignore the plastic-wrapped hypermarket specimens – you'd buy better French loaves back home. It all goes stale very quickly, so unless you can get it in a freezer promptly its not worth stocking up however delicious the freshly-baked specimens might be.

Similarly croissants can be very nasty from an inferior *patisserie*. 'Au beurre' are the richest and best, but cost a bit more.

Speciality bread shops selling dozens of different varieties of bread are a new breed in France, and still only to be found in big towns. I like the brown variety with hazelnuts embedded, but generally the traditional crusty white is too good to forego.

Take with You

Soap (only the grander hotels supply it) and a decent towel if you're heading for the S group and can't stand the handkerchief-sized baldies. If self-catering, take tea, orange juice, breakfast cereals, biscuits, Marmite, marmalade – all either expensive, or difficult to locate, or horrible.

Bring Home

Beer is a Best Buy and the allowance is so liberal that you can let it reach the parts of the car that other purchases fail to reach, i.e.: load up. Coffee is much cheaper; cheeses are an obvious choice if the pong is socially acceptable. If, like me, you have a weakness for *crème fraîche* and resent paying double at home, you can rely on it staying fresh for a week so long as its not confined to a hot car. I buy fresh fish if I see a boat coming in while I'm homeward bound, and early expensive vegetables like asparagus, artichokes, mange-touts and the wonderful fat flavoursome tomatoes. Electric goods are often cheaper, le Creuzet pans, glassware. Jancis Robinson's notes on p. 174 will help choose the best bargain of all – the wine.

Tipping

Lots of readers, used to the outstretched British hand, worry about this. Needlessly – 's.t.c.' should mean what it says – all service and taxes included. The only exception perhaps is to leave the small change in the saucer at a bar.

Changing Money

Everyone has their pet method, from going round all the banks to get a few centimes advantage, to playing it the easy and very expensive way of getting the hotel to do it. It depends on how much is involved and how keen a dealer you are as to how much trouble is worth it. I change mine on the boat, where I have always found the rate to be very fair. If you get caught outside booking hours, the *bureaux de change* stay open late.

Telephoning

Most of the public telephones in France actually work. You put your 1f. piece in the slot and watch it roll down for starters, then as many more pieces as you estimate you will need. If it's too much, out it all comes at the conclusion of conversation.

From October, 1985, the system of dialling has been changed. All French numbers now have 8 digits.

To dial U.K. from France: 19, wait for tone, 44, then STD code minus 0, then number.

Inter-departmental: 16, then 2-figure code, then number.

To dial France from U.K.: 010, pause, 33, 8-figure code.

Emergencies: Fire 18; Police 17; Operator 13; Directory Enquiries 12.

I am often asked how I go about the inspections: 'Do they know who you are?'. Well, generally, no. Never in the case of a restaurant and only where necessary in a hotel in order to see as much as possible. No question ever of special treatment. 'Do you go alone?' Sometimes and increasingly often. In the early days of 'F.E.1.' (which I realise now were a doddle) I needed friendly support and found no shortage of willing volunteers. As I got tougher and more sceptical, though, I found them too nice, enjoying every minute of this lovely break, and it became hard to spoil everything by criticism. Nowadays it is only family that I subject to the rigours of a much speeded-up routine. Only they, I feel, can be asked to put up with a heavy lunch when a beautiful day indicates a picnic, or a 'S' dinner when they feel like putting on the Ritz. Only they can be expected to work all day and stay awake all night because the mattress is so hard or the disco so noisy.

I can't say I like going it alone, especially in the evening, when there's no-one to grumble with over an awful meal or a one-watt bulb, but there's no doubt that this is when the eye is beadiest and the observation gains accordingly.

A special thank-you and dedication of F.E.5 to daughter Charlotte and husband Colin, who came not only for the ride.

Introduction to Brittany

Brittany – a rich and rewarding province, but a devil to research for a guidebook. The first thing I had to learn was that it was not a bit like next-door Normandy. Normandy, with its autoroutes, proximity to Paris, and industry, keeps going year-round, whereas most of Brittany dies for six months of the year. It's on and around the coastline that the essential flavour is to be found and there's a helluva lot of coastline to see in six months.

Of this time, July and August are out for casual booking – the regulars reserve a year ahead, and as their season is so short, hoteliers like you to eat in. So for the freewheeler, one-nighter, eater-outer, like me, the prospect is, to say the least, difficult.

Doggedly resolved to make some use of the fallow months, I tried some off-season sorties, but the power to write convincingly about best beaches, best views, best balconies, deserted me in the face of windswept rocks, sea fogs, peeling paint and stacked plastic recliners. A meal eaten alone in a frumpy dining room takes on an altogether different aspect from one on a sunlit terrace overlooking sparkling water.

Inland kept me going for a while. The autumn was a perfect time to explore the canals. I can't recommend too highly the pleasures of picking up a little boat at Redon or Josselin, or whatever other station appeals (details from the French Government Tourist Bureau) and proceeding at jogging pace through a green and lush Brittany – quite a contrast to the drama of the coast, and in many ways more real, more substantial. The lockkeepers' wives sold us vegetables as we waited for the water to change levels, the simple restaurants along the route were pleased enough to see us but generally relied on local trade more than tourists and cooked and charged accordingly. Cycling along the towpath, foliage draped with glittering cobwebs, for the breakfast baguette, buying and cooking the best of the local market's produce and eating it pulled up under a willow, is a very agreeable way to get to know Brittany. But as the leisurely pace tends to slow down to the point of inertia, it would take more time than I had available to cover the extensive canal and river network, and winter was setting in.

November was a good time for Rennes, though I grew to hate the drive down from Cherbourg in the early darkness and unkind weather. Still I found, shaking somewhat after manoeuvring round the *périphérique*, that I could be in my hotel room by six o'clock, and at any other time of the year I would recommend this timetable – the morning boat from Portsmouth and an early afternoon drive-off makes a very civilised start to the holiday.

Nantes is another good off-season choice – I did my Christmas shopping there. The most sophisticated of Breton cities, lively year-round, the best shops, good restaurants. And Dinan's mediaeval charm and diversions don't rely on summer weather; in fact without the traffic jams and tourists its probably nicer o.o.s.; but then of course you'd have to go again to have the pleasure of sitting out in a café terrace down by that picturebook port and to take that obligatory trip up the Rance.

Quimper and Vannes fitted in nicely to a spring visit but when I tried to tack on a few of the coastal resorts between them, I knew it wouldn't do. Without their visitors, some looked more attractive, some less, but none typical. I should have to come back later, stay longer.

And so the summer of '85. (What summer, you may well ask) was spent covering practically every resort, every point, every bay around the truly staggering coastline. I found such contrast of stark rock, soft dunes, pink granite, azure sea, fierce rollers, gentle estuaries, dizzy heights, boggy marsh, bleak moor, fertile farms, fishing village, jazzy resort, that it was hard to believe all this could be encompassed in one country let alone one province. Add a mystery of fairy legend, a history of relentless warfare, a glimpse of starched coiffes, a severity of bleak granite, an economy of fish and farm, and you just begin to get the flavour. I doubt if any foreigner gets more.

Because of this variety, Brittany is perfect touring territory. You can drive from rocky north to sandy south in a couple of hours, taking in a mediaeval village, a river, and a canal or two along the way.

Or you can stick to the coast and just keep on driving, left hand down, from Mont St. Michel to Nantes, which is the route I propose to detail now.

Two shortcomings I have to admit: Where does Brittany end? I had pictured the Loire as its south-eastern limit; when I asked people in the north some said yes, some said they didn't rightly know; when I asked those in the south they were sure it stretched across for a slice of the other bank too.

The Loire-Atlantique is a hybrid *département*, coming under the 'Pays du Loire'; by the time I had established that historically some of the south bank should indeed count as part of Brittany, it was too late to go back. So the SE limits for this book stop a bit short.

The other omission is at the opposite extreme, in the far north-west. I had left the Brest peninsula till last, and anyone who remembers what August '85 was like might perhaps sympathise when I explain that, with the westerly gales driving full and furious directly onto this unprotected land, with remote villages shuttered and scattered seaside resorts apparently deserted, there was little incentive to drive on. I struggled as far as Aber Wrac'h and listened with relief to local advice that if I'd seen the Crozon peninsula, I could imagine the Brest. As there are very few hotels in this least tourist-populated area I don't believe I missed too much.

The big industrial ports – Brest, Lorient, St. Nazaire – are deliberately omitted. This is a holiday book.

So, a brief summary from NE to SE to help plan the holiday:–

From **Pontorson** both road alternatives are bad. The N. 176 is both bad and dull, so take the coast road to **St. Malo** for preference. At least there is some interest in the oyster and mussel beds that line the flat coast from **Le Vivier** northwards.

Cancale is a charming little port and resort. From then on the drama begins, with rocks, cliffs, islands, to **St. Malo**, a No. 1. choice in and out of season. Across the beautiful river Rance **Dinard** has fine beaches and a Riviera setting.

Then along the **Emerald Coast** comes a chain of little family holiday spots, unsophisticated, good sands, spectacular views – **St. Briac, St. Jacut, St. Cast**. The coast dips into sand dunes at **Sables d'Or; Erquy** and **Le Val André** are small fishing harbours.

I have to say I do not care for the stretch between **St. Brieuc** and **Paimpol**. Diligently I followed most of the lanes leading off the D.786 to the coast and found often enough good sands and sheltered bays, at **Binic** and **Étables** for example, but they lacked charm; **St. Quays'** tawdriness I positively loathed. Worth making a détour from the fishing port of **Paimpol** to **Arcouest** and the **Île de Bréhat**, and from then on it all starts getting really interesting – undoubtedly one of my favourite regions. Hundreds of islands dot the seascape, rivers provide safe anchorages. **Tréguier** and **Trébeurden** are the pearls on this unique **Pink Granite Coast**; between them are dozens of beguiling bays and beaches. **Perros** is the biggest and noisiest resort, in a superb natural setting, **Lannion** is a pleasant inland market town.

Immense sandy bays follow one another from **St. Michel-en-Grève** westwards, with the nice little port of **Locquirec** facing all directions at the tip of the point. **Morlaix** is an old and interesting river port and the minor coast road from there to **Carantec** is a delight. More islands and lovely beaches here, up to **Roscoff**, a colourful port and resort, with the time-warped **Île de Batz** just offshore.

At this stage I would head inland and visit some of the unique parish closes (see pp. 18, 79 & 159) but if you stick to the coast it is back to sand dunes and a rather uninteresting stretch until **Brignogan Plage**, where the rocks take over again.

Then the remote area of the *abers* – creeks that cut deep inland – with few tourist amenities, round the wild west coast to the industrialisation of **Brest**. The **Crozon** peninsula is green and soft to the north, grey and harsher after **Camaret**, round to **Morgat**, a little fishing harbour.

Inside the **Bay of Douarnenez** are low sandy beaches, like **Ste. Anne-la-Palud**, round to the busy fishing port of **Douarnenez** itself, from whence it all gets mighty impressive, with high cliffs and crashing seas, around the daunting **Raz**. Softer again to the port of **Audierne**.

Then a dullish stretch, low and windswept, to the bleak fishing port of **St. Guénolé** and round the grim little harbours of the south of the **Bigouden** peninsula.

Sheer delight from then on, with the deep estuaries of green-banked rivers, **Odet, Aven, Belon, Laïta**, slicing into the Mediterranean-style foliage, and charmers like **Benodet, Concarneau** and **Pont Aven. Raguénés-Plage** has an unbelievably beautiful beach. The stretch between the pretty little port of **Le Pouldu** and **Larmor Plage** is a bit of a let-down, but beyond **Lorient, Port Louis** has charm and a good beach.

Everyone finds the **Quiberon** peninsula fascinating, with **Carnac's** contrasting attractions of megaliths and beach, and **Belle-Île** would be well worth a visit. **La Trinité** is a modern yachting centre.

Then another favourite area, full of interest, around the **Gulf of Morbihan**, with its dozens of islands and picturesque **Auray** and **Vannes** to explore. The little fishing ports of **Locmariaquer** and **Port Navalo** are the tips of the arms that enfold the gulf; the **Rhuys** peninsula to the south is only moderately interesting and I wouldn't bother to divert through the flat countryside to the little resorts in the sand dunes to the south, except perhaps for the rocky point of **Pen-Lan**.

The mighty river **Vilaine** is good to explore by canal boat, with **La Roche Bernard** an attractive town on its banks. Don't miss the walled **Guérande** on the way to sophisticated **La Baule**, with fabulous beach, light years away from the simple family holiday villages of the north. Take a drive to **Le Croisic**, a photogenic fishing port, to eat the freshest seafood, and then its foot down along the motorway to elegant **Nantes**, 'little Paris'.

Although I believe most travellers will be seeking coastal

holidays along the coast, or 'Armor' region, the 'Argoat' or inland regions, have their high spots too. I would pick for outstanding interest: **Dinan, Josselin,** the **Paimpont/ Brocéliande** forest, the **Regional Park of Armorica** and the parish closes of **Finistère**, and I have also tried to indicate stops along the main routes.

THE BRETONS

Ignored by industry, poor communications with the rest of France, a history of warfaring – its not hard to see why the Bretons are known for their spirit of independence. By clinging doggedly to regional dress, customs, legends, language, they have succeeded in maintaining a unique charm and interest that, combined with their extraordinarily beautiful coastline, has made Brittany the second most popular tourist destination in France.

    The costumes are passed down through the generations and are most likely to be seen in the south, at Quimper, Pont Aven, Pont l'Abbé, Plougastel, Douarnenez, Auray. It is worth planning a holiday around the 'Pardons', the colourful local religious processions, to see them being worn. Here is a list of the chief *pardons* and local events of special interest:

2nd Sunday in May	Quintin
May 19	Treguier
Whitsun	Moncontour
Whit Monday	Carantec
Friday before Trinity	St. Herbot
Trinity	Rumengol
June 23	St. Jean du Doigt
Sunday before June 24	St. Tugen
Last Sunday in June	Le Faouët
Last Sunday in June	Plouguerneau
Eve of 1st Sun. in July	Guincamp
3rd Sunday in July	Douarnenez, Blessing of the Sea
3rd Monday in July	Roscoff
4th Sunday in July	Quimper, festival of Cornouaille
4th Sunday in July	Bubry
July 25 and 26	Ste-Anne d'Auray
July 26th	Fouesnant
1st Sunday in August	Pont Aven, Festival of the Golden Gorse
August 15	Perros-Guirec
August 15	Plougastel-Daoulas
August 15	Guelven
Sunday after August 15	Carantec
Sunday after August 15	Ploerdut
Penultimate Sunday in August	Concarneau, Festival of the Blue nets
Last Sunday in August	Audierne
Last Sunday in August	St. Anne-la-Palud, Grand Pardon
1st Sunday in September	Camaret
1st Sunday in September	St. Nicholas-de-Pelem, Blessing of the Horses

September 8 or Sunday before	Le Folgoet, Grand Pardon
September 8 or Sunday before	Penhors
2nd Sunday in September	Carnac
2nd Sunday in September	Josselin
3rd Sunday in September	N.-D de Tronoen
Last Sunday in September	Hennebont
December 4	Le Faouët

Every Breton would claim that the Quest for the Holy Grail and the rest of the Arthurian legend centred on Brittany not Britain, as most of us supposed, and certainly in the Forest of Brocéliande around Paimpont, (see p. 100) the magic is potent, carefully fostered by the tourist board. Otherwise it is in the north-west that the Breton affinity for myths and fairy tales is most strong. The local saints, many of them monks coming from Britain in the 5th and 6th century, have villages named after them – St. Ivy (Pontivy), St Suliac, Île Tudy. The miracles they performed still work for the believers, the spells are still potent, the tabus formidable.

The Breton language in a written form is surprisingly evident but nowadays only a few of the older peasants in the remotest northwest villages do not understand French. There is a strong movement to re-introduce Breton to the young and it is taught in schools all over 'Lower Brittany' – the line from St. Brieuc to Vannes – where the feeling for independence is strongest. You can buy Breton dictionaries, but some of the most common prefixes are: *plou* (look at the list of place names in this book) = parish, *tre* = congregation, *loc* = holy place, *ker* = house, *gui* = town, *tro* = valley, *goat* or *coat* = wood, *lan* = sacred ground.

CHURCHES

It is not surprising that in an area as poor as Brittany was in the Romanesque period (11th and 12th centuries), when some of the outstandingly beautiful cathedrals were being built in Normandy and elsewhere, few churches of any stature were achieved here. It therefore comes as an additional shock of pleasure to find the startling richness of the Gothic and, particularly, Renaissance periods, when the wealthy Dukes were in power, in the interiors of churches often built in humble villages.

The parish closes – *enclos paroissiales* – (see Lampaul Guimiliau, St. Thégonnec) are the most outstanding example of what I mean and no-one visiting Finistère should fail to witness this unique Breton phenomenon of parish vying with parish over several centuries to produce the most glorious combined effect of triumphal arch, calvary, ossuary and brilliant church interior.

However the local material they had to work with on the exteriors was still the unmalleable granite and any delicacy and lightness was achieved with difficulty. The carvings often appear crude to the point of caricature, but are nonetheless fascinating in the stories they tell.

Calvaries

In the most famous, at Guimiliau, are 200 figures depicting

episodes of the Passion; at the other extreme is the simple cross to be found at the roadsides all over Brittany. The oldest remaining calvary is at Tronoën, dating from the end of the 15th century, but they were still built two hundred years later. Those in the late 16th century were intended to ward off the plague or as a thanksgiving to have escaped from it.

A LITTLE HISTORY

A common Breton phenomenon are the megalithic monuments of prehistoric times. Anyone interested in depth should make for the display and explanation in the Musée de Bretagne in Rennes, or the Museé Préhistorique Finisterien in St. Guénolé, but, very briefly; – dolmens mark huge collective graves dug at a time of a cult for worshipping the dead. Menhirs (lit. tall stones) probably mark a sacred spot but, in spite of many theories over the years, nobody has ever satisfactorily explained their existence. The puzzle remains too as to how they and the dolmens, some weighing over 100 tons, were erected at that time.

After the mysterious builders of the megaliths came, in the 6th century BC, the Celts, of whom the most powerful tribe were the Veneti, around Vannes. After much resistance, they were conquered by the Romans in 5 BC. Having drained the land by fierce taxation, the Romans left Armorica to degenerate again into savagery until about 460 AD when the first settlers arrived from Britain. These intrepid seafarers settled mainly in the North-west, often in communities ruled by the monks who later became locally sanctified and gave their name to their villages. They also gave a new name to Armorica – Brittany, or Little Britain.

Charlemagne's forces conquered Brittany in 799 AD but the Breton rebellious spirit hardly faltered and only 44 years later Duke Nominoë from Vannes defeated Charles the Bald at Redon and founded an independent ducal dynasty.

Here the sense of territorialism worked against the new country, for the Dukes persistently quarrelled amongst themselves and, divided, were an easy target for Norman invasion. William the Conqueror used Brittany as a buffer state between his England and his Normandy.

From the 12th to the 15th centuries, Brittany, a hub of maritime trade routes, was a prize coveted by both French and English monarchs, while powerful dukes, kings in all but name, whose names are commemorated in fortresses, villages and streets throughout the province – Montfort, Rohan, Clissons – were contending for control of the duchy. The weak duke Conan IV had to call in Henry II of England to help deal with his opponents and feebly ceded the throne to Henry in 1166, ensuring a period of chaos with no clear ruler. The War of Succession in 1341 had the French supporting one contender, Charles de Blois, and Edward III the other, Jean de Montfort. It was in this war that that indefatigable warrior, much revered by the Bretons, Bertrand du Guesclin, made his name (even though he was fighting on the losing side – the de Montforts won).

The Dukes of Montfort, virtually sovereigns, paid only scant homage to the King of France. Under their rule in the 14th and

15th centuries, Brittany enters its most successful period, economically and artistically.

In 1491 Anne, Duchess of Brittany, the best remembered of all Breton rulers, married Charles VIII of France, but on his death, seven years later, she returned to her duchy for a year (see St. Mâlo) before marrying another king of France, Louis XII (she seems to have had quite a way with her since both these monarchs had to repudiate previous wives to marry her, and she herself did some two-timing by rejecting her first proxy marriage to the future Emperor of Austria). When Anne died in 1514 her daughter, Claude, inherited the duchy and ceded it to France on her marriage to the future Francois I, finally linking the two states, but with a partially independant parliament for Brittany.

But the Bretons hardly ever stopped rebelling against irksome control, either from the French or from anyone else. When their Governor in 1588 tried to make a Catholic take-over, they rebelled against him too and called in the French for help! The Edict of Nantes in 1598 brought a temporary halt to the religious conflict.

The 17th and 18th centuries saw many other uprisings, against taxation, the Jesuits, the Republicans (from welcoming the Revolution as a defeat for autocracy, the Bretons came to resent the new disciplines as much as the old.)

The last rising organised by the colourful Duchesse de Berry (said to have invented sea-bathing) petered out in 1832 but the resolution to achieve a free Brittany for the Bretons has never faltered.

FOOD AND DRINK

This is no place for complicated gastronomy. With prime materials – other mens' luxuries like lobster and oysters, turbot and sole, artichokes and strawberries – what need, argued the wise forefathers, to taint the pure Breton lily with the superficial gilt of Paris elaboration. I believe they were right, and in my travels I came across very few successful examples of cuisine haute or nouvelle. But throughout the province is to be found some of the best seafood in Europe and I have yet to taste a dish more sublime than a lobster freshly plucked from Breton waters, plainly cooked to show off his freshness. The 'Armoricain' version (so often wrongly tagged 'Americain') has to be treated circumspectly. Rich and delicious in skilful hands, it is no dish for pretentious amateurs.

The *beurre blanc* sauce that hails from Nantes is a natural and delicious accomplishment to fish. (It incorporates two Breton products, dry white wine and butter; the wine is reduced to intensify the flavour and the butter judiciously whisked in.) Not as simple as it seems – it can end up swamping the plate and the flavour.

Perhaps this is the moment to clarify the great crustacean mystery. *Langouste, homard*, lobster, crayfish, crawfish, *écrevisse, langoustine*, Dublin Bay prawn, scampi, shrimp, *crevette rose*, not to mention crab, spider crab, *étrilles, tourteaux* and *crabe* become hopelessly confused in minds and on menus, and as most of them will be encountered some time in Brittany, a little light should be thrown.

Homard (lobster) rules O.K. The king of the sea, ink-coloured in the *vivier*, turns an angry red (who can blame him!) when cooked. *Langouste* is the spiny lobster or crawfish, covered in shell pimples, reddish brown alive, scarlet when boiled, not so fine a flavour as *homard*. Delicate *langoustine*, pale pink, with long spindly claws = Dublin Bay prawn = scampi, except that most 'scampi' are not scampi at all but glorified prawns – *crevettes* in French, shrimp in American. Are you still with me?

Crevettes roses look and taste delicious when pink and briefly boiled; on the fishmongers' slab they appear outer-spaceish, weirdly transparent. Baby shrimps caught in the rock pools are *crevettes grises* – fiddly to shell but with a unique salty flavour that brings just reward for the labour.

Écrevisses are freshwater crayfish, sometimes wrongly termed crawfish. Red-clawed, like miniature lobsters, they are a great delicacy, fashionable in the *nouvelle cuisine*.

Tourteaux or *crabes* are the kind we know back home, full of meat; *araignée*, the spiny spidercrab, has more flavour, less meat, and *étrilles*, the tiny grey swimming crabs have no meat at all but are good for soups. Do I make myself clear?

Fresh scallops, lightly poached in Muscadet or cider from the rocks around Erquy I particularly relish, and one taste of their pearly moistness is enough to make you foreswear their frozen aunties forever. Baby scallops are *pétoncles*. Local mussels and clams (*palourdes*) are cooked simply *à la marinière* or stuffed (*farcis*) on a half-shell (try the clams for a change).

Oysters are The Best Buy, especially if you can pick them up from the market stall or the stands along the coast at Le Vivier, Cancale, Le Pô, Bélon, and serve them yourself (having first purchased an oyster knife in the market). They are cheap enough to make you (a) understand why they used to be considered poor man's food in England, and (b) wonder how they can possibly be so expensive there now. Belons (see p. 34) are the best. Even in restaurants they will feature on inexpensive menus with a lavishness that makes the fancier's eyes glisten.

The fishing boats also bring in a good supply of flavoursome sole, turbot and bass, which I prefer any day to the modeish monk-fish. If you can find a good restaurant grill, who will stripe these fish over a hot flame and serve them simply with perhaps a sprinkling of herbs, lemon, butter, stick with it.

What *bouillabaisse* is to the Med., *cotriade* is to Brittany, except its potentially better because cold water fish have more flavour. Well-prepared, the drabness of its components (cheaper variety of fish, like mackerel, whiting, *eel*, plus potatoes) is relieved with the corals of mussels and scallops, the flavour sharpened with sorrel, enriched with cream; carelessly prepared, its a sorry grey mess, unmitigated with the saving saffron of *bouillabaisse*.

Lamb from the salt marshes – *pré-salé* – near Mont St. Michel or the Crozon peninsula is the meat to look for, ready salt-flavoured, killed pathetically young, served pink. The juices round a *gigot à la bretonne* comes thick with white beans. *Kig-ha-Farz* is a hotch potch that combines several courses in one – a sweetened buckwheat pudding with meat – beef, ham, oxtail – and vegetables. You have to be both hungry and brave to try that one. Duck from the Grande Brière region, usually described as *canard nantais*, is justly famous, often served with *petits pois*. From Morlaix comes the products of the pig – *andouilles, saucisson, jambon*.

Breton puddings – '*far*' – cater for hearty northern appetites. Heavy is the word I hesitate to use. '*Far breton*' is like a Yorkshire pudding with raisins (prunes from the Loire region are a better idea) *Gâteau breton* is a pound cake made with the slightly salted breton butter.

Brittany is one area in France where you need never have problems finding a snack. *Crêperies* abound, turning out the lacy pancakes and *galettes*, made from flour or buckwheat (*sarrasin*) and stuffed with every imaginable combination of filling, sweet and savoury. They used to provide the basis for a three course meal for the breton worker – the first crumbled into his soup, the second wrapped around a sausage and the third spread with sugar or jam. The aroma from the *galettières* – the open air griddles – in the markets, along with gaulois and garlic, is part of the instantly recognisable flavour of France.

CHEESES

Trust the Bretons to be different. Here is one of the few provinces in France where cheese is not revered. Only two indigenous species are likely to be tracked down: – '*Campenéac*', made by the nuns in the Campenéac convent, is similar to *St. Paulin*, round with a very smooth ochre rind and a light yellow inside, very fine holes and strongish flavour. 'A good buy' says Androuet. The other, also made from cows milk and similar in appearance and flavour, is the '*Nantais*' or '*Fromage du Curé*', because it was invented last century by a priest from the Vendée. This one is now factory-made, square with a straw coloured smooth rind, 'A fairly good buy'.

'*Maingaux*', (or *Mingaux* or *Mingots*) *de Rennes* is a combination of fresh and soured cream beaten together and eaten with sugar and perhaps fruit. It used to be a speciality of the crêpe-makers, each one of whom would jealously guard the proportions of the delicious filling for his pancakes, but I should very much like to know of any *marchand de galettes* nowadays who would take the trouble.

The local drink is cider, the best coming from Fouesnant, but generally inferior to the Norman variety. Muscadet is claimed as the local wine, but the vineyards in which the grapes from which it takes its name are grown spill over from the area around Nantes into the neighbouring Anjou. The best are to be found on the gentle slopes bordering the Loire.

The best sub-district within the *appellation controlé* is Muscadet-de-Sevre-Maine, another – Muscadet-des-Coteaux-de-la-Loire comes from outside the Brittany border. Gros Plant, made from the Folle Blanche grape (Gros Plant) is a VDQS from the area around Nantes.

Muscadet ages quickly and is best drunk young. '*Sur lies*' indicates that the wine has been left to mature in the cask on their lees, giving a distinctive fruity taste.

SPECIAL RECOMMENDATIONS

The hotel's and restaurants marked by an arrow ➤ have been selected for the following reasons:—

Arradon: *Les Venètes* (HR)M, superb site, near Vannes, comfortable hotel, congenial management.
Les Logoden (R)S, excellent simple country value.
Benodet: *Ferme du Letty* (R)M, unusually good food, delightful atmosphere.
Cancale: *Restaurant de Bricourt* (R)M-L, No. 1 restaurant in Brittany.
Combourg: *Hotel du Château* (HR)M, most popular hotel/restaurant. Strategic position.
Fouesnant: *Hotel d'Armorique* (HR)S, good value, honest cooking, welcome.
Guenrouet: *Le Relais St. Clair* (R)S, good simple cooking, off the beaten track.
Guincamp: *Le Relais du Roy* (HR)M-L, extremely comfortable, excellent food.
Josselin: *Hotel du Commerce* (HR)M, best restaurant in popular town.
Jouvente: *Manoir de la Rance* (H)L, superb site, supremely comfortable, friendly management.
Larmor Plage: *Le Beau Rivage* (HR)S, best seafood.
Locronan: *Le Manoir de Moëllien* (HR)M, Comfortable hotel.
Mordreuc: *L'Abri des Flots* (HR)S, superb site, outstanding value.
Nantes: *Hotel du Château* (H)S, best site in interesting city, outstanding value.
L'Hotel (H)M-L, same site, luxury accommodation at reasonable prices.
Pacé: *La Griotte* (R)M, good value, near Rennes.
Paimpont: *Le Manoir du Tertre* (HR)M, excellent food in charming setting.
Plélo: *Au Char à Bancs* (R)S, best crêperie.
Pleugueneuc: *Château de la Motte Beaumanoir* (R)L, outstandingly beautiful rooms, something different.
Pointe du Raz: *Hôtel de la Baie des Trépassés* (HR)M, excellent seafood, comfortable hotel in popular tourist area.
Pont L'Abbé: *La Bretagne* (HR)M, Hotel of the Year in Medium Category.
Pouldrezic: *Le Moulin de Brenizenec* (H)M, stylish, convenient, friendly owner.
Le Pouldu: *Ster Laïta* (HR)M, individuality, pleasant position, charming rooms.
Raguenès-Plage: *Men Du* (HR)M, superbly-sited beach hotel.
Redon: *La Bogue* (R)M, good food.
Riec: *Auberge de Kerland* (R)M, excellent cooking in superb site.
Ste. Anne-d'Auray: *L'Auberge* (HR)S, good cooking, comfortable rooms, excellent value.
St. Malo: *Le Villefromoy* (H)L, supremely comfortable, good position.
La Duchesse Anne (R)M-L, long-established favourite, best position in popular town, good cooking.
St. Ouen La Rouerie: *Château des Blosses,* unusual, good accommodation in strategic position, friendly owners.
St. Thégonnec: *L'Auberge de St. Thégonnec* (HR)S, Hotel of the Year in Simple Category.
Trébeurden: *Ti al Lannec* (HR)L-M, Hotel of the Year in Luxury Category.
Tréguier: *Kastell Dinech* (HR)M, charm, good value food.
Vannes: *Le Lys* (R)M, excellent cooking at reasonable prices in popular town.

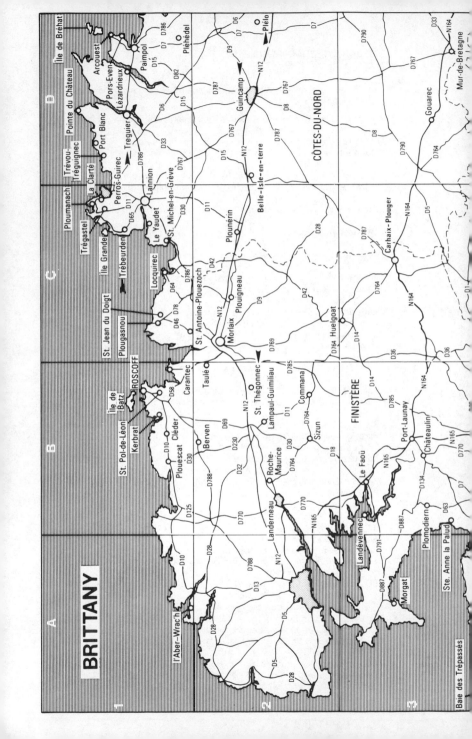

BRITTANY

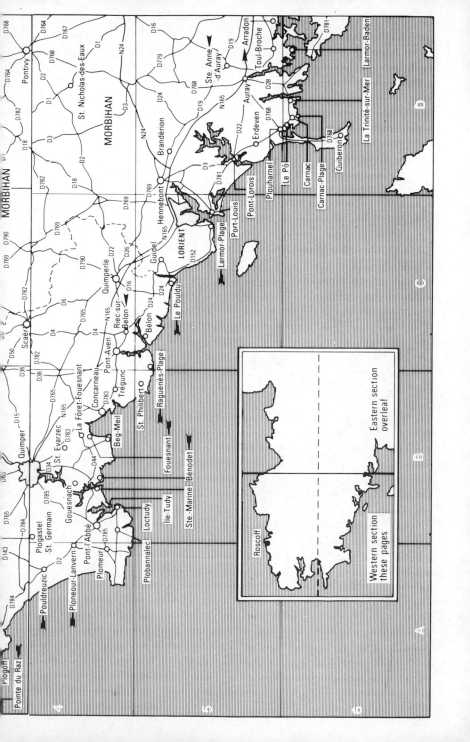

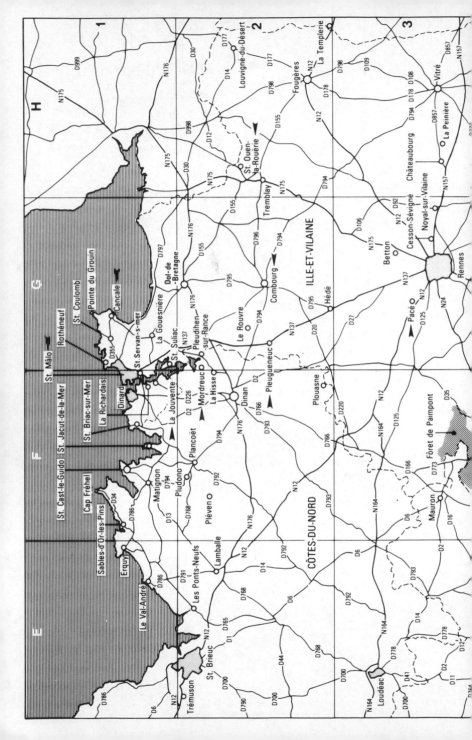

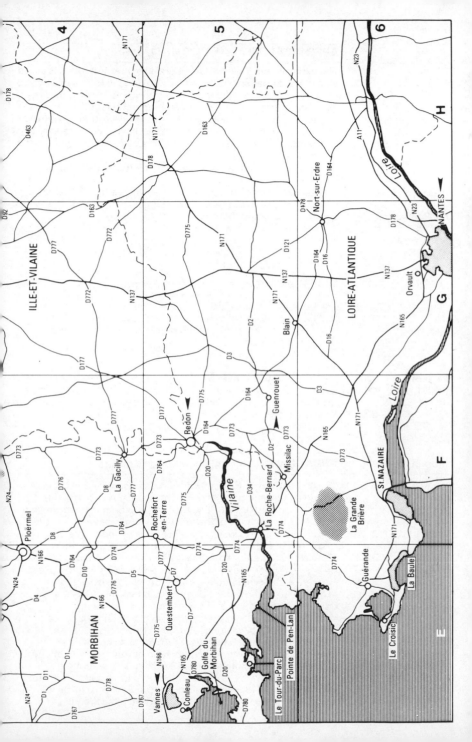

ABER WRACH (Finistère) 28 km N. of Brest

The extreme north-west coast of Brittany, low and rocky, is sliced by wide estuaries known as 'abers'. No ports or big towns around here, just a few unsophisticated holiday spots and tiny harbours, with little in the way of accommodation or restaurants.

Aber Wrach is attractively sited on a wide estuary, useful for sailing. The hotel I went to look at, the Bellevue, was desolate and shuttered, and apart from the activities of a sailing school, not a lot was going on, even in August.

On the road to the pretty village of **Lannilis** at **Paluden**, is:

Relais de l'Aber
(R)S
rte. Plouguerneau
(98) 04.01.21. cl.
Nov. and Mon.
AE DE EC.

A little restaurant with a good view down over the Aber. Not specially exciting otherwise, but the best I can do in this gastronomic desert. Menus from 50f.

Map 1D

ARCOUEST (c. du N.) 6 km N of Paimpol

The point of Arcouest is the depot for the boats that leave every half hour to the Ile de Bréhat (see p. 39). Even better is to take one right round this enchanting island, or along the coast and up the river Trieux.

Right on the point is:

Le Barbu
(HR)M
(96) 55.86.98.
Closed 15/11–15/3
AE, DC, V.

Dignified, creeper-covered, with a large hydrangea-filled terrace from which to observe all the activity; smashing views from the front bedrooms – 280f with bath. The cheapest double is 200f. Very good menus from 65f.

Map 5D

ARRADON (Morbihan) 7 km SW of Vannes

The gulf of Morbihan loops and curves and juts, with as many promontories and bays as there are islands. Any of the side turnings off the D101 will lead to water and boats, and often to a little hotel or bar. One of the most pleasant is down to the Pointe d'Arradon, which is just a cluster of houses and a little dinghy harbour. Via sea walls and beaches you can walk for miles around this stunning bay. One golden autumn evening I did just this, from Arradon towards Vannes, and met only half-a-dozen people — children dawdling on the beaches, a fisherman sitting in his pulled-up boat, an elderly couple walking their dog – in an hour's perambulation at the water's edge, with island succeeding island over the sparkle, and only the chatter of halyards and an occasional phut-phut to disturb the calm.

We liked it so much that we returned for a second look, arriving on a hot Saturday in June and hardly believed our eyes at the sight of our quiet little bay overrun with sunbathers, promenaders, windsurfers and all. Dying for a swim after a long sticky ride, I had to pick my way over the bodies to reach the decidedly murky water. Another favourite bites the dust?

But no, next morning was cooler and the beach stayed reasonably free all day. During the marvellous weather of the week that followed, spent exploring this exceptionally beautiful area, we had it all to ourselves and the conclusion must be that anywhere as attractive as Arradon, so near to a big town like Vannes, must be busy at peak periods. Still a lot of calm to go round, and with the bonus of:

►**Les Vénètes**
(HR)M
(97) 44.03.11
Closed 1/10–1/4
R. closed Tue.

 H
R

The Vénètes were the earliest Armoricain seafarers, rough and crude — not a bit like this smart little hotel. Right on the water's edge, with terrace and dining room enjoying the view.

The rooms vary a lot in size and price but all are extremely well-fitted, bright and cheerful. Those on the front, with balcony, are well worth the 272f, but all have some view of the sea, and a tiny one at the side was perfectly agreeable at 180f with bath.

The brothers Tixier, Jacques and Henri, who run the little hotel, are exceptionally friendly and helpful and although they have a most attractive restaurant (menus from 78f), there were no sour looks when we ate out.

The combination of superb site, comfortable hotel and congenial management make this my no. 1 choice for Morbihan and a certain arrow.

From the Tixiers came the recommendations for another winner:

►**Les Logoden**
(R)S
(97) 44.03.55
Closed Wed; Thur.

The Logoden are the humpbacked islands opposite Arradon, and M. and Mme Gabriel Pellan are true Morbihanais. Their delightful little restaurant opposite the Poste in the bourg of Arradon, 2 km away from the Pointe, was the find of the week.

Les Vénètes

We went initially because it was open on the difficult Sundays and Mondays, but would go back any night of the week for such exceptional value.

There are perfectly good menus at 44.30f and 55.30f, including oysters and seafood, but the 79.50f menu was irresistible. For me, a huge platter of *langoustines*, home-made mayonnaise; for husband, six fat oysters, grilled and scattered with almonds. Then *saumon cru mariné* — a kind of gravadlax — and *coquelon de pêcheur* — scallops and white fish gratinéed in an excellent sauce. The third-course sole covered the plate and would have justified the menu price alone, and husband's herbed beef, cooked on skewers over the charcoal fire, was served exactly as he requested. The cheese-board far exceeded normal expectations for a modest country inn, and the strawberries were lavish and served with *crème fraîche*.

Gabriel Pellan is more than just an adequate patron-chef, and is not content to dish up the standard fishy menus, admirable but undemanding, of the area. If you want a plain *sole meunière*, you can have one here for 49f — one of the lowest prices for this fish I found — but he will also offer it with a lobster stuffing. And sorrel soufflés like his don't come ten a penny in many un-sung Breton villages. Go soon.

Map 4A

AUDIERNE (Finistère) 15 km E of the Pointe du Raz, 35 km W of Quimper

---

A big fishing port, especially for tuna and crayfish. Sheltered from the west, it nestles in the estuary of the Goyen, approached from a bridge from the Plouhinec side, with the beach. Overlooking the port is:

Le Goyen
(HR)L
(98) 70.08.88
Closed mid Nov.–
mid Dec.; Mon.
o.o.s.

I found it all a bit grand and impersonal, with an intimidating *patronne*, but some of the rooms are extremely comfortable, tastefully furnished, with balconies overlooking the water, and good value at 240f. Others are nowhere near as nice, so it pays here to go for the best or forget it.

But the main reason for staying at Le Goyen would be for its delightful restaurant, bay windows making the most of the view, to sample M. Bosser's superb cooking. He combines the best of both worlds of traditional and *nouvelle cuisine*, using prime local ingredients with imagination and flair. Particularly valuable to come across one such as he in this area, where it is just possible, even for me, to tire of plain seafood twice a day, every day. I am always begging for the flavour of fish to be allowed to speak for itself but M. Bosser's lightly poached *coquilles St.-Jacques* and lobster, presented in the flaky pastry for which he is famous, lost nothing by being served in a *cardinale* sauce whose richness was spiked with tarragon, and, once the luxury of eating oysters on modest menus has become taken for granted, it is wonderful to find them here in a new guise, hot on a bed of *crêpes*, cooked in Sancerre. His most popular dessert involves pastry again — a *mille feuilles* served warm, enclosing whatever fruits are in season.

The 105f menu is a bargain (not Sundays) and merits a

considerable detour, but otherwise the bill can get out of hand, especially if the temptation to take advantage of the impressive wine list becomes irresistible.

| Map 5D | **AURAY** (Morbihan) 18 km E of Vannes |

An enchanting town, split into two distinct parts by the river Auray, on which in high season you can take a *Vedette Verte* out to the Gulf of Morbihan.

The little port of St.-Goustan, once one of the busiest in Brittany, is pure picturebook, with its cobbled square and old grey stone houses brightened with masses of flowers. Benjamin Franklin landed here in 1776 to seek French support for his country's War of Independence.

We sat there, under one of the multicoloured parasols, one hot summer day and watched the local children dive from the old bridge into the fast-flowing river, to be carried along, squealing happily, to the far river bank, or hang on to the bridge supports to get a free jacuzzi from the powerful stream.

On the other side of the bridge a path zigzags upwards through the trees to the Promenade du Loc, for a good view of the colourful harbour from the other, more down-to-earth Auray, with shops, a market square and the Office du Tourisme. The 18th century St.-Gilda's church is up here, with a fine reredos behind the high altar.

Nearby is:

Hotel de la Mairie
(HR)S
24 pl. de la Mairie
(97) 24.04.65
Closed Oct.; Sat.
p.m.; Sun. o.o.s.

An unpretentious little Logis, much used by locals, whose patron, M. Stephant-Guidelo, cooks good-value meals from 58f and has rooms from 76.50 to 161f with bath.

I didn't think there were any hotels down by the river, since none proclaim their existence, not even:

L'Armoric
(HR)S
(97) 24.10.36
Open all year

It says only 'Restaurant' very firmly on the awning above the terraced tables, but it does have rooms, mostly overlooking the river, at 85f a double. Only a one-star hotel, but the rooms are quite large and comfortable and there is one with a splendid view of the port for 93.50f.

I would say that this position would be quieter than in the town, but perhaps the popular bar below might prove me wrong. Anyway, at this price, in this privileged position, it's a good bet.

| Map 1B | **ÎLE DE BATZ** (Finistère) 1.5 km off Roscoff |

A truly enchanting place, permeated with a serenity that is catching. No one hurries or flusters on Batz, not even the weather which is as calm and mild as its inhabitants. Mediterranean plants — mimosa, figs, oleanders — thrive alongside the early vegetables which are transported to the mainland once a day on the bulky carrier ship that returns with the islanders' supplies.

The ferry from Roscoff crosses every half hour, or thereabouts — they tend to wait for their regulars who may not have quite finished lunch or depart a bit early if someone's got a train to catch. It takes fifteen minutes to reach the 3 km-long island, with a choice of twenty little *plagettes* to decide upon, according to the wind direction and inclination for solitude or company.

Walks are marked around the island, through narrow streets lined with grey cottages, flowers a-tumble everywhere, down to the little fishing harbour where the boats land the shellfish that proliferate on the surrounding rocks, to the beaches where the other 'industry' of the island — seaweed gathering — is carried on by the fishermen's wives.

 Just by the landing stage is the inaptly named **Grand Hotel** with a terrace overlooking the water, and I highly recommend an excursion to this lovely island combined with a platter of *langoustines* eaten here or in the large bustling dining room. For 90f (other menus at 60f) we ate a huge perfectly fresh quantity of these crustaceans, followed by a delicious seafood *feuilleté*, followed by sole, followed by cheese and dessert. Not at all smart, very French *familial*.

M. Morvan has simple rooms available too, but in August they were all full and unviewable. A weekend here would certainly be away from it all.

Mme Ressot's *crêperie* **du Port** makes a good cheap snack alternative, open every day from April to October.

Map 6E | **LA BAULE** (Loire-Atl.) 136 km SW of Rennes, 58 km W of Nantes – *Mkt: Tues, Fri, Sun*

Of the many youthful memories of La Baule — stylish/mostly pine trees/expensive — only the last, sadly, is valid today. The pines have retreated one by one further from the beach, invaded by the inexorable march of the apartment blocks. A street or two away from the prom they are still to be found, shading the little hotels and causing the quiet roads to twist around them.

The chic has departed with them, it seems. the main street goes in more for jeans than Balenciaga, cafés and fast foods are easy to find, good restaurants are not. The 'best beach in Europe' is still very fine indeed, but now that the backdrop green has gone, so has a lot of its character.

Jam-packed on sunny weekends, entirely deserted on grey days after mid-September, it's hard to hit it right. Most hotels shut up firmly for six months and charge enough for the other six to compensate. Those that do stay open are full if the weather is good, and in fairness it often is – La Baule enjoys a microclimate that gives it more sunshine than its latitude would seem to expect.

Restaurants are a big disappointment. Here's a case I think for resignation — it's going to be expensive anyway, so make sure it's worth it. It should be at:

Castel Marie-Louise
(HR)L
espl. Casino
(40) 60.20.60
Closed 30 Jan.–6 March
P. AE, DC, V.

I call 140f a bargain, in this town or anywhere else, for the chance to sample the sublime cooking of Henri Reverdy in this odd Gothicky 'villa' set in the pine trees on the Esplanade. The dining room is not large and you must certainly book, since I am not the only one to appreciate the excellence of his *gâteau de pintade et de jarret de veau* or his *marinière de lotte aux artichauts*, his irresistible pastries and even the home-made breads, all served in surroundings as elegant as one would expect from a member of the *Relais et Châteaux* chain.

The bedrooms are expensive — from 345f to 845f — but so comfortable and with such perfect service that the cost might seem justified, especially if full use were made of the swimming pool and tennis courts.

L'Espadon
(R)L
2 av. de la Plage
(40) 60.05.63
Closed Oct. and from 21/9–1/2 Sun. p.m. and Mon. o.o.s.
DC.

Still in luxury mood and still a bargain. M. Cova offers a 74f menu which makes nonsense of the over-priced rubbish in the town.

Again the dining room is not large and you must book to get a table with one of the best views along the entire coast. **L'Espadon** is on the fifth floor of a modern and luxurious Résidence du Golfe. It's the kind of restaurant that it's worth dressing up for — you'd certainly feel all wrong if you didn't.

The food is superb, based heavily on fish — *bar rôti à l'ail sauce au fenouil, les petits rougets à la menthe fraîche* — but with interesting meat and poultry dishes too. Desserts perhaps not so distinguished as at the **Castel Marie-Louise**.

Even if you stick to the cheapest menu (and there is another, even more alluring at 128f), what with wines and service this will not be a cheap evening, but what value!

Le Petit Duc 🦢
(R)S
42 av. des Ibis
(40) 60.48.09
Closed Sun. p.m. and Mon.

One of the very few moderately-priced restaurants I could find not geared to the holidaymaker exclusively. This one stays open all year round and the locals eat here. Its not on the main drag up to the prom, but in a side street leading to the market.

The menus are straightforward steaks, grills, fish, but the quality is good and so is the value — menus start at 50f.

An alternative is to drive out to Le Croisic and choose from the numerous restaurants there, all serving better and cheaper fish (see p. 54) than anything in La Baule.

La Palmeraie
(HR)M
7 allée Cormorans
(40) 60.24.41
Closed 1/10–1/4
AE, DC, V.

You name it — Gault-Millau, Michelin, Logis de France, Bottin Gourmand — and many more guidebooks laud **La Palmeraie**, so it's not easy to get in. Certainly an attractive little hotel, in a good position a few quiet roads back from the promenade, set in pine trees. It recently won a special prize for being more 'fleuri' than any other hotel in France; the front garden is ablaze with colour, around a dazzlingly white courtyard, with steps leading up on to a well-equipped terrace. And the palm trees are no idle boast — very lush and healthy they look and as polished as the rest of the horticulture. Little white balconies are clapped on to most of the rooms, from which to survey the pleasant scene below.

Inside, the riot of colour and pattern continues — all a bit too busy for my taste, but still patently clean and shining. Outside it's great but in such a midget-sized room, where one occupant has to stay in bed while the other gets dressed, it all gets a bit oppressive. The plumbing here is unavoidably near your ear and too raucous to be used nocturnally without the certainty of waking up your neighbours. In the morning rush-hour the building nearly got lift-off.

It's a very noisy hotel altogether in fact — that gleaming white terrace got harshly scrubbed at a very early hour with unacceptable cheerful chatter, and gallic cops and robbers shot it out irrepressibly in the TV room beneath our bedroom to an audience of (deaf?) elderly residents.

We were the only eaters-out and crept guiltily down those steps, to escape the no-choice menu of the day — cauliflower soup, poached fish, ice cream: 80f. Perhaps it was more exciting than it sounded, but it didn't seem worth the risk.

So — clean, central, not expensive (140f a double) but best for the hard-of-hearing dwarf.

Délice-Hôtel
(H)M
19 av. Marie-Louise
(40) 60.23.17
Closed 23/9–15/5
P.

All modern, bright and cheerful, set in a quiet road not far from the front. Good sized bedrooms, all with bathrooms, are from 178f with shower to 256f for four beds, with variations of bath; twin beds, in between. No restaurant.

Hôtel Ty-Gwenn
(H)S
25 ave. de la
Grande Dune
(40) 60.37.07
Garage

In La Baule-les-Pins, at the southern end of the bay. The little old-fashioned-style hotel is in a quiet road, in a garden, and chosen because it stays open all year round. The rooms are simple, but warm and comfortable. From 90f to 180f.

Map 4B

BEG MEIL (Finistère) 19 km W of Concarneau by D44 and D45

They said it had been ruined, they said I'd never recognise it, but it hasn't and I did. A nostalgia trip is always a risky business but I can still see perfectly well why we loved Beg Meil so much in the bucket-and-spade days and indeed am prepared to love it again for different reasons. Then, parking hot cars in pines, hung about with potties, parasols and picnics, we stumbled down what seemed a very long flight of steps and sank exhausted on that marvellous beach, don't remember stirring further than to the water's edge, or to the or to rocks to aid the shellfish quest.

That's all exactly the same and if I had young children today I'd make straight for the unbeatable combination. But fresh attractions now reveal themselves. Unencumbered, how pleasant it is to take a walk in those pine woods and how sensible of the people of Beg Meil not to cut them down for lucrative flats. For the first time I walked round the cliff edge by the lighthouse, and found the other delightful sandy beaches, inaccessible at high water, facing across the glittering bay to Concarneau. So sheltered are they from the westerlies that, on a indifferent Easter day, bikini sun bathing was feasible there. In fact, whichever way the wind blows, there will be a bay sheltered in that direction.

OK so it's all busier, less select now, and they tell me the beaches and pines are packed for the dreaded six summer weeks, with cars queueing to get in, but that leaves a lot of year and a lot of beaches still to go round.

Finding a hotel though doesn't get any easier. Time was when the Rolls dropped off their elegant owners at the **Grand Hotel** to dine in discreet splendour there or in the nearby private villas; the villas are still there, some fading, some still prosperous in well tended gardens, but the days of the big hotel are over. In fact the days of all hotels in Beg Meil are over it would seem.

Ever since I can remember the **Thalamot** has been a reliable and unchanging institution for generations of British families. Looking at it again with fresh eyes, I find it's a let-down. The Brits still come, taking over the bar at drinks time and the shady garden for tea, swapping their connections and travel stories and showing off their intimacy with Madame, but the recently renovated rooms are tiny, characterless and dull. Ours had no curtains, not a picture to relieve the plain walls, uniformly plastic, with a view over a corrugated roof. Ash remained in ashtray, bath remained uncleaned, the single towel was transparently thin, and packaged breakfast arrived half an hour late. Not good enough to cash in like this on position, not, as claimed, *sur la plage* but one row back, with no view.

Map 2D	**BELLE-ISLE-EN-TERRE** (C. du N.) 10 km W of Guincamp

Turn off the busy N12 motorway just one km. to find this pretty peaceful little village, whose name derives from its site – an island between the rivers Léguer and Guic.

Le Relais de l'Argoat (HR)S
(96) 43.00.36
Closed Feb; Mon.
EC, V.

A pleasant little Logis, run by Colette and Pierre Marais, with comfortable rooms and bath for 140f. The menus are excellent value, with regional specialities, like *brochette d'Argoat*, included. They start at 49f but I would go for the 79f version — four good courses of straightforward country cooking, with tasty *terrine du chef*, generous *entrêcote marchande*, cheese and pud.

Map 4C	**BÉLON** (Finistère)

The Bélon is an enchanting river. Trees grow right down to its edge, reflecting their green in its deep waters. It twists and turns disorientatingly so that each vista is a new one, urging you on to discover the next. Little settlements, some just a few houses and as many boats, punctuate the water line. One of these is the **Port du Bélon**, where, near the bottom of a steep hill, with sublime views round a wide sweep of water dotted with yachts, and across the river to **Chez Jacky** (see Riec), you'll find a most unusual bar:

La Cabane
(R)S
(98) 71.04.74

Stone walls, sailing photos, flowers inside for cosy dark days, benches out for sunny ones admiring the view — a very upmarket cabin indeed.

Its menu is simple and perfect. Situated on the best oyster river in France what should it offer but *bélons*? The finest cost 60f a dozen but a plateful of *creuzes* at 40f would make a good *dégustation* too; or there are mussels for 25f, and if you order ahead, their famous *cotriade* (a fish stew) for 55f.

A really super little place for a quiet excursion, guaranteed to charm.

The whole area is full of treats; my favourite beach is at **Kerfany les Pins**, where the sand and rocks are backed by pine trees in which to picnic. There's a *crêperie* there for modest refreshment. Wonderful cliff walks.

Map 4B

BÉNODET (Finistère) 16 km S of Quimper

I must declare a weakness here — if I had to pick one holiday spot in the whole of Brittany, it would be Bénodet. Not particularly clever this — the Brits (me among them) discovered the little town on the mouth of the Odet (Bén-Odet) years ago and have colonised the place ever since. It's like saying you've found a little French resort called Cannes to recommend Bénodet to an Englishman. It's obvious and not even particularly French. They say in summer (when I refuse to see for myself) the population swells from 2500 to 35,000 and it must be another story then from my experiences at Easter, in June, in September, which have been pure gold.

Particularly pure gold in that the resort faces due west and when Ste.-Marine across the estuary is dark in shade, gets the benefit of the evening sun, so that late strollers along the river path, around the point, past the old lighthouse, towards the little port and maybe even as far as the marina, continue to bask in the unusually warm air and spectacular sunsets.

There are splendid sandy beaches to the south but the intrusion of concrete beach huts into the pine trees does not please and I prefer the river aspect, where the coves are still sandy, more sheltered, and more interesting, with the never-ending fascination of water traffic. It all reminds me very much of beloved Salcombe.

A boat trip up the beautiful river Odet makes a most agreeable excursion, from Bénodet to Quimper, or vice-versa. I've never tried the lunchtime or dinner gastonomic trip but I'm told they're good value for money and certainly the restaurant looks classy. Personally I'd rather sit outside on the upper deck for a better view of the variety of scenery passing by.

From wide estuary, dotted with yachts, under the Pont de Cornouaille, the river shrinks to ford-like proportions, still and very deep, then widens into a lake just short of Quimper. Always tree-lined, herons posing along its banks, châteaux to admire, the river offers a peaceful way to spend a couple of hours. An alternative trip on a calm day is to the offshore islands of **Glénan**.

Le Minaret
(HR)M
(98) 57.03.13
Closed 30/9–25/3
P.

A strange white building, prominent with the odd tower that gives the hotel its name. They say it was built by some eastern potentate for the local doctor who had saved his life. The interior carries out the theme with oriental carpets, a tapestry or two and the odd gong. No, it's not for the incongruous decor, nor the bedrooms which anywhere else I would reject as on the small side and poorly furnished, nor yet the spartan bathroom, that I would return to the Minaret whenever able. It's the position that wins hands down. To sit on the balcony with all that truly fabulous panorama of sea, river, rocks, boats, gardens, lighthouse, spread around is worth a lot. A lot in this case is from 200–300f depending on aspect, and here it's worth going for the best.

The elegant dining room also makes the most of the view but, as I had heard poor reports of the food, we didn't eat in. Now, at least so I hear, it is vastly improved, but herein is the snag — between June and September demi-pension is insisted upon, and if the food is only indifferent, what starts off as a very good deal indeed becomes insupportable. I enjoy eating in occasionally but neither want (nor am able) to do so every night, so for me the Minaret can only be an o.o.s. experience (other reports welcome), but that's when Bénodet is at its considerable best anyway.

There is a lovely formal garden to walk through en route for

Le Minaret

beach just below, shady pines to park in and a new pagoda-like tea-room, which I would have liked even more had it not been for the dreaded pop deafener.

Ancre de Marine 👍
(HR)M
(98) 57.05.29
Closed 1/11–1/3;
Rest. closed Mon.
o.o.s.

Overlooking the port, with an especially good view from the pleasant dining room. Menus from 75f have a good local reputation but the cool *patronne* has not.

Modern bedrooms, functional, clean, at 230f for a double with bath in the main building, or 100–160f in the annexe across the road, with no sea view.

➤ **Ferme du Letty**
(R)M
Letty
(98) 57.01.27.
Closed 1/10–20/10;
Wed.; Thurs.
lunch.
Too expensive

2 km SE on the D44 and VO. **Letty** is on an almost enclosed inland sea between the **Pointe de Bénodet** and the odd strip of land that spits out from **Moustelin**. Known as the Mer Blanche, the peaceful lagoon, perfect for fishermen, is now a popular sailing centre, with the shallow water providing ideal conditions for falling into.

The best meal we had in Finistère was eaten at this old stone farmhouse now cleverly converted into a smart restaurant without going over the top tapestry-chair, heavy-drape-wise. Here one can still be cosy and romantic, rustic definitely, while appreciating the classy *couverts*. French windows open on to a summer terrace, log fires burn cheerfully in winter, flowers everywhere and Quimper pottery on the walls. Very nice indeed.

And the food! No menu, but a very reasonable bill — say 120f — emerges at the end of a three course meal, helped no doubt by the bargain wine list, with excellent house wine at 26f or Muscadet at 29f.

I ate an inspired *crêpe*, stuffed with *mousserons* (wild mushrooms) and crab, then an escalope of *lotte* with an interesting creamy red pepper sauce, while husband tucked in to a dozen oysters, thoughtfully produced as two half dozens in sequence, so that the debris shouldn't get out of hand, followed by the cheapest item on the menu — a farm chicken roasted on the spit over the fire, for 35f.

But the justly famous course at the **Ferme** is the dessert. Mme Bilot wheels round a vast lazy-Susan apparatus on whose tiers are strewn the kind of puds that weaken even the most dedicated dieter. Noting that all the locals chose at least three, we felt able to do as the Romans do and allow Madame to serve generous protions each of a wonderfully tangy *tarte au citron*, a dark and rich chocolate mousse cake and a *bavarois* of orange. With dollops of *crème fraîche* . . .

I liked particularly the atmosphere, with parties of locals, all obviously regulars, being greeted by name by M. and Mme Bilot, locals themselves, who have clearly made a huge success of this project – once a modest *crêperie* I understand. A future Michelin star would not surprise me. Meanwhile an arrow from me will have to do.

Domaine de 👍
Kereven
(HR)M
rte. de Quimper
(98) 57.02.46.

Peacefully situated a km or two north of Benodet. All very pristine and straightforward and no surprise to learn that the owner is Dutch (I think — or was it German?). Anyway he speaks unusually good English and is exceptionally friendly and helpful. No complications about the prices either — the

comfortable well-equipped rooms, each with its own good
bathroom, are 220f and the menus are 70f. They prefer demi-
pension but do not insist out of season. There is a terrace, a
salon and a nice dining room; all so nice and respectable and
blameless that if all French hotels were so exemplary I should
have nothing to write about.

Map 2B	**BERVEN** (Finistère) 20 km W of Morlaix on the D19, 11 km SW of St.-Pol-de-Léon

The 16th-century church here attracts art lovers to its lantern
dome, the first of its kind in Brittany and the model for several
others. Its parish close has a fine triumphal arch.

Les Voyageurs
(HR)S
(98) 69.98.17
Closed 15/9–15/10;
Sun. p.m.; Mon.

A nice little old stone building in the centre of the village. Really
pretty inside, warm and welcoming, with friendly *patronne*,
Mme Simon, who is also the chef.
   She cooks super-value meals at 36f, 45f and 70f, the last
offering, for example, *melon au porto, langoustines
mayonnaise*, roast beef and dessert.
   The attractive rooms have only washbasins and bidets (the
shower is along the corridor) but they are better furnished and
more comfortable than in many a more expensive hotel, at the
bargain price of 72ı, or 92f for three people.
   First choice for a cheap stay in the area, well placed for both
coast and inland exploration, and a prospective arrow.

Map 3G	**BETTON** (I. et V.) 9 km N of Rennes – *Mkt: Sun*

Take the N 776 road north out of the city and turn left at the
traffic lights in the village of Betton (Sunday market) to find the
river Rance and canal, running side by side. Just before them is:

Hôtel de la Levée
(HR)S
r. Amérique
(99) 55.81.18
Closed Sun. p.m.;
Mon.

A simple country Logis, whose modest décor is more than
compensated for by the friendliness of the owners M and Mme
Louazel. She speaks some English and they welcome regulars
each year, who make this a convenient and cheap stop-over on
the road from Normandy to the South.
   The value is excellent; a double room is 82f or 85f with a
shower; a three course simple meal is 36f, but for 65f Jean-
Claude shows what he can do — *pâté de saumon maison aux
deux sauces* or eight *huîtres portugaises chaudes, beurre à l'ail*,
followed by *lièvre marinadé* or *canard à l'orange*.

Map 5G	**BLAIN** (Loire-Atl.) 22 km N of Nantes, 75 km from Rennes – *Mkt: Tues*

Not a lot to recommend the town itself — the only Logis being
on a noisy main road and the shops unusually dull, but lots of
interest all round, since it lies in the heart of a deeply wooded
area, rare in Brittany. To the north is the forêt de Gavre, where
wild boar and stags are hunted, and nearer the town the forêt le
Groulais makes for cool picnicking.
   The 14th-century castle stands guard over what was once a

Breton frontier town (*Blain* means limit). I cycled from the canal one early morning down the lane, over the massive drawbridge bordered by massive towers, into the courtyard, where a dignified old man sold me tomatoes and peaches. He let me choose the best to pick straight from tree to basket — a kilo for 3f — and we ate them for breakfast, our boat tied up on the quayside opposite the château on the mirror-surfaced water. Alongside and therefore useful for canal trade is:

Hôtel du Port
(HR)S
(40) 79.01.22

Like the town, recommendable primarily for its site. The menus at 35f and 47f looked good value and the *carte* and wine list most impressive, but we unwisely picked the 77f menu and ate our way through crab, moules, duck and apple tart. I can't claim this was a great gastronomic experience. Better stick to the oysters and mussels and the cheapest menu, and with house wine at 20f and a view over the water you can't feel cheated.

Rooms are basic but quiet and overlooking the canal. At 80f they should not be grumbled at.

Map 5D

BRANDÉRION (Morbihan) 7 km W of Hennebont

Leave the *Voie expresse* at Landévant, heading west, on to the N165.

Hotel l'Hermine
(H)M
(97) 32.92.93
cl. 5/1–15/3

A practical choice for those who might wish to eat at Locquénolé (see p. 73) but are not prepared to pay the exorbitant price for a room. The nine rooms here are immaculate, not very large, comfortable, and quiet if you ask for one at the back away from the main road. At 230–250f they are not a bargain, particularly as the grooming of the terrace and garden has cost the owners little or nothing, but a reliable contingency choice.

Map 1D

ÎLE-DE-BRÉHAT (C. du N.) (see Arcouest, p. 28)

For me, a magical island, partly due perhaps to an arrival by sea one evening, after a fretful storm-bound week in St.-Malo, to find the glowering sky and sea suddenly yield to a spectacular sunset, deep blue water, pink rocks and pine trees. Anchor dropped in horseshoe bay, we swam ashore, feeling like Robinson Crusoes.

That must have been September because I remember a powerfully golden light and the stillness and shadows of late summer. This July it was a more prosaic approach by packet from Arcouest, accompanied by scores of twittering schoolchildren. There was barely room enough on the sand of the little beach for Man Friday to leave his footprints, but still the charm was there. The climate is so oddly mild that oleanders and palm trees flourish, the rocks really are pink, the water just as blue.

You arrive at little **Port Clos**, where there are bars and a hotel and walk through narrow car-free lanes smelling of broom and hydrangeas to get to the beach. Or, as I did, hire a bicycle and explore all 3 km of what is really two islands, joined by a causeway. In the centre is a lively little *bourg* centring on a square for boules, stalls, craftwork.

I wouldn't at all mind the chance of staying the odd night in the Logis de France here:

La Vieille Auberge
(HR)S
(96) 20.00.24 👍
Closed Nov.–
Easter

You eat at a central courtyard under the trees, and the hotel itself is set back well away from the main thoroughfare. The rooms are more modern than you might suppose; with dinner and breakfast they cost 225f per person.

Map 1G

CANCALE (I. et V.) 14 km E of St. Malo, 59 km from Avranches – *Mkt: Every day*

A picturesque little fishing port looking east across the Bay of St.-Michel. Wonderful walks along the cliff edge, via the old Customs Officers' path, as far as the **Pointe du Grouhin** (see p. 68) For centuries Cancale has been famous for its oysters, which used to be the finest in France. A mysterious disease decimated the population some twenty years ago and now the young spat comes from Bélon (see p. 34). Stocks are building up again and there is no shortage in evidence in the numerous cafés and stalls round the harbour advertising stand-up *dégustation*. Like Southend but classier. There's a very jovial atmosphere to be induced by strolling about the harbour, out along the jetty to watch the fishing boats unload, and then partaking of a little refreshment, both liquid and marine-based. Plenty of choice down here:

Continental 👍
(HR)M
au port
(99) 89.60.16
Closed 7/4–11/11;
Rest. closed Mon.
V.

The best position in the town, overlooking the harbour, with smart yellow awning to sit under and watch all the activity. The bay must twist round here to face west because it gets all the evening sun and it is so pleasant to settle down for a meal on the terrace that the slowness of the service shouldn't annoy; when the food does arrive, it's excellent. 84f buys nine oysters, sole, cheese and *pâtisserie*, but for 155f you get lobster for the second course.

The rooms are very pleasant too, especially if you get there early enough to pick one with a good view; with bath, it will cost 266f. The cheapest is 85f. Good value altogether.

Ty Breiz
(R)M
quai Gambetta
(99) 89.60.16
Closed 15/11–1/2;
Tue.
AE, V.

A smart little restaurant that the locals recommend. 95f for four courses, including a huge *sole meunière*, or 115f if you like langoustines grillées as much as I do.

La Bisquine 👍
(R)M
4 quai Gambetta

Newer, and as yet untried, but said to be particularly promising. Certainly looks most attractive, with Art Deco décor. Fishy menus start at 75f.

These are good of their kind, but for something quite exceptional it is necessary to leave the port, drive up the hill to the town:

▶ **Restaurant de Bricourt** 🏠 🏠
(HR)L
r. Duguesclin
(99) 89.64.76
Closed 30/11–1/3;
Tue.; Wed.
V.
Now with rooms

My No. 1 restaurant in Brittany. An elegant old manorhouse, with antique furniture, gilded mirrors, chandeliers, and two small dining rooms, whose tables are set with beautiful china.

One is led through the house to an unexpected garden behind, to sit under the parasols by the pond and contemplate the delights of the menu.

Mine was truly a test case here, since I fulfilled all the least favourable criteria for a restaurant: a female, alone, who chose the cheap menu, ordered no aperitif and only half a bottle of one of the least expensive wines on the impressive list. And I couldn't have wished for better service or welcome.

The menu I chose is quite extraordinary value. 82f (not weekends) for cooking of this quality must be the gastronomic bargain of the year. It could have started with ten oysters but I ventured to try *Béatilles de veau*. These proved to be a mixture of calves' sweetbreads and brains lightly fried in butter, so that the crisp outside contrasted with the melting tenderness within, served on a salad of lamb's lettuce and curly endive and little chunks of concassed tomatoes dressed with raspberry vinegar. Sharp, rich, tender, crunchy, fresh — the kind of plate that should make those who dismiss the *nouvelle cuisine* out of hand think twice. That is what it's all about — quality without skimping, eye appeal without irrelevant decorating, skill without fuss.

Then *mélange de poissons*: three *solettes*, three *rouget* fillets, arranged as spokes round a hub of just-cooked shredded cabbage, on a sauce of *beurre blanc*, herbed with chervil. Imaginative perfection. Then *terrine de chocolat* — a chilled slice of dark deliciousness, studded with hazelnuts, surrounded by a sauce of coffee beans and fresh mint. Then the best *petits fours* anywhere, each one a trifling masterpiece — tiny fresh strawberry tartlets, miniature almond crescents, baby *profiteroles*.

Impeccable service, efficient and smiling, and a mighty wine list that still included lots of modest half bottles for the likes of me. Even were one forced to eat *à la carte*, the price is reasonable for this standard — around 160f I would say for three courses.

Chef Olivier Roellinger is a mere stripling yet and there's no limit to his increasing confidence and expertise. Only one Michelin star so far, but I wouldn't mind betting . . .

Map 1G | **ST.-COULOMB** (I. et V.) 3 km W of Cancale on the D 355

Ferme de la Motte-Jean
(R)M
(99) 89.00.12
Closed 29/9–17/10;
6/1–30/1; Thurs.
lunch; Mon. and
Tue. Nov.–Mar.
Wed. 19/9–30/6

In other words this delightful old stone farmhouse, down a track off the St.-Malo road, really caters for weekenders. If you do happen to coincide with a mid-week opening day you qualify for a 55f menu; otherwise the cheapest is 75f but go for the 95f if you can, to get a good range of dishes, some *nouvelle cuisine* but all really interesting, i.e. lots of oysters in different guises, unusually good desserts.

A very pleasant outing — peaceful, tables outside to enjoy the preliminary drink, rustic simplicity inside and the talents of a clever chef. Choose it if you want something different.

| Map 1B | **CARANTEC** (Finistère) 15 km N of Morlaix |

Follow the highly scenic D73 from Morlaix along the river Frout, through Locquénolé to the estuary, up to Carantec, a charming little holiday resort on a peninsula, with beaches and bays in all directions. Smashing views from Pen Lan point, but you have to leave the car under the pine trees and scramble down a long sandy tack to see the panorama of Île Louët, the 16th-century Château du Taureau built on a reef, and numerous small islands, part of a bird sanctuary.

Excellent walks abound, like those to La Chaise du Curé, a promontory overlooking the Baie de Morlaix, the estuary of the Penzé, St.-Pol-de-Léon and Roscoff, but it is more fun to discover some for yourself — no matter which road you take, past gardens full of hydrangeas, it is bound to end up with a rewarding seascape.

The little town itself is lively and very busy; I was driven away by mind-blowing pop music relayed from every corner, but I hope that was just an unlucky one-off. Its chief industry, apart from oyster-farming, is tourism, and very popular it is too. The several hotels are all full in the season and demi-pension is generally obligatory.

Pors Pol
(HR)S
(98) 67.00.52
Closed 20/9–16/5

A family hotel with a nice garden overlooking the little beach of Pors Pol. Good value cooking earns it a red R in Michelin for its 51f menu. 40 rooms from 120–140f, but all occupied so I could not check. Children particularly well cared for. Demi-pension is 95–256f per person.

La Falaise
(HR)S
(98) 67.00.53
Closed 15/9–1/5

Large Gothic mansion overlooking the beach of Keleur (means a hollytree). They are gradually doing up all the 26 rooms so that some are currently much more comfortable than others, reflected in the price range from 74–150f. The food is said to be so good that demi-pension at 110–126f would be no hardship.

| Map 3C | **CARHAIX PLOUGUER** (Finistère) 44 km SW of Guincamp |

It wasn't until I started to research Carhaix that I realised that La Tour d'Auvergne was a man not a building! He was this dairy market town's most famous son, campaigning for the Breton language in the 18th century. On June 27 and 28 Carhaix still celebrates his name.

Once a Roman settlement, still the hub of five main roads, Carhaix makes a good base from which to explore the pleasant country of the Argoat, the Montagnes Noires to the south and the Regional Park of Armorica to the north, but accommodation in this area is unfortunately sadly limited. The best I could find is:

Gradlon
(HR)M
12 bd. République
(98) 93.15.22
Closed Jan. Rest.
Closed Sat. o.o.s.
AE, DC, V.

An aggressively modern hotel in the centre of the town, offering a strictly functional possibility for an overnight stop. Rooms are 180–220f, menus from 60f.

'In my opinion this hotel warrants three stars in view of its standard of comfort and efficiency. The 5-course dinner at a mere 85f was in quality, quantity and service the most outstanding gastronomic feast of our journey. Carhaix and its amenities deserve your further research.' Eric Sheldon.

Auberge du Poher
(R)M
(98) 99.51.18
Closed Feb.; Mon.
EC, V.

6 km to the south on the D769, a pleasant ride through wooded countryside to a pretty little restaurant specialising in Breton dishes, like *tripes Bretonne* and local *andouilles*.

Large helpings of traditional cooking on the 57f menu earns it a red R in Michelin. Stick to this, or other menus at 84f or 94f, since the à la carte prices are prohibitive, and the wine is not cheap.

Map 6D

CARNAC (Morbihan) 13 km SW of Auray on the D768, on the bay of Quiberon

---

Divided into two distinct and very different areas — the Carnac of the historic monuments and the Carnac-Plage that cares more about Ambre Solaire than *alignements*.

Flaubert said that Carnac has had more rubbish written about it than it has standing stones and, as there are 5,000 stones, I shall not add to the rubbish. A specialist guidebook is clearly necessary for the serious *dolmen* fancier. I admit I find the serried rows of crude megaliths whose origins are lost in time — some say religious some say astronomical — sinister rather than inspiring, and a short visit to the scrubland at the entrance to Carnac town, dotted with almost as many *meinherren* as *menhirs* (sorry) enough, but it is certainly an excursion that everyone will want to try for themselves.

I made my own discovery in Carnac. Poking around the back streets behind the Office du Tourisme, I came across:

Mme André Raynaud
(H)S
6 chemin du Douët
(97) 52.04.71
Closed 1/10–15/5

Through a pleasant courtyard with tables and parasols, to Mme Raynaud's spic and span house for an excellent value stop. She has four large double rooms in her annexe, all shiningly new and well-equipped, for 160f, which includes breakfast for two, or two slightly smaller ones in her house for 140f.

Mme Raynard is friendly and efficient and I think that a stay under her roof would prove not only more comfortable and cheaper than a hotel equivalent, but probably a deal more interesting. She also has a smashing new flat to let, sleeping 6–8. Details from her.

Just across the road is:

Le Râtelier
(HR)M
4 chemin du Douët
(97) 52.05.04
Closed Oct.; Nov.;
Tue.
V.

A nice old stone building in a quiet corner, flowery and appealing. It was a Tuesday when I visited it, so I have little to report except that the menus looked good, from 60–130f and that there are ten rooms from 180f with bath. Mme Raynaud recommends the food.

La Marine
(HR)M
4 pl. de la Chapelle
(97) 52.07.33
Closed 1/10–1/4
DC, V.

A bright and cheerful modern hotel recommended by locals, with friendly management from the Gehière family. In the centre of the town, but with a nice terrace for outdoor eating and good food prepared by *père et fils*. Rooms from 138–209f, menus from 83f.

Lann-Roz
(HR)M
35 av. de la Poste
(97) 52.10.48
Closed 15/11–15/
12; Rest. Closed
Wed. o.o.s

On the outskirts of the town, set in a particularly flowery garden, and usefully open for most of the winter. Unusually good food, but the cheapest menu is 100f. Pretty flowery bedrooms are 207f or 223f for three beds.

Map 6D

CARNAC-PLAGE (Morbihan) 3 km SE of Carnac

Only 3 km away, altogether another world. A smart little modern resort, with a beach that rivals La Baule's — pale fine sand curving round the vast bay. Not much of a heart to the place yet — shops and boutiques are still being built and you'd have to go to the other Carnac to find any Gallic atmosphere — but if its just wholesome sun and sand you're after, Carnac-Plage is probably one of the best bets in this area.

Lots of summer hotels, nearly all modern, functional. In June it was not easy to find a room with a sea view, and we ended up paying more than envisaged at:

Hotel Diana
(HR)M–L
21 bvd. de la Plage
(97) 52.05.38

Here is a frankly sybaritic hotel that earns its keep. For 330f we got a spacious room, furnished with better than average taste, luxurious bathroom and large balcony overlooking that gorgeous beach.

No stinting with the extras. By the time we'd had the expensive chaises-longues and parasols carried down to the beach (name *Diana* prominent so that no-one should miss that here was the quality), washed off the sand in the kind of shower that gushes not trickles, hair protected by their bathcaps, soap by courtesy ditto, dried on blissfully dense white towels and descended refreshed to sip something long and cool on more expensive terrace furniture, we came to believe we were getting our money's worth. Pleasant efficient service and good breakfast reinforced the feeling.

The restaurant looked fairly international/boring, but there was no pressure to use it, so taken all round in this area, **Diana** is not a bad idea at all.

Les Genêts
(HR)M
45 av. Kermario
(97) 52.11.01
Closed 25/5–28/9

An older hotel, quieter, classier, set one road back from the beach, peacefully amongst the pine trees. The rooms, some with sea-views, are larger and have more character than those of most of the beach hotels, there are good lounges and restaurant and the patronne is as elegant as her furniture. Perhaps not a family hotel — more for a rest than a frolic. A double costs 115–224f and full pension from 380–540f.

Les Rochers
(HR)M
Port de Plaisance
(97) 52.10.09

Another older hotel, with views of the yacht harbour from all its bedrooms, lots with balconies. Not so conventional as the others but good value — 93–197f for a double, 290f per person full pension in July and August. A particularly pretty dining room, all pink and pastels, and lots of comfortable cane chairs on the terrace.

Ajoncs d'Or
(HR)S
(97) 52.32.02
Closed Nov.–Feb.

In deep peaceful countryside a few kilometres outside the town, well-marked off the Erdeven road, an old stone farmhouse, very pretty, with simple rooms at 150f and menus from 51f. Logis de France, and popular, so book.

See Le Pô (p. 113).

Map 3G

CESSON-SÉVIGNÉ (I. et V.) 6 km E of Rennes – *Mkt: Sat*

From Rennes take the Paris road, the N157, and Cesson-Sévigné is signposted to the left. Although the autoroute is very near, the village character has somehow been retained.

Germinal
(HR)M
9 cours de la
Vilaine
(99) 62.11.01
Closed 1/8–19/8;
21/1–4/2; Rest.
closed Sun.
P. V.

A unique setting, on an island in the middle of the river Vilaine, qualifies this hotel as a member of the *Relais du Silence* chain. I think it may once have been a mill — the stone façade would suggest so, but the rear is modern, as are the majority of the rooms. Their styles therefore are in several distinct variations, those on the front being particularly pleasant. Most of them, back or front, look out over the surrounding water.

This takes care of two of my prime concerns, location and comfort, and I would rate it even more highly were not the other two – welcome and cuisine — sadly deficient. Distinct lack of welcome, with unsmiling manager watching us hump heavy cases unaided (wife very much more pleasant next day) and the worst food encountered so far in Brittany (chips soggily absorbing floury sauces, tinned beans, minute portions, canned fruit and commercial ices, and this on a 110f menu).

The whole hotel is being refurbished ready for 1985 and I only hope that the old character will not be sacrificed to the plastic expedient. It does make a peaceful agreeable base from which to explore Rennes, which has plenty of restaurant choice, and almost next door is:

La Fourchette
(R)S
(99) 62.11.21
Closed Mon.

A little restaurant with an equally good view over the river, serving good grills and fish at modest prices. Sit out on the terrace in fine weather for a drink or tea.

'Setting on the river very pleasant and the 61f four-course meal was worthwhile, with plenty of fish dishes. My assiette du pêcheur *had oysters, cockles, mussels, shrimps, prawns and crab, all as a starter.'* — Ken Bell.

Auberge de la Hublais
(R)M
28 r. Rennes
(99) 62.11.06
Closed 1/8–22/8
P. V.

A useful stop on the main Paris road, with menus from 53f.

'Just a short distance from our hotel Ibis. A very good French meal for 53f.' — Ken Bell.

Map 3H

CHÂTEAUBOURG (I. et V.) 21 km E of Rennes

Included as an example of how Michelin symbols can mislead. How does the following strike you?: 'An old mill, built of stone and wood, full of character, set in its own magnificent grounds, through which flows the river Vilaine. Wide terrace, huge fireplaces, elegant dining room. Bedrooms with every amenity from 124f, rocking horse in Michelin for tranquillity. Situated in the old town of Châteaubourg, just off the autoroute, a few miles from Rennes.' Well-nigh perfect? And all absolutely true but. . .

I had placed **Ar Milin** top of my list for visits in this strategic area. Until I saw it for myself that is. What on paper looks so promising, in reality is all I do not want from a hotel. What the symbols don't tell you is that it is now part of a chain, more interested in conferences than individuals. The old interior has been devastated and now plastic rules supreme. All is uncaring pretension, from the bored unsmiling reception to the expensive food. The rooms, relentlessly modernised, are mostly double the advertised starting price, due no doubt to the inclusion of extras like colour TV, which in France I would willingly swap for a chat with a friendly patron. Ideal for many, no doubt, but no thanks.

For an alternative see **La Peinière** (see p. 103).

Map 3G   **CHÂTEAUGIRON** (I. et V.) 16 km SE of Rennes, on the D463 – *Mkt: Thurs*

A pleasant little town, steeply sloping around its impressive castle. In the Middle Ages, Châteaugiron was one of the most important towns in Brittany, its lords having the right to serve as Grand Chamberlains to the Duke. Many of the houses date from that period, lining narrow streets, gabled, beamed, delightfully crooked. The castle was much-besieged, destroyed and re-built, with every century from the 13th to the 18th leaving its mark. The NE keep is the oldest part.

Cheval Blanc et Château
(HR)S
(99) 37.40.27
Rest. closed Sun. p.m. o.o.s.
P.
EC.

A pleasant old hotel in the town's main street, which would make a useful overnight stop — not expensive and strategically placed on the N–S route, by-passing Rennes. A large twin-bedded room with its own bathroom at the back of the hotel, well away from any possible traffic noise costs 125f, but the cheapest double is only 85f. Wide range of menus starting at 42f, all perfectly adequate, but a happy combination would be an economical bed here and an extravagant dinner across the road at:

L'Aubergade
(R)M–L
(99) 00.41.35
Closed 2/1–16/1; Sun. p.m.; Mon.

An old town house, heavily beamed and rough-cast, with accoutrements as elegant as the cooking. The Rennais drive out here for a better meal than any to be found in their city, and booking is wise. Chef Jean-Louis Casse, offers inventive variations on both the new and traditional cuisines. *Fricassée de gésiers* (giblets), *choux confits*, is recommended for the adventurous, or maybe smoked duck served with home made pasta, but for more conservative tastes the fillets of sole surrounded by a delicate green sauce contrived from the hearts of lettuce would be an equivalent treat. Superb wine list. Menus are 70f, 110f and 150f, but à la carte would cost around 230f.

Map 3B	**CHÂTEAULIN** (Finistère), 31 km N of Quimper, 48 km S of Brest – *Mkt: Thurs*

Astride the river Aulne and a great centre for salmon fishing. So important did the city fathers rate the noble fish that they included it in their coat of arms. Very pleasant to stroll along the wide sweep of the river on the tree-lined banks,

High above the town on the Quimper road, loftily looking down on the river's meanderings is:

Auberge Ducs de Lin
(HR)M
(98) 86.04.20
Closed 4/3–23/3;
16/9–5/10; Sun.
p.m.; Mon.

A popular and well known little restaurant, not only because of its excellent food but because of its modest prices, which earn it a Michelin red R. Louis le Meur relies primarily on local produce and especially the salmon fished from the river far below. Try it simply grilled over the charcoal fire for a taste of the real thing, not over-sauced, not cut into dry thin strips in the name of nouvelle cuisine, but reminiscent in its curdy moistness of the salmon of my youth. Pastry is M. le Meur's other speciality so go for any *feuilletés* for starters, or *pâtisserie* for dessert. Menus start at 76f.

The rooms I thought too expensive for the comfort offered — 210f for a double; all rather dark because of aggressive wood panelling and small windows and approached via a distinctly un-vacuumed corridor. But Mme le Meur emphasised that they look upon themselves as a restaurant with rooms rather than a hotel, and it is clear where their heart and talents lie. Fair enough. They reinforce their priorities by insisting that the rooms are only available to those who dine at the auberge.

See **Port Launay** p. 120).

Map 1C	**LA CLARTÉ** (C. du. N.) 2 km E of Perros-Guirec

Le Verger
(H)S
La Clarté
(96) 23.23.29
Closed Sept.–
Whitsun

La Clarté is a hamlet and **Le Verger** is opposite the interesting old church. (Look at the coloured carved Renaissance figures of the saints in the porch.) It's an old stone farmhouse, with a nice green garden and its simple double rooms cost 90f each. Not at all a bad stop, only five minutes from numerous beaches, all very calm and peaceful, with no demi-pension compulsion. Two cheap restaurants are within walking distance.

Map 3A	**CLÉDEN CAP SIZUN** (Finistère) 10 km NW of Audierne

A pleasant alternative to the tourist-crowded D784 leading to the Pointe du Raz is to take the little D43, running further north through hamlets and past grey farmsteads to the village of Cléden. It's worth it anyway to see the astonishing church, with strange carvings of lichened monsters on the main porch and fishing boats lovingly portrayed on the west wall and south porch. Face to face with the gargoyles across the narrow street is:

L'Étrave
(R)S
(98) 70.66.87
Closed 29/10–25/3;
Wed.

A shock in a sleepy little village to push open the door of this tiny restaurant and be met with a babble of local voices all vociferously appreciating their Sunday lunch outing. You step down into a dark little room, with a handful of tables, shake the hand of the *patronne* behind the bar and settle down, perhaps to a no-frills splendid *langouste* on a 98f menu, or the 52f three courser, inclusive of wine. Wise to book.

Map 1B	**CLÉDER** (Finistère) 4 km W of St.-Pol-de-Léon

Le Temps de Vivre
(R)M
9 r. d'Armorique
(98) 69.42.48
Closed Mon.; Wed.
p.m.
EC.

It calls itself a pub-restaurant but that gives entirely the wrong impression. Jean-Yves Crenn's little restaurant may not look much from the outside, but inside ~~NEW MANAGEMENT~~ history and he is one of the most professional ~~NEW MANAGEMENT~~ district; this will be a sophisticated ~~NEW MANAGEMENT~~

Take the ~~NEW MANAGEMENT~~ menu at 90f (others at 45f or 140f) and try his specialities like *salade de ris de veau aux artichauts* the best of the fish catch. House Beaujolais good value.

Map 2G	**COMBOURG** (I. et V.) 24 km SW of Dinan, 37 km N of Rennes – *Mkt: Mon*

At the hub of six roads, a strategic staging post for many a voyage.

The mediaeval pile of a castle, where Chateaubriand lived as a youth, dominates and gives considerable character to the town. As does the lake to the south, so that the best approach is from the Rennes road, where the castle can be seen, looking down on the water, from some distance away; the pleasant leafy square beneath it, where Chateaubriand's statue stands brooding, is a good place to abandon the car. Decision time — watch the car passengers dart across the square to consult the menus of the establishments on either side before the important choice is made. About the hotels I have no doubt:

►**Hôtel du Château**
(HR)M
1 pl.
Chateaubriand
(99) 73.00.38
Closed 15/12–30/1;
Sun. p.m.; Mon.
o.o.s.
P. AE, DC, V.

I thought the rooms to go for here were those in the annexe, tucked away in a nice old stone building behind the hotel. Furnished with lots of character and good bathrooms, they are well worth 270f, but a reader who was there last year disagrees:

'We had a beautiful room for 155f with bath etc. — by far the largest bedroom we have had in any hotel. It was at the back, so no danger of noise. We could have paid more for a room leading out on to the garden, but why bother when Room 28 was such good value.' . . . Why indeed?

Very smart dining room, with big log fire in winter and substantial menus at 88.50f —

I had spider crab and my husband chose pâté, *then we had* porc à la crème *with a lovely sauce. A good cheeseboard, followed by* bavarois *and chocolate mousse.'*

There is also a boules pitch, terrace, children's games, so this represents a good-value comprehensive deal, and is arrowed accordingly.

'We stayed for a week and everything was right. The half-pension menu offered at least four different choices each day in both starters and main course and free choice of desserts and cheeses. The house wine we enjoyed was a very good claret. Mme Pele was a charming hostess and she has a happy and hard-working staff.'

Hôtel du Lac
(HR)S
2 pl.
Chateaubriand
(99) 73.05.65

A cheaper and very pleasant alternative is to eat here across the road, with a better view, right on the water's edge. Stick to the cheaper menus and you will be well pleased. They even do a 32f basic quick traveller's lunch — tomato salad, lamb chops with lots of *frites*, pud, all perfectly good — but it is the 64.60f version that I recommend. I'd keep it simple — my *terrine de saumon de mer, sauce cressonière*, proved a bit too ambitious, with an offputting khaki sauce, but husband's more cautious choice — six oysters, generous *gigôt d'agneau* and an untraditional *crème caramel* (delicate egg custard served with separate toffee sauce) was voted excellent value. I wouldn't stay there though — the bedrooms did *not* appeal.

La Charrette
(R)S
pl. de l'Église
(99) 73.00.60
Closed Wed. p.m.

Another cheaper and altogether different alternative at the other end of the town, more French, less touristy, all gingham, log fire, tin tables outside. Substantial menus start at 45f and go up to 110f for five generous courses. There are rooms, but I have not inspected, and I suspect the neighbouring church clock might be a sleep-disturber.

Map 2B

COMMANA (Finistère) 25 km SW of Morlaix

An isolated village in the foothills of the **Monts d'Arrée**, a strange wild region of rock and heather, rising abruptly from the surrounding flatness. Roc Travezel offers a rare panorama.

This is natural material for the Breton fondness for legends, and where else would you see a Will o'the Wisp or come across a *Kannerezed an noz*, a washerwoman condemned to spend eternity washing shrouds? If you should hear a strange tinkling, do not be tempted to investigate. It will be the Devil himself luring the avaricious by the clinking of coins.

The village is chiefly known for its fine *enclos paroissiale* (see p. 8) but there is another attraction:

Boutique du Bien-Manger 🦶
(R)S
pl. de l'Église
(98) 78.90.68

A row of dingy dwellings fronts the church; in one of them is my favourite Breton crêperie. Duck inside the door to find everything much as it must have been a hundred years ago; wood floors, scrubbed tables, benches, dressers, bunches of dried flowers and wicker baskets hanging from the rafters.

Their batter recipe is a secret — one I would dearly love to know — their fillings simple, the cost minimal. They also do other Breton specialities, like *Kig ha Fars* (a kind of *pot au feu*) and *poulet au cidre*, and sell rather upmarket preserves and honey.

Their card encourages lodging with the villagers, and the little tourist bureau a few doors away confirmed that this was possible in half a dozen cottages thereabouts. A double room with breakfast costs 80f – guaranteed to be an out-of-the-ordinary experience.

Map 4B

CONCARNEAU (Finistère) 24 km SE of Quimper – *Mkt: Mon, Fri*

A town of several faces: France's second fishing port,

particularly concerned with tunny, so it's lively year-round, with lots of real fish restaurants that don't have to depend on tourists. Its west-facing aspects across the bay are fringed with beaches and hotels, turning their backs on the industry going on behind them; its other completely self-contained attraction is the picturesque *ville-close*, a town within a town built on an island linked to the mainland only by two narrow bridges. Walk across them and enter a third altogether different world.

Deep inside the massive walls, built in the 14th century and completed in the 17th by the military architect Vauban, there is no feeling of a life outside those narrow twisting streets, old houses, souvenir shops and *crêperies* which cater for the snap-happy visitors, but take a walk round the ramparts (by ticket only, at Easter, then from May 1 to September 30) and the jig-saw slots together, with glimpses of channel, two harbours and town falling into place. Inside a former prison in the r. Vauban is the Fishery Museum, with a fascinating display of boats, marine creatures and 'preserved fish containers' (not always cans, since the first sardine preservers used glass not tin).

The Americans love the *ville close*; they also love the restaurant that nestles so attractively at the end of the main street:

Le Galion
(R)L
(98) 97.30.16
Closed 3/12–11/12,
4/2–7/3; Sun. p.m.,
Mon.
AE.

Well you have to laugh. Or else you'd cry at so large a bill for so little fill. For deriders of the *nouvelle cuisine* (not always me) this is a must for ammunition.

First impressions are totally disarming — **Le Galion** is a charming old stone building, full of flowers and warmth, discreetly elegant. The welcome is efficient as is the service — too efficient it turns out since all the rushing about up and down stairs and flourishing of trays laden with more flowers than food proves wearying. And the charm of having the chef personally to conduct you to your table and discuss the menu melts a little with the thought that he might be better employed in the kitchen.

The 110f menu has two starters — *poisson cru* and *mousseline de poissons, coulis de cresson*. Whichever one you don't choose, you get for free as *amuse gueule*. My *gueule* was not so much amused as assaulted by the fierce acidity of the raw monkfish, so I was pleased to have chosen the *mousseline* for the serious bit. Well, not serious perhaps — no-one could take the transparent slice, with dab of very solid *coulis* as a serious starter, so the arrival of second course *cuisse de canard* was keenly anticipated. That was the biggest laugh of all — a matchstick of a bone with the two adhering forkfulls of duck soon despatched.

From then on the amusement came from watching other diners' faces as their meagre lots were set before them. That of one bluff Yorkshireman we had met the previous night tucking with evident enjoyment into a vast *plateau de fruits de mer* at some humbler joint, was especially memorable as he poked dubiously at the two strips of *poissons mélangés en papillote* (monkfish again!) swallowed them in one go and sat back blinking in astonishment at the sheer cheek of the thing.

Hot goat's cheese was of the same liberality — a teaspoon on a *croûte* — and the *gâteau aux poires* wasn't generous either, even with its flamboyant flambéeing, but it was so nasty that it didn't really matter.

Evidently to eat real food one must abandon the rarified atmosphere *intra-muros* and cross back to the bustle of the town. As an antidote to the chi-chi I would recommend:

La Pêcherie
(R)S
20 quai Carnot
(98) 97.02.12
Closed Wed.

Refreshingly simple décor, all navy-blue and white, fishing nets draped on walls. No-nonsense fishy menus at no-nonsense prices, i.e. from 45f. The recommended 80f version offers langoustines, seafood brochette, etc. A plate of excellent mussels costs 24f.

La Coquille
(R)M
1 r. du Moros
(98) 97.08.52
Closed 20/12–20/1;
Sun. p.m. o.o.s.
AE, DC, V.

In the 'new' port, right in amongst the cargo ships, with a ferry to skip across from the *ville close*. The classiest of Concarneau's fish restaurants, but still good value, with a cheap menu at 65f. Tables outside and a terrace from which to watch all the harbour activity. Very pretty inside too, in a rustic kind of way, all beams and oil lamps.

La Douane
(R)M
71 av. Alain Le Lay
(98) 97.30.27
Closed Sun. p.m.

Locals are a bit miffed that their favourite caff has now gone upmarket, thanks to a rave in Gault-Millau. It's still a faintly seedy building, in a distinctly seedy street near the fishery sheds, and the decor is horrible — lurid coloured glass illuminating very basic basics, but nowadays Jean-Marc Peron calls his café *"restaurant gastronomique"* and proposes recherché dishes like *mignonette de lotte au poivre et pâtes vertes* alongside the straightforwards.

For those who not so long ago remembered Granny sitting in the corner knitting liners for sabots, and vast platters of seafood for next to nothing, the news is not good, but for those of us who never knew its salad days, **La Douane** offers a chance to sample excellent fresh fish (and some other dishes) interestingly served at comparatively reasonable prices. Good menus at 70f.

Chez Armande
(R)S
15 bis av. Dr
Nicolas
(98) 97.00.76
Closed Sun. p.m.;
Mon.

By the yacht harbour. Old-fashioned, with waiters in black jackets, and M. and Mme Dupais genial hosts to the many locals who regularly patronise this old reliable favourite. Good value straightforward dishes, mainly fish, all fresh and cheap.

Ti Clémentine
(R)S
quai de la Croix
(98) 97.21.05

A *créperie* facing outwards to the sea. It won the Gault-Millau gold medal a few years ago but I can't say I thought it extra special – just a good-enough *créperie*, but in a pleasant quietish position, tables outside and rustic within, particularly convenient for those wanting a late cheap meal.

For an extra good cup of tea, *pâtisserie* and ices, try **La Duchesse Anne**, 14 ave. Pierry Guey, not far from the Tourist Office in the harbour.

HOTELS

Nothing special in the town, so I made for the beaches. To the south is **Le Cabellou**, with a choice of sands, facing towards the town (blowing a gale) and out to sea (so sheltered that bikinis were feasible in May). On the former stands the well-known **Belle Étoile**, which I thought outrageously expensive even in its luxury bracket. An unexciting double cost 530f, with breakfast a steep 40f each on top, and the menus are just not worth the 150f starting price. Across the road in a quiet garden is the much more modest **Bonne Auberge**, a Logis de France, with rooms at 80–110f, but I stupidly missed the chance to look round, so first-hand reports particularly welcome.

Right at the opposite end of the town, facing across the bay of Concarneau on the Plage des Sables Blancs is:

Ty Chupen Gwenn
(H)M
(98) 97.01.43
Closed 6/5–12/5;
Dec.; Sun. o.o.s.

An unequivocally modern hotel, of the kind I usually shun as being boringly plastic. This one I have to admit has a lot going for it. The rooms are functional but graced with real furniture, discreet wallpaper and lots of personal touches. Most have a splendid balcony overlooking that marvellous view across the bay, and the white sands are just below. Not a large hotel — only 25 rooms — and so the management has time to be friendly and helpful. No restaurant either, so that full advantage can be taken of Concarneau's unusually good range of eateries.

Sea views cost 300f a double, rooms at the rear 200f, all with baths.

Map 5E

CONLEAU (Morbihan) 3 km S of Vannes, 109 km from Rennes

Take the Arradon road, D101, SW of Vannes, or follow Conleau signs from the port, to arrive at a little promontory in the Bay of Morbihan.

You can catch the ferry boat from here to the **Ile d'Arz**, if you don't have time to do the complete excursion round the bay — a very cheap way of getting at least a glimpse of the fascinating scenery. Set among the trees is a pretty chalet-like hotel:

The Roof
(HR)M
(97) 63.47.47
Closed 8/1–18/2;
Rest. closed Tue.
o.o.s.

It takes its name not from the present building but from the original, built at the turn of the century, whose multi-coloured roof was eccentrically steeply pitched.

We were unlucky with our room — this is a popular little hotel and even in late September it was full. Ours was hideously khaki/orange, poorly furnished and expensive at 260f, but even so the view outside redeemed the interior. When I managed to check the others, better furnished, some with better views and balconies, and all cheaper (180f) I realised we had paid for two extra unwanted beds. So ask for one on the first floor with balcony and avoid No. 10.

Le Roof.

Of course I don't know how over-crowded this might be in high summer — probably a favourite Vannois excursion, but I can heartily recommend it in the autumn. The food is particularly good — it really is more a restaurant with rooms than hotel — and you should certainly book a table in the pleasant dining room overlooking the water. There is an adequate menu at 65f, but we ate oysters, bass, good cheese and puds on the 100f version and were well pleased.

Map 6E   **LE CROISIC** (Loire-Atl.) 10 km from La Baule – *Mkt: Thurs*

A favourite excursion from the beaches, casino, sophistication of La Baule, across the strange and eerie salt marshes, is to the little fishing port of Le Croisic, which has managed to retain a good deal of the character, if not the importance, of bygone days. To the north of the spur of land that juts out from the Guérande peninsula is the busy harbour, divided by three islands into several basins. Sardines and crustaceans are the port's specialities but those with the will to be in the fish market before 10 a.m. will witness all manner of sea creatures being auctioned off.

A bustle of colourful fishing boats, a screech of scavenging gulls, and a promenade of holidaymakers is guaranteed, and very agreeable it all is too. At noon everyone crosses to the other side of the road to inspect the menus of the numerous restaurants and bars that face the water. One is spoiled for choice and indeed it is hard to go wrong, so obvious are the credentials of the fish served up fresh and simple all along the quays. By far the most enjoyable procedure is to stroll along with the crowd and make your own decisions, based on how much you are in the mood to pay for, décor, and at which end of the harbour you happen to be when the legs give in (quite a stroll from end to end).

We followed Michelin's recommendations and ate at **Filets Bleus** and **La Bretagne,** but I think we could have done just as well rather more cheaply had we followed the French families to any one of the more plebeian eateries. A biting wind was the cause of the best discovery, when at the extreme end of the harbour we turned in thankfully to the fug of:

L'Estacade
(HR)S
4 quai du Lenigo
(40) 23.03.77
Open all year
V.

Unpretentiously old-fashioned in the brasserie genre, full of families all tucking in to mounds of *moules,* plates of steaming fish and teeming *plateaux de fruits de mer.* Excellent value menus from 43f. The rooms are clean and cheap, at 66f for a simple double, to 120f with bath, but personally if I wanted to stay in the area I would cross the neck of the narrow peninsula to the south-facing **Port Lin.** A good sandy beach, and built right on the rocks looking out to sea is:

Grand Hôtel de l'Océan
(HR)M
(40) 42.90.03
Open all year

Generally thought of as a restaurant, and certainly an exceptionally attractive one with splendid ocean panorama and splendid ocean produce (allow 100f minimum), but I discovered a bonus in 19 elegant and unusually well furnished rooms, all with private baths for 194f.

I think the combination of such a comfortable base, superb food available in the restaurant, with a choice of alternative price-ranges nearby, the attractive site on the water's edge, with wild rocky coastline to explore, and the animation and local colour at Le Croisic, make a combination infinitely more attractive than La Baule's brassiness; I suspect an arrow as soon as I have some first-hand experience.

Hotel Les Nids
(HR)S
(40) 23.00.63
Closed 30/9–Easter
V.

A good, cheaper alternative, not nearly so smart as **l'Océan,** and lacking its sea views, but with a friendly family atmosphere and a pleasant peaceful garden. M. Audonnet has won first prize in the *Tours Gastronomique* contest in the category of *patron artistique* and there's no doubt that he feeds his guests imaginatively and copiously, on menus that start at 55f. It's a pleasant chalet type hotel, with balconies to most of the rooms, which start at 87.50f and rise to 190f for a double with bath.

Map 2F

DINAN (C. du N.) 51 km from Rennes, 187 km from Cherbourg – *Mkt: Sat & Thurs*

The 'Welcome to Dinan' sign on the approach road states firmly 'Ville médiévale, mérite une longue visite' and that's quite right. A gem of a town, one of the most attractive and interesting in

Brittany, and not to be rushed through on any account. Not that it's easy to rush in Dinan — in the main thoroughfares too much traffic crawls helplessly, in the old town the uneven cobbles and narrow pavements enforce a leisurely pace, with irresistible frequent stops to stand back and admire.

Dinan.

I would put Dinan top of my list for an out of season break, when coastal hotels are desolate. Always lively, with plenty of restaurants, dozens of *crêperies,* it is ideal for a long weekend without too much driving, as it is of course as a staging post on a longer journey into Brittany.

From very first view (try to make it from the Rennes road across the suspension bridge), thanks to its unique hilltop site overlooking the Rance, 'impressive' is the word. Ten bulky towers and four gateways punctuate the mainly 14th-century ramparts. A two mile walk to complete the entire circuit is highly recommended but if that daunts, for views of the surrounding country, the port and the river far below, a 'must' is the section enclosing the English Garden; on the site of an old cemetery, it makes a cool and pleasant spot to picnic in summer and even in February the mimosa trees are in unseasonable bloom.

If time, extend the walk to the Promenades of the Grands and Petits Fosses – ditches built in the 12th century to protect the city walls. The Grands Fosses from the Porte St.-Malo to the Tour St.-Julien is the best preserved section with gardens in the moat, and the Petits Fosses from the Town Hall to the Castle is now a cool avenue of lime trees, with a view over the Val Cocherel.

Penetrate further into the heart of the old town with camera well-loaded, record the photogenic crooked gables, pillars, beams of the old houses built for 15th-century merchants, whose trades are echoed in the street names – *Cordeliers, Merciers, Lainerie, Poissonerie.* In the rue l'Apport you can see the three types of half-timbered houses typical of Dinan: *à porche,* with upper stories supported by pillars, *à vitrines* with high casement windows built by ships' carpenters and recalling the sterns of ancient sailing ships, and *á encorbellement* with stepped out upper stories. The rue d'Horloge is one of the most picturesque, with its strange 15th-century clock tower enclosing four bells, one of them a gift from the ubiquitous Duchesse Anne. Stallholders used to sell their wares in the shelter of the arcades formed by the stubby granite pillars supporting overhanging upper stories; nowadays the fish market is open every day in the narrow rue de la Chaux, part of a tangle of a little streets round the Old Market.

The main market takes place on Thursday on what used to be a mediaeval fairground, the Places du Champ and du Guesclin, full of parked cars on other days. Hard to imagine now that this was the site of a famous duel between the renowned local warrior Bernard du Guesclin and Thomas of Canterbury, representing the Duke of Lancaster who had treacherously captured du Guesclin's brother. Du Guesclin spent most of his career in combat with the invading English, nearly always successfully, as in this case. So popular was he that after his death in 1380 four different towns claimed parts of his corpse, but it is in Dinan's St. Sauveur's church that his heart lies. In the gruesome business of sharing out the mortal remains, he is one up on the kings of France whose members only get distributed three-ways.

When the delightful meandering round the old city is

complete, take a closer look at the port, (where the pleasure boats take off for a fascinating trip up the Rance to St.-Malo in summer) by walking down one of the most beguiling thoroughfares in Brittany. It leads from the English Garden, via the rues du Rempart and Michel, into the rue du Jerzual and its extension, the rue de Petit Port, winding through the 500-year-old Jerzual Gate, between elegant houses now owned and restored by craftsmen, right down to the water.

Here refreshment is at hand, supplied by one of several pleasant bars and restaurants:

Les Terrasses
(R)M
(96) 39.09.60
Closed Nov.; Tue.

The best position, with tables outside making the most of its water's edge site. In winter the bar is animated with vociferous locals and the 65f menu is good value and the cheapest of these short-seasoned restaurants.

Le Relais Corsaire
(R)M
(96) 39.40.17
Closed Sun. p.m.;
Mon.

Opposite the Terrasses, classier, with a *vivier* and most attractive interior, all dark and beamy, and menus from 80f.

Les Merveilles des Mers
(R)M
(96) 39.86.54
Closed Tue.

The best food of the three to be found here, living up to its name with splendidly fresh seafood. Newish and highly recommended by discerning locals. Menus, which include oysters and sole, start at 98f, but this would be an excellent place to take a lunch of just a dozen oysters at 35f or a *soupe de poissons* for 25f.

Back in the town:

D'Avaugour
(HR)M–L
1 pl. du Champ
(96) 39.07.49
P. outside or in car park opposite
AE, DC, EC.

It must be twenty years since I first found the **d'Avaugour** and M. Quintin had already been its patron ten years by then. Not a lot has changed, which is good — 15th-century character un-plasticised, loads of charm still evident — and bad — silk moiré on bedroom walls could do with a re-cycle, bathrooms unlovely. The rooms are tiny for the 260f price tag and the plastic breakfast is a let-down, but it would still be my first choice in this enchanting town.

The food, too, is good in parts. Not expensive if you stick to the perfectly adequate menus at 80f or 100f, and of prime quality, but M. Quintin is over-generous with his sauces and the flavour of my succulent calf's liver was drowned in a sea of sweet orange sauce. Likewise the raspberry *coulis*, dark and delicious though it was, completely nullified the welcome sharpness of the fluffy blackcurrant soufflé.

This lavishness is praiseworthy when appropriate — to find eight scallops and a generous salad as an entrée on a 100f menu is remarkable, and my husband's 80f version with leek-stuffed blinis followed by *blanquette de veau* and *chausson de pommes* was all good and well balanced — but a little more restraint would make this a winner. Impressive wine list, with a good house wine, a red Saumur, at 40f.

However the vibes are good and M. Quintin achieves

miracles, rushing between kitchen and restaurant, with peculiar rocking gait induced by his unrelenting clogs. In fact, footware, grubby apron and over-involvement made me feel he would have been much more at home running a simple rustic bistro rather than the elegant **d'Avaugour**, which takes some living up to.

He's certainly trying hard though — in his pretty green-trellissed bar there is a 50f lunch menu on offer (65f with wine and coffee), whose no-choice three courses take some beating at this price, and in the summer he opens up another restaurant, **La Poudrière** (39.07.49) in a tower of the ramparts in his garden. There one will be able to eat the 80f menu in the cool of the 15th-century arched stone walls, or sit and sip at a garden table in the heart of the town.

I asked M. Quintin's advice for a cheaper base and he directed me to:

La Duchesse Anne
(HR)S
10 pl. du Guesclin
(96) 39.09.43

Pierre Malbet has recently taken over this dilapidated old black-and-white hotel on another side of the square and is giving it a complete re-fit. All the rooms are being re-decorated and equipped with modern shower rooms, and if they turn out to be as bright and cheerful as the downstairs restaurant, already re-vamped, they should prove a good buy at 100f a double. Demi-pension will be 140f per person or the menu is 42.50f. Reports welcome.

La Marguerite
(HR)M
29 pl. du Guesclin
(96) 39.47.65
Closed Jan.; Sun.
p.m.; Mon. o.o.s.
AE, DC, EC

A few doors away from the **d'Avaugour**, a spacious, bright Logis de France. Elegant restaurant with log fire in winter, serving menus from 47f. Comfortable modern rooms from 76–188f, but those at the front could be noisy. Good value for position and quality.

Hotel des Remparts
(H)M
6 r. du Château
(96) 39.10.16
Garage.

Built into the ramparts on the hill winding up to the Porte du Guichet, with hazardous parking and unloading. However, once inside, the hotel is unexpectedly modern and stretches spaciously back and away from the main road noise. All the rooms face away from the gear-changing. They are bright, clean and comfortable and cost from 109.50–173f a double, with cheerful management thrown in.

La Caravelle
(R)L
14 pl. Duclos
(96) 39.00.11
Closed Oct.; Wed.
o.o.s.
AE, DC.

Pass through an ordinary little public bar to find the attractive restaurant, starred by Michelin. If you are lucky enough to pick a good day, the 90f menu is an excellent choice, cooked by M. Marmion, a talented chef, but if, as was our fate, the no-choice dish of the day is a potentially boring grilled lamb chop (who knows — it could have been inspired?) you have a problem, since the *à la carte* prices are prohibitive. Most of the main courses are over 100f, and, what is even more unacceptable, so are the desserts.

There remains one other intriguing alternative — 36f *menu grillade* which I have yet to try. It seems incredible that for such a modest sum, in such an upmarket establishment, one could dine on grilled ribs of beef, preceded by saffron soup and followed by a choice of desserts (*can* they be the same 100f offerings?) but that's what the menu says, and for dinner as well as for lunch. If it's prepared to the *Caravelle's* usual high standards it must be the bargain of the year and it would be interesting to know of any experiences here.

Mère Pourcel
(R)M
3 pl. Merciers
(96) 39.03.80
Closed 22/12–1/3;
Sun. p.m. o.o.s.;
Mon.

Cannot be missed, in the centre of the old town, and worth visiting for the unique old staircase, dark like a liquorice stick, that forms the centrepiece of the elegant dining room. It's a lovely old-fashioned ambiance, with lots of service for your money and glowing displays of *tartes* and fruit to whet the appetite. The cheapest menu is 91.50f, except at lunchtime, when a 50f version offers three light courses – exactly what I would wish for at that time of day.

'We sat outside but would have been in the comfortable dining room if the weather had not been so good. We thought the four items on the first course were choices, but we got them all. They would have been sufficient for a midday meal' — Dennis Osborn.

Le Dauphin
(R)S
11 r. Haute Voie
(96) 39.25.66
Closed Wed.

The best cheap restaurant in the heart of the old town. *Cadre rustique* and friendly patron-cooking. the 45f menu offers six oysters or terrine of rabbit for starters, followed by three main dish choices, veg., cheese and dessert; for 52f you get nine oysters or stuffed *amandes* on the entrée choices, and the 78f version is a real blow-out with three main dishes and salad included. Locals' favourite and rightly so.

Map 1F | **DINARD** (I. et V.) 22 km N of Dinan – *Mkt: Tues, Sat*

A town of changing fortunes. Little over a century ago Dinard was a simple fishing village, but its sheltered beaches, gentle climate and magnificent natural setting at the mouth of the Rance enticed rich Americans and English to build expensive villas there among the palm trees and camellias, and it soon became the most fashionable resort not only along the Emerald Coast but in the whole of Northern Europe.

The villas, a little faded perhaps, are still there, and the luxuriant vegetation and the spectacular sands, but what would the Edwardians have made of the Grande Plage now, with its hot dog and ice cream stalls, plastic cafés and transistors? How unthinkable that the modesty of bathing carriages should have given way to the (almost) ultimate 'topless'.

The town is still a favourite with the Brits and I heard more English spoken here than anywhere else in Brittany. The cafés and souvenir shop accommodate their requirements. Only one luxury hotel remains — the outrageously expensive **Reine Hortense** — no starred restaurants, but plenty of bars and more modest accommodation

The building of the dam over the Rance in 1967 made access from St.-Malo by road a whole lot easier; an alternative is to take the ferry across. For my taste this approach from the eastward side of the town is the best, with the ramparts of St.-Malo and the old Solidor tower to look back upon and the splendid beaches of le Prieuré and l'Écluse, slightly less crowded than the one by the Casino, to view from the sea.

Arriving by car, park by the yacht club and take the utterly delightful walk along the water's edge — the Promenade du Clair du Lune — to get an idea of the past elegance and tranquillity of the place. Round a sudden bend, the Pointe du Moulinet, lies unexpectedly a deep and sheltered beach, the Plage de l'Écluse, unsophisticated and somehow rural, in contrast to the brashness of the main Plage de St.-Énogat just round the point. Not a lot there except:

Hôtel de la Vallée
(HR)M–S
6 av. George V
(99) 46.94.00
Open all year

An old-fashioned Logis de France, with good views of the water from the dining room and lots of expensive and very comfortable terrace chairs. A good place for at least a drink, if not a meal. Rooms from 97f up to 250f for one with bath and balcony. Menus from 70f.

Hôtel de la Paix
(HR)S
6 pl. de la
République
(99) 46.10.38
Closed 15/11–15/3

Right in the middle of the town and quintessentially French — slate roof, green shutters, rustic red dining room — even though nowadays the waiters all have to speak English. The terrace overlooking the main square is full of happy beer-drinking Brits, but a lot of locals recognize that this is probably still the best value eating in town, and once the serious business of lunch gets under way, there is no doubt about nationality. Interminable menus, starting at 48.90f. Rooms at 63–168f, but since everyone's attention was fully engaged in lunch, I didn't look at them. Could be noisy.

La Plage
(HR)M
3 bvd. Féart
(99) 46.14.87
Closed Wed.

A pleasant middle-of-the-road Logis de France, modern, light cheerful, not far from the main beach. Some of the best rooms (250f) have sea views, all are well-equipped. It has the bonus of an unusually good restaurant **Le Trézen**, with menus from 55f, so demi-pension here would be a good bet at 212–243f.

Altaïr
(HR)M
18 bvd. Féart
(99) 46.13.58
Closed 15/12–15/1;
Wed. o.o.s

Yet another Logis, of very different character. This one is in a nice old town house, very French. It is best known for its restaurant — the no. 1 in Dinard. The food is simple but interesting — *flan de moules, truite rosé aux deux sauces* — on menus which start at 51.70f for three courses, up to a piggy 195f for six that includes half a lobster, but the 73.55f version is the one I would go for. All are served in a dining room full of polished old furniture, with an apéritif perhaps on the sunny terrace.

The rooms, which I asked to look at as an afterthought, were a pleasant surprise. All very different, some modern, some (nos. 2 and 4) delightfully antique, at 86–190f. Friendly and helpful chef-patron M. le Ménager.

Map 2G

DOL-DE-BRETAGNE (I. et V.) 26 km NE of Dinan, 54 km N of Rennes, 175 km from Cherbourg – *Mkt: Sat*

An ancient frontier town, where the severity of Breton architecture mingles with the softer Norman influences. The oldest house in Brittany is here, along with several other noteworthy mediaeval and 17th-century buildings, in the Grand'rue des Stuarts. St.-Samson, named after a 6th-century Welsh saint, is a vast granite cathedral, rather grim on a grey day with its blank western face and uncompleted tower, but indicating the erstwhile importance of the town. John Lackland burnt down the original cathedral in 1203, and, overcome with remorse, paid for its reconstruction. Inside gets better, with its Great Window of 13th-century glass and 14th-century choir stalls.

Locals say that an underground passage links one of its towers to Mont Dol, the hump rising oddly out of the fertile polders below. Prehistoric mammoth, elephant, and rhinoceros bones have been dug up on this strange mound which was once an island, when the sea lapped the escarpment on which Dol is built.

One of the most impressive dolmens in Brittany is to be found just a mile or so south of Dol on the Epiniac road. It fell out of the sky, legend has it, to divide the armies of two aggressive brothers, waging such bloody war that the field is known as Champ Dolen, or the Field of Suffering. They say it sinks one inch every 100 years and when it disappears altogether the world will come to an end, so hurry hurry — only another 31 ft to go.

I find Dol a sad town nowadays, mourning its past perhaps, but there's no doubt it's strategically a valuable stop, on the way west or south, and I was particularly anxious to find a likely hotel here. Not a lot of excitement though.

La Bresche Arthur
(HR)M
36 bvd. Deminiac
(99) 48.01.44
Closed 1/11–1/12
AE, DC, V.

Used to be everybody's favourite but now a bit plasticised. Rooms are clean and good-sized, however, from 160–180f. M. Faveau is keen on regional specialities, and there is a cheap quick lunch menu at 49f.

Hotel de Bretagne
(HR)M
pl. Chateaubriand
(99) 48.02.03

Outside looked highly promising but the interior is shabby and gloomy.

I did make one find though — a restaurant that would certainly cheer up the journey:

Les Roches Douves
(R)M
80 r. de Dinan
(99) 48.10.40
Closed Mon.
AE, DC, V.

Exceedingly pretty in an old beamy kind of way, with a huge stone fireplace dominating the tiny dining room. Splendid 80f menu offering interesting combinations of mostly *nouvelle cuisine* ingredients, including expensive items like *pleurottes* (wild mushrooms) enlivening guineafowl or *saumon cru* marinaded in lime.

Map 3A — **DOUARNENEZ** (Finistère) 22 km NW of Quimper

Mkt: Mon, Fri, Sat

Powerfully fishy. No doubt that its heart lies around the harbour; this part is vibrant and full of atmosphere, the rest of the town grey and drab. If, like me, you love watching fishing boats arrive, screeching gulls convoying, unloading their glistening heaving catch on the quays, or wandering round a busy fishmarket in the morning, wondering at the size and variety of the specimens, make for Rosmeur to the east of the town. Connected by a bridge to the west, narrow little Tréboul is for pleasure craft.

In the beautiful bay of Douarnenez they say lies the drowned city of Ys. Listen hard when the air is still and you may hear its bells ringing after fifteen centuries of submersion! The King of Cornouaille, Gradlon, reigned here, over a debauched population, who modelled themselves on his licentious daughter Dahud. So incensed was God at the immoral goings-on that he handed over the town to the Devil, who lost no time bedding the larky princess and persuading her to open the sluice gates which held back the tide. King Gradlon escaped on a galloping horse but Dahud got her come-uppance at last — she disappeared for ever beneath the foaming waters.

The legend persists in many forms — when the tide is at its lowest you have only to look for yourself to see the remains of Ys buried in the sands. Which should work up an appetite for:

Bar de la Criée
(R)S
Terre-plein du Port
(98) 92.43.43
Closed 1/10–1/4

Just as I'd hoped — a real, no-messing, honest fish restaurant in the port. This one has a surprising position. You enter what looks like a bleak office — it's the port authority building — climb bare tiled stairs to the first floor and there, encircling the building, is a room with a view and a half, over the harbour, across the bay, and out to sea. The view is the décor. Comfortable homely ladies — the patronne is Mme Reyrat — bustle about delivering vast *plateaux* of the freshest seafood (250f for two). Serious lunchtime eating starts early, finishes late.

The 50f menu includes 8 oysters for starters, you get *lotte* on the 98f and *langouste* on the 150f, then cheese, then pud. *Cuvée de la maison* (house wine) is 18f. The separate bar is open in the evenings too. Highly recommended for serving its purpose so well.

Le Feu Saint-Elme
(R)M
17 r. du Port
(98) 92.37.05
Closed Sun. p.m.;
Wed.

New, small, and very pretty, in a side street just above the port. Friendly young owners specialise in *langouste*, so this could well be the place for a special at 38f for 100g. Order lobster in advance at 200f for 600g, otherwise there is a good lunchtime menu at 55f (not Sun.) and others at 70f and 135f.

I have a hunch this might be a star, but have yet to eat there myself, so all reports particularly welcome.

Closed

Le Tristan
(R)M
25 bis r. du
Rosmeur
(98) 92.20.17
Closed Wed.

Bag a table by the window for the best view over the harbour from this little restaurant by the port. Seafood of course, on a 70f menu. Popular and small, so booking advisable.

Interesting hotels found I none, but perhaps in any case Douarnenez is more a place to visit than to lodge in.

Auberge de Kerveoc'h (HR)M *(98) 29.07.58 Closed 1/11–1/4* V.	5 km from Douarnenez, signposted west off the D765 Quimper road. A lovely old stone farmhouse converted into a comfortable hotel, with fourteen rooms, at 175f, rather over-furnished in the grand style, with swagged curtains around the bed and flock wallpaper. The dining room is more in keeping with the farm origins — stone flags, log fire, rush seated chairs and beams, and the menus start at a modest 55f, with the usual predomination of fish. Cooking is traditional, unflashy.

Demi-pension is insisted on during the season but any time this would make a relaxing quiet retreat, with green surroundings, pond, terrace, from which to explore the whole of Cornouaille, and I suspect it only lacks a confirmatory visit to earn it an arrow. Reports particularly welcome therefore.

Map 5D **ERDEVEN** (Morbihan) 9 km NW of Carnac

Auberge du Sous-Bois (HR)M *(97) 55.66.11 Closed 16/10–1/4*	1 km on the Port Lorois Road. A granite building set in the pine trees. Straightforward grills in the restaurant (from 52f) and clean functional rooms at 180f.

Map 1E **ERQUY** (C. du N.) 40 km NW on Dinan

A little fishing port, famous for its scallops, nestling under a spectacularly beautiful headland. Rather disappointing as a resort, but around it lie ten beaches to choose from, according to wind direction and inclination for fine sand, as at Caroual, or more private rocky coves. The best bit is around by the harbour, where lots of cheap cafés serve simple fresh fish. Saturday morning market.

L'Escurial (R)M *bvd. de la Mer (96) 72.31.56 Closed Tue. p.m.; Wed.* AE.	Most unpromising first impression — yellow plastic sign, in a block of flats by the dingy harbour, with a flashy mermaid to greet you at the door, but press on if you wish to eat the best scallops, straight from the boat. Usefully open on Sundays and Monday, and in winter too, when the seafood is reinforced with game.

Menus start at 66f and creep up to 265f for five courses including the lot, *via* apéritif, through lobster, best wines chosen to complement the food, coffee and *digestif*.

Map 3B **LE FAOU** (Finistère) 19 km N of Chateaulin, on the N170 Brest road – *Mkt: Sat*

Side by side on the wide market square, with its 16th century covered *halles*, stand two very popular hotel/restaurants, recommended to me by more than one local gourmet/ gourmand, the **Vielle Renommé** (98) 81.90.31, Closed Sun. and the **Relais de la Place**, (98) 81.91.19, Closed Fri. The first is old and famous and the second has a Michelin red R, so they obviously merit a good look; alas, so popular are they that I have failed to get in to either of them, so reports particularly welcome.

We had to settle, much disgruntled, for:

Crêperie la Malle Poste
(R)S
(98) 81.00.08

As so often happens, a virtue appeared out of necessity and here was a find. 'Find' is the *mot juste* because the **Malle Poste** disguises itself behind an antique shop in an ancient slate house in the main street leading to the bridge. You have to strike out down an alley, through a dubious door and up some dark stairs to arrive at a pleasantly raftered room with copper pans, dried flowers, wooden floors. All very basic, but so cheap and good.

The savoury *crêpes* come in two varietes, dark (*blé noir*) or light (*froment*), and range from 5f for a simple *au beurre* to their speciality, *fruits de mer*, at 27f, but most of the French eating there were tucking into the menu, which, at 43f, offered splendid value — *soupe de poisson* or *moules*, steak or pork, *tarte aux pommes* (and a good one). *Moules* were 25f, as was a ham omelette or a pork chop, steak was 35f and the kids had *omelette* and chips for 12f. So you can see what a good family stop it is, especially as a *pichet* of house wine set our personal price record low at 7f.

Map 4B

FOUESNANT (Finistère) 15 km SE of Quimper on the D44

Mkt: 3rd Fri.

The best Breton cider of all comes from Fouesnant, surrounded as the little town is by apple orchards. There is a festival of the apple trees on the first Sunday after July 14, which is a good time and place to see the traditional costumes of Fouesnant, as is the July 26, the *pardon* of Sainte-Anne.

Hotel d'Armorique
(HR)S
33 r. de Cornouaille
(98) 56.00.19
Closed 7/10–1/4;
Mon. o.o.s. P.

A splendidly French little hotel in the main street, run by the famille Morvan. Go through the popular bar to an unexpectedly charming dining room, giving on to a courtyard, with a great wall of hydrangeas, whose summer colour spills over into the room.

Comprehensive menus at 56f, 64f and 85f include plenty of shellfish. On the middle price we ate six oysters, two generous *rougets* crumbed and pan-fried in butter, and a home made *crème caramel*. M. Morvan cooks straightforward food and plenty of it, all excellent value, plus several Breton specialities, like a vast *cassoulet Breton*. Try the local cider, of course.

The bedrooms are fine; old-fashioned ones are in the main house and newer with all mod. cons. in the annex in the garden, from 80–205f. Good for families.

I cannot fault this one in its modest class for value for money, good honest food and smiling welcome, and the arrow is well deserved.

Arvor
(HR)S
pl. de l'Église
(98) 56.00.35
Closed Nov., Thur.
o.o.s.
P. V.

Do not despair if the **Armorique** is closed. Further up the main street on the other side is a nice old building, the **Arvor**, where good rooms cost from 95–180f and menus start at 48f. Lunch only o.o.s.

Map 2H	**FOUGÈRES** (I. et V.) 40 km S of Avranches – *Mkt: Sat*

Even the 'new' Upper Town is dominated by the massive castle dating from the 12th century down in the valley of the Nançon. Situated on the border of Normandy, it was obviously an important mediaeval fortress and it was the surrounding lakes and marsh land that secured its impregnability.

It's a fair old puff up to the Upper Town, the centre of a shoe-making industry. Some of the streets and houses here are old and interesting too, with a colourful covered market in the rue Nationale, leading to the best view of the mediaeval town and valley from the park, the Place aux Arbres, a good place to get your breath back and perhaps enjoy a picnic. You can complete the tour by taking the rue des Vallées and the Escalier de la Duchesse Anne down the side of the valley, crossing the bridge to the Place de Marchix, the town's oldest and most interesting quarter.

All very fascinating and obviously well-sited for an overnight stop but I have yet to discover a lodging possibility. The **Hotel des Voyageurs** near the central parking could be noisy and one reader points out that there is no sitting-room and only the bar to breakfast in.

I could recommend its restaurant, however:

Restaurant Les Voyageurs
(R)M
9 pl. Gambetta
(99) 99.14.17
Closed 17/8–6/9;
Sat. o.o.s.
AE, V.

A red Michelin R for the 60f menu, popular with the locals (but then there doesn't appear to be anywhere else to go!)

Map 4B	**LA FORÊT-FOUESNANT** (Finistère) 16 km SE of Quimper

A village at the head of La Forêt Bay, busier nowadays because of the vast yacht harbour opened up at Port-la-Forêt across the estuary. Market day Tuesday.

Hôtel de l'Espérance
(HR)S
pl. de l'Eglise
(98) 56.96.58
Closed 11/10–25/3

A little Logis set back from the road, behind a garden and terrace. It manages to retain a lot of character — white shutters, stone-walled dining room — along with the mod. cons., and is popular with locals and regular tourists alike, so booking advisable. A simple double room costs 99f and the most expensive, with bath, 189f. Menus start at 50f.

Auberge St.-Laurent
(R)M
6 r. de Beg-Menez
(98) 56.98.07
Open all year

2.5 km E of the village on the Concarneau road. The prettiest restaurant in the neighbourhood, flowery of windowbox, cosy with log fire, and authentically beamed. A can't-fail stop, with menus at 55f and 107f, more enterprising than most; good value (ten oysters for starters) and interesting *quenelles d'homard*.

Manoir du Stang
(HR)L
(98) 56.97.37
Closed mid-Sept.–
mid-May

Signed off the D783 heading north. A stunningly beautiful 16th-century manorhouse, set in a hundred acres of parkland. You can feel the green tranquillity settling as you approach through an avenue of ancient oaks. A *stang* is a large lake; here there are several and their watery vistas dominate the view from house and garden. Roses and hydrangeas abound, climbing round the house and set in formal, very French, flowerbeds. 'Idyllic' is the only word. When I did a sneak Easter preview the drive was carpeted with primroses, the trees in early bud and the birds noisily celebrating; I think it's a pity that the hotel doesn't open its doors to the public until so late in the year.

The rooms vary enormously in size and aspect, as you would expect from a building not built as a hotel, but all those I saw were utterly charming, furnished with antiques and gentle colours, *toile de Jouy* curtains, good bathrooms. Demi-pension is obligatory, at 720-920f for two people per day. The food is unremarkable, but well-served, in a pleasant atmosphere.

A lovely place to spend the odd couple of luxurious days, and with 26 rooms it is often surprisingly possible to get in on short notice.

Map 1F

FRÉHEL (C. du N.) 50 km NW of Dinan

The highest point on the Emerald Coast, with probably the most spectacular views in Northern Brittany. To approach it from Sables d'Or at sunset is a never-to-be forgotten experience, since the colours of the porphyry and red sandstone cliffs, towering 225 ft above the water, glow with technicolour intensity; dark shapes of wheeling migratory birds, for whom this is a natural sanctuary, punctuate the brilliance. The coastal panorama stretches from the Cotentin peninsula to the Ile de Bréhat, with the Channel Islands visible in particularly clear weather. Round the Anse de Sévignés is the mightily impressive fortress, the Fort la Latte, almost entirely sea-girt, mediaeval origins, more wonderful views. Ten minutes walk away is:

Le Relais de Fréhel
(HR)M
(96) 41.43.02
Closed 15/11–15/5

Originally an old Breton farmhouse, stone walls, mansard roof, into which are set some of the rooms, none of them large, but offering simple calm comfort. From 100–140f, but demi-pension is obligatory in high season at 145–290f. The food concentrates on grills and seafood; menus from 70f.

Map 4F

LA GACILLY (Morbihan) 58 km SW Rennes, 16 km N of Redon

We discovered La Gacilly by chance; some of the canals were shut for their winter clean-up and we were asked to return our boat not to Malestroit, whence we had first set off, but to La Gacilly. This enforced détour gave us one of the most attractive stretches of water to explore — the narrow, peaceful little river Aff. It also gave us the opportunity to spend a night in the basin by the falls in La Gacilly, a charmingly picturesque and flowery artists' town. Their workshops line the narrow streets — the woodworker, the jeweller, the weaver, the basket-maker and the leatherworker, all beavering away unselfconsciously in view of the perambulating visitors, for whom La Gacilly is obviously a favourite excursion. There are several bars and small restaurants to assuage the pangs brought on by all this exercise. The best is undoubtedly:

Hôtel France et Square 🔼
(HR)S
(99) 08.11.15

A simple old-fashioned hotel in the main street, serving simple old-fashioned meals at 38f and with rooms here and in its smarter annexe at 66f to 138f.

Map 3D

GOUAREC (C. du N.) 118 km W of Rennes on the N164

Mkt: 2nd Sat

Nothing special about this little town on the intersection of the Nantes–Brest canal and the river Blavet, but if, following the Nationale, on the way west, an overnight stop were required, here is the answer:

Hôtel du Blavet 🔼
(HR)S
(96) 24.90.03
Closed 29/10–
23/12; Feb.; Sun.;
Mon. o.o.s.
P. AE, V.

A pleasant little hotel overlooking the Blavet, with friendly patronne, Mme Le Loir. The bedrooms are all comfortable and well-furnished, but no. 6 is a joy. Four-poster, bath, view over the river, all for 211f. Cheaper rooms from 80f.

The dining room also enjoys the soothing water aspect and M. Le Loir dishes up his traditional specialities — no skimping here — on menus from 50–220f. Recommended and potential arrow.

Map 4B

GOUESNACH (Finistère) 6 km N of Bénodet

Aux Rives de l'Odet
(HR)S
(98) 54.61.09
Closed 20/9–29/10;
Mon. o.o.s.

First reaction was annoyance that this little Logis had misled me by its name into expecting something pretty on the banks of the river Odet; in fact it is a dull little building in a dull little village, with no riverbank in sight. On reflection, though, I am including it as a rare example in these parts of a really simple, really French hotel/restaurant, only ten minutes away from gorgeous beaches. The fact that it stays open in winter is significant — it feeds locals not tourists.

I went back a second time to see what was on offer and found one of the best value meals around, cooked by patron M. Le Nader. No choice and different every day; 50f bought home-made soup, *langoustines mayonnaise, foie de veau* and dessert. Simple rooms cost 70–125f.

Map 1G

LA GOUESNIÈRE (I. et V.) 12 km SW of St.-Malo

Hotel Tirel
(HR)M
(99) 89.10.46
Closed 17/12–17/1;
Rest. closed Sun.
p.m. o.o.s.
AE, DC.

1½ km north of the village on the D766 Cancale road, opposite the station, this is the **Hotel Gare** but known to all the locals by the name of its owners, the Tirels. Not sure I would have picked it without the guidance of a Michelin star, but I'm very glad I did.

The large dining room is the kind of plush the French love, velvet swags, tassels, awful oil paintings, tented draped ceiling, fake panelling, fake brick, fake marble, but definitely not fake food. Set in the middle of nowhere, it's a pleasant surprise to find it always full, warm and lively.

No need to look beyond the excellent 80f menu, but the most

popular order around was undoubtedly the lobster, for which the hotel is renowned. As I can never work out how much the grams are going to cost me, I stuck to the menu and was delighted with my *terrine de trois poissons Guillaume Tirel, foie de veau de vieux vins*, superb cheeseboard and blackcurrant mousse with fresh raspberry sauce. Home-made bread full of nuts and the *feuilleté* nibbles arrived in great profusion, even though I was clearly not going to be the night's big spender. My modest bottle of Bourgueil cost 53f, but the elaborate wine list included bottles in the 900f range.

The hotel part, in another building at the back, is ultra-modern. Someone has gone mad with the wall-to-ceiling carpet, but it's all very comfortable and well equipped, and good value at 180f with bathroom (cheaper rooms from 90f). The staff, mostly family, are friendly and efficient and the whole set-up is a pleasant experience, but it's all bigger than you'd think and 50 rooms means party bookings, so prior reservation for both hotel and restaurant is wise.

Map 6F **LA GRANDE BRIÈRE** (Parc Régional) N. of La Baule

If any proof were needed of Brittany's infinite variety, I would point to the Regional Park of La Grande Brière. Within a few kilometres of La Baule's sophisticated sands, a mere half hour's drive from the wild cliffs of the Croisic peninsula, or St.-Nazaire's industry, or the popular yacht harbour of Roche Bernard to the north, lies this strange other world of marsh-canals; granite islands support whitewashed cottages whose peasant owners have cut reeds to thatch their own roofs and journey by flat-bottomed punts (*blains*), not automobiles.

The coming of spring and the draining of the flood waters are signals for myriads of wild flowers to cover the rich low-lying land. Fields of yellow iris precede the exotic waterlilies. All around there is an explosion of flora and teeming of wildlife. Birds and fish literally abound.

Since many of the young Brièrons are deserting to the towns, a problem facing the remaining inhabitants is how best to maintain the delicate balance between encouraging tourism and continuing their simple peasant-style existence, living off the land, carrying on traditional occupations of thatching, breeding ducks and geese, cutting peat. The natural charms of this unique area could so easily be swamped. Some of the residents are happy to take you for a boat ride and it's a time-warp experience to glide through the expanse of glittering water along labyrinthine routes known only to the locals, with just the plop of the puntpole and sometimes the whirring of powerful wings overhead to break the depth of the silence.

A few roads cross the marshes and one of them, the D50, north from Montoir de Bretagne, leads to what is probably the best preserved village, Fédrun, entirely surrounded by water. You can visit a traditional Brièron cottage here, white and thatched, and engage a boatman guide.

Map 1G	**GROUIN, POINTE DU** (I. et V.) 5 km N of Canale

A finger pointing NE into the Bay of Mont St.-Michel, with the Mount swimming on the horizon to the right and a panorama of rocky headlands as far as **Cap Fréhel** to the left. The offshore **Ile des Landes** is a bird sanctuary and the inhabitants can be well observed by the energetic who care to take the marvellous walk towards Cancale, *via* the beaches and sheltered bays of **Port-Mer** and **Port-Pican** down to the little cove of **Port-Briac**.

Hôtel Pointe du Grouin
(HR)M
(99) 89.60.55
Closed 30/9–
Whitsun; Rest.
Closed Tue.

The privileged position, with views from all its windows across the bay, brings this well-known Logis a steady stream of customers. The impression, I have to say, is that it is too steady, and not a lot of *accueil* need be extended to ensure a full house.

With those views, those beaches, those sheltered coves, I think I'd be happier with a picnic, but the hotel is all very well-groomed, with an elegant dining room where excellent seafood menus start at 78f for four courses, rising to 109f for five. Rooms, none with bath, are from 98–220f. Booking definitely advisable.

Map 5F	**GUENROUET** (Loire-Atl.) 21 km SW of Redon, 86 km from Rennes on the D2

A very attractive section of the river/canal system that lattices Brittany is south of Redon on the wide river Isac. Dense foliage, writhing roots, a certain stillness, kingfishers blazing a shining darting trail, all confuse the senses. Tarzan-territory, Breton-style.

This is a favourite stretch for fishermen, who line the banks, hunched in silent contemplation, or sit back to back like bookends in ancient flat-bottomed boats.

The odd modern roof in the trees surprises by its incongruity — villages are rare in these parts and not particularly attractive. Guenrouet has a church, a *boulangerie*, a couple of *charcuteries*, a bar and a plastic restaurant, but down by the water, a step from our night's mooring we found a treasure:

►**Le Relais St.-Clair**
(R)S
(40) 87.66.11
Closed Tue. o.o.s.
P.
DC, EC, V.

A new patronne, Mme Geffray, has made this little restaurant by the bridge on the D2 into one of the most agreeable stops along the waterways. The first-floor dining room has a splendid view over the water, with a smart little rustic bar and white tables on the patio — a good choice for an *omelette* or *crêpe* lunch.

Classy place settings, smiling efficient service and excellent value. For 43f we ate perfect *soupe de poissons*, grilled country ham or fresh river trout, good vegetables, salads and pud. House wine is 32f and there is more ambitious food on 78 or 130f menus.

Arrowed for good value, pleasant situation, helpful staff.

Map 6E	**GUÉRANDE** (Loire-Atl.) 6 km N of La Baule – *Mkt: Sat*

One of the most delightful aspects of Guérande is its unexpectedness. Rising unpredictably from the strange chequerboard of the salt pans is this encapsulated mediaeval town.

An unbroken coronet of 15th-century ramparts, ten towers, four gates, surrounds highly photogenic old streets, squares and churches. Stroll from the Place du Marché au Bois to St.-Aubin, *via* the rue St.-Michel, which leads into the heart of the mediaeval town. The church was founded in 852 but was rebuilt between the 14th and 16th centuries, with a strange exterior pulpit flanked by two angels' heads.

Not difficult to guess from a look at the map that Guérande must be a popular excursion for holidaymakers seeking diversion from sand and sea, and there are plenty of cafés and little restaurants to refresh the tourist. There is also a perfectly delightful little hotel:

Roc Maria
(H)M
r. des Halles
(40) 24.90.51
Closed 11/10–1/4
V.

Cross the square from the church and look left to find, tucked away in a cul de sac, the picturesque old house in a flowery courtyard. Simple rooms are 165f and there is no restaurant, but that should prove no problem. You could try:

Fleur du Sel
(R)M
r. de la Juiverie
(40) 24.79.39

An attractively light restaurant in another street of old timbered houses. Interesting menus start at 72f. For a light lunch, my *terrine de poissons aux trois sauces* met the bill (28f) very nicely.

Map 5C

GUIDEL (Morbihan) 12 km NW of Lorient

La Châtaigneraie
(H)M
(97) 65.99.93
V.

Well signposted 1 km W on the D162. Drive down a leafy avenue to reach this smart little manorhouse, all spic and span, in a rose-filled garden. It is immaculately furnished in Directoire style, and the bedrooms, though small, are attractive and well equipped with modern bathrooms. At 280f (all double beds — no room for twins) it is not particularly cheap but does have many advantages. Only 5 km from the beaches, blissfully quiet, no restaurant so no compulsory eating in, and, with only ten bedrooms, room for the personal touch from the nice and friendly patronne. A safe inland bet.

Map 2D

GUINGAMP (C. du N.) 32 km W of St.-Brieuc

On a steaming July Saturday, with the colour of the market stalls vibrant in the sun, there was more of an air of gaudy Provence than grey Brittany in the square; here were fountains, lime trees, awnings protecting great piles of Cavaillon melons and peaches limp in the airless heat, and plump farmers' wives fanning themselves with newspapers. Even the frightened rabbits forgot their trauma and dozed in their hutches.

Very pleasant was Guingamp then, with its cobbles, old houses, cathedral viewed from a café table complete with cool beer; it had looked altogether different in winter, on a non-market day, uniformly grey, with through-traffic clogging the square. The one constantly agreeable factor:

►**Relais du Roy**
(H)M, (R)M–L
42 pl. du Centre
(96) 43.76.62
Closed 1/9–15/9;
Sun. p.m. o.o.s.;
Mon.
AE, DC.

A 17th-century grey stone house facing the market square, with a wonderful Rennaissance door inside its courtyard. Lots of other ancient features discovered in unexpected quarters, like the stone carved chimney breast in the corridor. Which leads to the seven rooms set in the quiet of the rear of the building. All are furnished elegantly and well equipped with modern bathrooms — good value at 200f.

The whole establishment is smart and well-run, with M. and Mme Mallégo very much in attendance in their attractive dining room. They resolutely maintain that it is possible to serve traditional cuisine that is not boring, enlivened with a certain individual touch. This generosity of quantity and quality would make the **Relais** an ideal base out of season when heartier appetites need satisfying.

Lots of meat as well as seafood appear regularly on the menus, which leap from 85f to 160f. If the cheaper menu, no-choice, happens to suit, you'll get a bargain, but if you weaken towards the *carte* it will cost around 200f, so it's worth checking to see what's on offer. Certainly on my last visit the braised pork *plat du jour* would not have appealed on such a sultry day.

An arrow for cossetted luxury at a reasonable price and superb traditional cooking.

Map 2G

HÉDÉ (I. et V.) 23 km N of Rennes on the N137 – *Mkt: Mon*

It takes eleven locks for the Canal d'Ille et Rance to climb up to the hilltop village of Hédé, whose ruined castle, old houses and colourful gardens cling precariously to a rocky ridge. Below, the Valley of the Windmills makes a tranquil respite from the main road, with lovely walks along the canal banks.

Vieille Auberge
(R)M
(99) 45.46.25
Closed 25/8–31/8;
Feb.; Sun. p.m.;
Mon
AE.

Tucked away from the Nationale among the popular trees, with a pleasant terrace where you can eat on fine days, is Marcel Leffondré's little inn. His cooking is skilled but unfussy, ingredients superbly fresh — red mullet served with a mousse of sorrel and a sharp blackcurrant ice cream melting imaginatively into warm apple slices. I recommend the 109f menu.

Hostellerie Vieux Moulin
(HR)M
(99) 45.45.70
Closed 15/12–31/1;
Sun. p.m.; Mon.
V.

You'd think, wouldn't you, that two inns in the same community would see to it that they didn't close on the same days, but no — the dreaded dead Sun. p.m. and Mon. prevail. For the rest of the week this one is also old, also very picturesque, with attractive dining room serving less-upmarket, cheaper menus than the **Auberge**, starting at 65f. It does have fourteen rooms, from 90–150f, which I have not yet managed to look at.

Map 5D — HENNEBONT (Morbihan) 137 km SW of Rennes

Château de Locguénolé
(HR)L
(97) 76.29.04
Closed 16/11–1/4;
Rest. closed Mon.
P.
AE, DC, EC, V.

 R

 H

Outrageously over-priced accommodation. Our modest back room cost 540f, a bad buy only surpassed by that of our friends, whose attic walls were livid with vinyl flowers of species unknown to nature — a far cry from the classy French wallpapers and elegant bedchamber they had been looking forward to. An absence of hot water at bath time and holes in the stair carpets made us even more convinced that a stay here was not a good idea.

A pity, because the setting is magnificent. The squat bulk of the not-very-ancient château, more impressive than beautiful, commands a striking view through the wooded hills, down the rough-cut lawns to a wide sweep of the river Blavet. Little boats and water-skiers animate the view in many an American lens. The grounds otherwise are a disappointment to English gardeners, all unpruned rosebeds and straggly grass, with the swimming pool's temperature uninvitingly chilly.

So forget the bed and concentrate on the board. Altogether another story. Here is money well-spent indeed. The two cheapest menus at 190f and 280f looked only moderately interesting, and the 370f version is designed for those on a restricted international diet — *foie gras*, lobster, fillet steak and out of season strawberries. So we felt entitled to eat *à la carte*. The four hours from eight to midnight passed ecstatically, the 'oos' following the 'aahs', preceding the 'mms'. Will those who feel ill/disgusted/jealous please turn the page:

Amuses-bouche (gratis) — almond-shaped mounds of salmon mousse, pigmy shrimps of a translucent coral petalled daisy-style round the (porcelain) plate, a baby galantine of cubed ham, flecked with sweet peppers and herbs, set in an aspic gentle of texture, rich in flavour, a wine glass of minted melon balls, peach-coloured, wine. And more to come one might well ask? Ah yes . . . a cold *entrée* of sole fillets, swiss-rolled around a fishy/herby mousse, garnished with crayfish, sharpened with a crunchy tomato *coulis*, or a palette of white and green turbot in a sorrel sauce, artichoke hearts and stuffed baby lettuce parcels. Then a great flourish to remove the silver domes protecting the main course — a whole shoulder of pink baby lamb between the two of us, coated with herby crumbs, stuffed with black olives, whose smokiness permeated right through the tender slices.

The sweet trolley! Our unstinted selection of chocolate *marquise*, wild strawberry tart, *fromage blanc* mousse and nectarines coated with apricot sauce was arranged with such consummate artistry that we felt not greedily guilty but self-congratulatory at our clever selection.

The bill was astronomical and worth every penny.

Map 2F — LA HISSE (C. du N.) 7 km NE of Dinan by the D57

Just a couple of bars by the little yacht basin, where the bridge crosses the Rance, and some very pleasant walks along the river banks. High above the river is:

Auberge du Val de Rance
(HR)S
(96) 39.16.07
Closed Sept.

Amazing value in this little country inn, with friendly young owners. 33f for the dish of the day, or 46f for three courses, including eight oysters! the bedrooms are in a separate stone building, clean and attractively furnished in country fabrics; 70f for a simple double or 110f, with shower. Highly recommended, but Mme Lemoine did say that she receives lots of English in the season from a nearby camp-site, so I can't vouch for its exclusivity.

Map 3C | **HUELGOAT** (Finistère) 24 km S of Morlaix

Mkt: 2nd & 4th Thurs

The most popular inland tourist attraction in Brittany, as the lines of coaches and parked cars testify. They come to this area of mammoth mossy rocks, cool beechwoods, rushing streams heard not seen between the piled boulders, not only for the beauty of the place but for its atmosphere. The tourist authorities have taken full advantage of the legends that have proliferated since the days of King Arthur, and there are well-signed routes to follow to the Devil's Grotto, the Trembling Rock, the Rock Chaos, the Virgin's Kitchen, the Chasm, and many more attractions. Maps and ideas from the tourist bureau for short strolls or more ambitious hikes, all fascinating but populous.

The town centres on a lake, which used to be more romantic before someone built a housing development on its banks. The wide main street is charming and very Breton, with its old grey houses and colourful market stalls most days of the year.

I didn't think much of the restaurant and hotel scene — so often disappointing in tourist centres. **Ty Douz** has a good setting overlooking the lake, but the food was banal and the service harassed, and the **Hôtel du Lac** looked very tired indeed. There is a little hotel, **An Triskell**, up the hill on the Plében road, but the orange vinyl wallpaper and the weedy garden put me off. The **Auberge de la Truite**, 7 km away at Locmaria Berrien, is a famous restaurant with rooms (and a Michelin star) but sadly Mme Le Guillon is now in her eighties and changes are afoot.

I suggest a day visit only, with a picnic to eat in the woods.

Map 4B | **ILE TUDY** (Finistère) 10 km SE of Pont l'Abbé

A narrow spit of land that juts out into the estuary of the Pont l'Abbé river, with a good view of all Loctudy's fishing boats opposite and of the Anse de Bénodet to the right. The *haute marée* is most impressive from this vantage point, when the spring tides flood the narrow winding alleys of the little village.

This is a real fishing village, not an instant holiday resort, and is correspondingly picturesque. It tolerates the tourists at summer weekends, accepting that some of its residents gain their livelihood through them, but once the parking lot is empty, it settles back happily to the serious business of putting the world to rights in the bar of:

Hôtel Modern
(HR)S
9 pl. de la Cale
(98) 56.43.34
Closed Sat. o.o.s.

Lovely, scruffy not-so-modern hotel on the front, where the fishermen noisily congregate. Splendid cheap menus and not so splendid cheap rooms. Sit outside on a hot day for a lunch of *langoustines* (50f) or *moules* (25f) or indoors for a prolonged wet Sunday comforter of three courses for 56f. Other menus are 70f and 82f and a room costs from 80f to 120f. Full pension is 185f.

There are several other bars and a *crêperie* to choose from but the **Modern** is the friendliest and liveliest.

Map 4E

Mkt: Sat

JOSSELIN (Morbihan) 72 km E of Rennes on the N24

A more attractive approach from Ploërmel than the main road is to take the D122 and D123, which follow the canal through pleasant wooded countryside. Josselin is a delightful little town, familiar from many a poster showing the turrets of the Rohan family's home, half palace, half fortress, reflected in the river Oust. Josselin de Rohan-Chabot, the 14th Duke de Rohan, has been the town's mayor for over twenty years.

They say the best viewpoint is from the Redon road but I can assure you that it's only from the pit of a small boat tied up in the castle's shadow that its full immensity can be realised. Those towers rear up for ever.

From the river they make an impressive example of mediaeval military architecture, but the façade over the main courtyard is altogether different, extremely elegant, ornamented with lacy stonework on balustrades and window frames. Look for the letter 'A', crowned and surmounted by the emblem of Queen Anne — a girdle — and accompanied by the royal fleur de lys. The castle is open 2–5 p.m. in summer every day, and on Thursdays, Sundays and fêtes from April to June.

Josselin.

Old slate-roofed houses climb the steep hill to the basilica of Notre Dame de Roncier — Our Lady of the Bramble. Legend has it that eleven hundred or so years ago a peasant found a glowing statue of the Virgin in a bramble bush that never lost its leaves, winter or summer. He carried his prize away but the next day it was back in the bramble bush. Twice more he removed it, twice more it returned, to indicate firmly the place where the Virgin wished a chapel to be built in her name, The present basilica is mostly Flamboyant Gothic; it is renowned locally for the great *pardon* which centres on it on September 8, and whose strange name of the Procession of the Barkers also concerns the Virgin Mary. It seems she once asked, in the guise of a beggarwoman, for a glass of water from some Josselin housewives, who turned her away. As a punishment she condemned them to bark like mad dogs at Whitsun and on September 8. Their barking and frothing only ceased when they were brought into the basilica and made to kiss the holy relics. Since then many epileptics are said to have been cured by similar tactics.

For the less spiritual refreshment, Josselin is well equipped. Following local recommendations, we bypassed the more obvious claim of the **Hôtel Château** and climbed the main street, to find a little Logis:

►**Hôtel du Commerce** 🏠 🏠
(HR)M
9 r. Glatinier
(97) 22.22.08
Closed Mar.; Tue.; Wed.

Surprisingly elegant inside, with delightful dining room high above the river, full of French. Big log fire in winter, copper pans, strings of garlic confusingly assorted with smart tapestry chairs and expensive *couverts*.

M. Blot (*maître-rôtisseur,*) is chef–patron. All his menus are interesting and the 48f version particularly good value. For 77f he offers three different kinds of oysters for the first of four courses. Husband took his neat — nine giants — one friend ate hers grilled with almonds and pronounced them as delicious as they looked and the other enjoyed his hot, stuffed with herbs and garlic, while I, allergy-restricted, had to content myself with a *terrine de poisson* (no hardship). Double rooms are from 85f–160f.

Recommended for good value, good food, in a charming town.

Hotel du Château
1 r. Général de Gaulle
(97) 22.20.11
Closed Feb.; Sun. p.m.; Mon. o.o.s.
P.
V.
🏠

How right we were to follow local advice rather than all the other guidebooks. The **Château** has the prime position, right opposite the castle, dining room overlooking the river, but this of course makes it the obvious tourist attraction. If you get a table in the window you do get a good view, but the aspect is north and no sunlight penetrates into the vast and gloomy room. The welcome is just as cold.

The menu at 55f wasn't bad but in no way comparable with the **Commerce**. I found it all so depressing I didn't penetrate as far as the bedrooms, but there are 36 of them, from 120–200f.

Map 1F   **LA JOUVENTE** (I. et V.) 7 km S of Dinard

Take the D114 immediately after crossing the barrage, signposted La Richardais. La Jouvente is a hamlet well marked to the left.

►Manoir de la Rance
(H)M-L
*Château de
Jouvente,
Pleurtuit, Dinard
(99) 88.53.76
Closed in winter
except by prior
arrangement*

This one I really am tempted to keep to myself. Till now it has been bliss to telephone Mme Jasselin and be fairly confident that there will always be a room for me, preferably no. 2, which to date is my favourite hotel room in France.

It is not philanthropy that persuades me to tell all, but the sad conviction that the truth will out, and if I don't spill the beans, someone else will soon take all the credit for having discovered the Manoir and Mme J.

The view from her house I find hard to describe purple-prose-less. The wide river Rance lies just beneath; left, right, or centre there is a choice of vistas of sparkling green-fringed water, bobbing boats, beaches, coves, in infinite variety. I do it less than justice.

It used to be known as Château de Jouvente but there is nothing grand about its *châtelaine*, my favourite, indefatigable, Mme Jasselin, who bobs about tirelessly tending her beautiful English garden, all old-fashioned roses, lily of the valley and Mrs Sinkins pinks — not at all garish French-coloured. There are espaliered paths contrived with tantalizing glimpses of the water below, a tented retreat should the midday sun glare and, best of all, the terrace, glass-sheltered from the wind, so that

Manoir de la Rance.

even on doubtful days the tan can be acquired while reclining on expensive *chaises longues*, appreciating that view.

The house gleams. From the burnished copper in the hall to the polished antique furniture, to the modern bathroom fittings, elbow grease has not been stinted. Flowers everywhere. When did I last find a welcome of fresh garden roses in my hotel bedroom?

All the rooms are lovely, but no. 2 is the best. The view of the river below encircles the occupants, filtered through the tall windows draped with elegant blue *toile de Jouy* curtains. Yellow bedspreads on twin beds, grey carpet, antique furniture, spacious bathroom. I could not wish for better.

Dead on the appointed hour, be it ne'er so early, breakfast arrives, Mme J. puffing a little from carrying laden tray up the beautiful yellow carpeted staircase. At last a real breakfast! Home-made apricot jam, a pot of farm butter, lots of coffee and hot milk, hot croissants and brioches, all served in pretty china.

I try hard to find a fault, and fail. No restaurant, which means no bar to enjoying St.-Malo and Dinard down the road. Drinks and coffee readily served on the terrace and permission to picnic there at lunchtime. Absolute tranquillity, and what a site!

It amused me to read that the Oriental Hotel in Bangkok had been elected as the Best Hotel in the World. I can only conclude that the judges have never visited the **Manoir de la Rance**. The rooms are twice as large, twice as comfortable, the river below ten times more beautiful; as for the service — I'd put my money on Mme J. beating any Thai flunkey up the stairs. All at a fraction of the price (200–320f).

A close runner-up for ''L' Hotel of the Year.

Map 1B	**KERBRAT** (Finistère) 5 km SW of Roscoff
	A truly beautiful beach, with sheltered sand dunes and a stream running through.
Le Ressac (R)M *(98) 29.90.34* *Closed Thurs.*	A smart little restaurant, with views over the water, newly opened by Odile and Christophe Bouvet. Their predominately fishy food is not particularly cheap, with menus starting at 90f, but there are surprisingly few seafood restaurants in the area and none in so attractive a site; the locals tell me it is well worth the money.
Map 3B	**KERLAZ** (Finistère) 5 km E of Douarnenez on the D107
Chez Tante Jeanne (R)S (98) 92.28.11	A nice little bistro, none too common in these parts, open every day and usefully on the main road, making a good stop for, say, a splendid platter of mussels or a comprehensive 55f menu.
Map 2E	**LAMBALLE** (C. du N.) 40 km W of Dinan by N176
Mkt: Thurs	The Tourist Office now occupies the 16th-century executioner's house facing on to the Place du Martray (Graveyard Square) in the centre of this important livestock market town. Horse lovers

will no doubt wish to visit the National Stud, from 12.30 to 4.30 p.m. 'except during the covering season', which I am informed is from 10/2–15/7, when the stallions go off on a prolonged orgy all round Brittany.

Not far away from the Stud the Gothic-Romanesque church of Notre-Dame de Puissance stands on the promontory once occupied by the castle, with a fine view over the valley of the Gouessant.

The popular old **Hotel Angleterre** is now part of a chain but still retaining a lot of individuality is:

La Tour d'Argent
(HR)S
2 r. Dr. Lavergne
(96) 31.01.37
Closed 8/6–23/6;
12/10–27/10; Sat.
o.o.s.
AE, DC, V.

The hotel part is in a side street off the main square, away from traffic noise. Simple comfortable bedrooms from 82–200f. Some 500 yards away down the hill by the roundabout is the black-and-white restaurant. Once inside the ancient building, though, the picture changes; through the cheerful bar there's a smart new dining room and menus, popular with the locals, from 42f. Relais Routier give it a casserole for good regional cooking.

Auberge du Manoir des Portes
(HR)M–L
La Poterie, 2 km on
D28.
(96) 31.13.62
AE, V.

Our Coldest Hotel of the Year. In an unseasonable March snowstorm there was no heating turned on in the bedroom when we arrived, chilled and weary, at tea-time. Leaving the electric radiator to do its best, we thought tea by the fire in the lounge might do the trick, but the whole conversion from old grey stone manorhouse to hotel has been done so much on the cheap that the wind howled around the ankles, and bellow at the reluctant embers though we might, it was an overcoat-round-the-knees hour perforce.

Along the vinyled corridor of the wing across the courtyard the rooms are depressingly dark and cramped, with tiny high windows and plywood fittings — rotten value at 250f — but the water was hot in the midget-sized bath and we cheered up a bit at the prospect of dinner.

Not much warmer in the dining room, though, and perhaps that made it harder to evaluate the food fairly. Certainly the menu was disappointing: *hors d'oeuvre*, singularly flavourless *gigôt,* poor cheese-board and a fair *tarte aux poires.*

The best bit was the huddle round the fire afterwards. All the guests were English (it's in every known guide) and we huffed and puffed sociably to persuade the logs to glow and settled down with a cognac or four. The general consensus was; service friendly, rooms poor and overpriced, menu boring, but *à la carte* excellent. Those who had eaten fish were particularly pleased.

So the advice here is not to stay unless you're desperate, but consider eating *à la carte* (allowing 200f), in summer, when the courtyard and surrounding rural calm can be appreciated.

Map 2B | **LAMPAUL GUIMILIAU** (Finistère) 4 km S of Landivisiau

I had not intended to write at length about the *enclos paroissiales* and churches of this region, and indeed could not as far as those of Lampaul Guimiliau are concerned, since no words of mine could do them justice. If you wish to see but one example, I can only urge you not to miss this little village, buy a guide in the ossuary-turned-bookshop, and prepare for a very special experience inside the church. Allow plenty of time to take in all its treasures, from the first blast of colour to the detailed craftsmanship of the font, rood beam, astoundingly beautiful reredos, Entombment, and Pietà, whose six faces I guarantee will stick in your mind long after any gastronomic experience I can lead you to.

 There is a modest little modern hotel here, **l'Auberge de l'Enclos,** but I spent so much time in the church I never got round to looking at it.

Map 2B | **LANDERNEAU** (Finistère) 44 km SW of Morlaix

The estuary of the Élorn narrows here and is crossed by the picturesque 16th-century Rohan Bridge, one of the few in Europe on which there are occupied houses. It takes its name from the ubiquitous Rohan family who held the town in fief, and joins two bishoprics, Léon to the north, and Cornouaille to the south. The quays are named after them.

It's an agreeable town, with a lively Saturday market and many old houses, especially around the church dedicated to St. Thomas of Canterbury, a reminder of the trading links with England. Take a stroll along the quayside and perhaps some refreshment at the bar built out over the water, all most civilised on a fine sunny day.

Le Clos du Pontic
(HR)M
r. Pontic
(98) 21.50.91
Rest. closed Sat.
lunch; Sun. p.m.;
Mon.
EC, V.

An odd turreted house set peacefully in a shady garden some ten minutes walk (uphill!) from the town centre. Unexpectedly at the rear is an uncompromisingly modern wing with 32 bedrooms each with all mod. cons. and bath, at 180f.) Pleasant restaurant and interesting meals from 62–188f.

L'Amandier
(HR)M
55 r. de Brest
(98) 85.10.89
Rest. closed 1/8–
15/8; Sun. p.m.;
Mon.
AE, EC, V.

Even more aggressively modern but in discreet taste and of higher quality. This one is on a main road but the entire hotel was restored in 1984 and all the rooms are soundproofed, even the ones at the back. Well-equipped, they cost from 160–250f. Nice little green courtyard and lounge, and smart dining room, with good menus for 60f.

Restaurant de la Mairie
(R)S
9 r. de la Tour
d'Auvergne
(89) 85.01.83
Closed Tue.

Behind the lively bar there is a delightful restaurant with an appealing menu at 49f, offering several Breton specialities. I wouldn't mind betting this one merits an arrow, but as it is so far, alas, unvisited by me, it will have to wait for confirmatory reports.

Map 3B	**LANDÉVENNEC** (Finistère) 33 km NW of Chateaulin

To the north of the Crozon Peninsula take the D60 off the D791. Well worth making this diversion to the little hooked peninsula to appreciate the contrast of its soft greenness and freak Mediterranean climate, which allows even palm trees to flourish, with the harsh greyness of the rest of the area. But that's not the only reason; Landévennec is an instantly charming villlage, starting on a hill above the bend of the wide and gentle river Aulne, and flowing down past the old lichened church to the little landing stage, with pleasant vistas of estuary and trees all the way. Good walking country, with suggested routes well signposted. There's an old ruined abbey there, with the tomb of the once bawdy King Gradlon, converted to Christianity and a life of sobriety here by St. Guenolé, son of a 5th-century British nobleman. It was Guenolé who founded the monastery that was to become Landévennec.

Abundant atmosphere brings discerning tourists and so does:

Beauséjour 🚩🚩
(HR)S
(98) 27.70.65
Rest. closed Mon.
p.m. P.
V.

Friendly M. Renard runs this little family hotel, with splendid views from most of the bedrooms and the restaurant. For 169f you get a double room with bathroom and that absorbing frame of river and boats, but cheaper rooms come at 85f. Menus (fishy of course) start at 65f, and the restaurant is very popular locally so booking is wise.

A possible future arrow, I feel, lacking only a few more favourable reports.

Map 1C	**LANNION** (C. du N.) 63 km NW of St.-Brieuc – *Mkt: Thurs*

A most agreeable town on the river Léguer, with a wonderful Thursday market, that spills over from the river banks and extends up the steeply climbing old streets. Worth arranging your holiday schedule around this weekly burst of colour. At any time it is a pleasure to explore the pedestrianised area, lined with old houses, that leads up to the pl. Général Leclerc. Not particularly worth the effort, except for the masochist is to climb the 142 steps (I counted 'em all out and I counted 'em all back) to the church of Brélévenez, a Templars' church, remodelled in the Gothic period, where the promised view doesn't include, as I had hoped, a panorama of river and estuary, but only the more recent roofing of this ancient town.

Park by the river and discover **Jean-Yves Bordier**, the cheese shop *par excellence.* Allow at least fifteen minutes to wait while the young and knowledgeable owner shakes each customer's hands and discusses his needs. Tell him when you want to eat your favourite cheese and he will select it for you accordingly. Light worlds away from picking up a hunk of Irish Cheddar in the local Co-op.

Just opposite is:

Le Serpolet
(R)S
1 r. Félix le Dantec
(96) 46.50.23
Closed Sun. p.m.;
Mon.; Sat. lunch

A nice old stone restaurant in a quiet street just by the parking on the Quai de Viarmes. Small, dark, cosy, with charcoal fire, perhaps best on colder days.

Alain Gloud calls his cuisine *'traditionnelle soignée'* but perhaps he's too young to remember the time when salmon didn't come in escalopes and raw fish was not on every menu. However, he certainly mingles the two disciplines charmingly and the value he offers is superb. You get two courses for 49.50f or three for 66f and these include oysters, and the said salmon, which was served *à l'oseille* and very tasty too. Husband's *pièce de boeuf* was a bit tough but otherwise we could find little to fault and where else would you get a generous *salade aux asperges et noisettes* on a 66f menu for starters? *Porc aux abricots* came with the best of both worlds, fanned out attractively, *noove* style, but of a quantity rarely found in the more expensive restaurants that deviate from the traditional.

Cheese came from across the road, impeccably chosen by Jean-Yves Bordier, and the raspberries with a *coulis* of strawberries were extravagant and refreshing.

The relaxed welcoming atmosphere is much appreciated by the young-married age group (most of whom were intent on the 130f menu) so booking advisable. Recommended as unusually interesting food in this price range.

Otherwise the restaurant/hotel scene is not brilliant in Lannion. Two possibilities, uninvestigated, are the brand new **La Gourmandine**, up by the cinema, an old stone building lovingly restored by the charming young couple who run the *crêperie* on Trébeurden beach. Just charcoal-grilled meat, *crêpes*, ices, but open attractively late in a town drastically short of evening diversion; or there's **Les Pastorales**, another pretty little new restaurant not far from the Mairie in r. du Mal. Foch. They do a special children's lunch for 45f which speaks worlds about French children's tastes – 6 snails, home made *terrine*, lamb chop or roast chicken, then *tarte aux pommes* or sorbets, with a glass of fruit juice thrown in. Grown-up specialities like *pigeons en bécassine* on menus from 60f.

Hotels are dismal. Better make for Le Yaudet (see p. 173).

Map 6D

LARMOR BADEN (Morbihan) 16 km SW of Vannes

A little fishing village on a promontory, facing south, with splendid views towards the entrance of the Gulf of Morbihan. From here you can take the boat to the **Gavrinis** tumulus, said by Michelin to be 'The most interesting megalithic monument in Brittany and perhaps in the world.'

There is a better-known, smarter hotel in the village, but with an infinitely better position is:

Les Isles 🍴 🍴
(HR)S
(97) 57.03.31

Water laps the terrace when the tide is in; when it recedes there's a little beach below. The hotel is faded, somewhat scruffy, but so peaceful, with such a unique view, so very cheap, so very friendly, that shortcomings should be forgiven. A double room costs 70f, or if you can run to 140f (try!) you get a private bath and a balcony from which to observe that fantastic panorama of islands. Food is simple and predictably fishy on menus from 55f and locals like both the restaurant and the bar.

Map 5C

LARMOR-PLAGE (Morbihan) 6km S of Lorient

The seaside escape for the Lorientais and fast becoming their dormitory suburb. However the village still has a pleasantly unsophisticated air about it, with a large market place centring on a Gothic church, with some remarkable 16th-century polychrome Apostle statues in its side porch. A charming ancient custom is still respected: whenever a warship leaves Lorient on a long tour of duty, it salutes Our Lady of Larmor by guns, and Our Lady replies by hoisting tricolour and saluting the ship with bells.

A pleasant beach curves round the bay facing across to the citadel at Port Louis; I don't think I would suggest a holiday here, but if you find yourself in the area when a meal or bed are indicated you could certainly do worse than make for:

►**Le Beau Rivage**
(HR)S
(97) 65.50.11
Closed 1/11–10/12;
Rest. closed Sun.
p.m.; Mon.
AE, DC, V.

Overlooking the water, pleasantly old-fashioned, very French, very popular with regulars and I don't blame 'em. It's *the* place for fish – any fish, cooked any way you wish. You name it — they've bought it fresh from the boat that day — bass, brill, sole, turbot, *langoustines*, oysters, mussels — prepared and cooked with utmost distinction even in this area of good seafood. The clever patron, M. Roic, knows of course that the best way to show off the freshness of his fish is to serve it unadorned, but he is not averse to adding pure gold to the lily with a perfect *hollandaise, béarnaise, sauce au beurre*, or indeed to cooking his scallops in Sancerre. He even chances his arm by combining *langoustines* with home made *foie gras* and pine nuts, and gets away with it.

Stout ladies in pinnies push the sweet trolleys round. The puddings are simple — *îles flottantes*, fresh fruit salad – and the cheeseboard is good, but nothing to overshadow the fish.

No concessions, even to décor — plastic rampant — it's serious eating here. Only the certificates of gastronomic merit round the walls indicate something special. The lights fused halfway through dinner, which didn't matter a bit. Everyone lit their own candles, which improved the décor immeasurably, and went on eating.

Menus at 59f, 70f, 125f, 150f and 175f, so you can make it as cheap or memorable as you feel inclined. *Gros Plant* costs 35f.

We needed an antidote to the previous night with Carnac Plage's international luxury — a little Gallic simplicity — and had no difficulty finding it here. Coveting the best front rooms (with bath 150f), we firmly put in our place — 'booked months ago' — and sure enough on all five balconies sat a smug French couple complacently viewing the seascape. For us it was a hump up three flights to the last available attic room, with equally fantastic view but no balcony. No bath either, but the shower was efficiently fierce and at 85f we were happy enough

to forget the cold lino. Certainly I couldn't have staggered much
further after taking full advantage of M. Roic's cooking.

A simple no-frills place, arrowed for superb good-value.

Map 1D	**LÉZARDRIEUX** (C. du N.) 5 km W of Paimpol

Mkt: Fri

By the bridge that crosses the wide estuary of the river Trieux,
up the hill into the wide market square, where nothing much
seems to happen, and left on to the Pontrieux road:

Du Trieux 🏆 🏆
(R)S
(96) 20.10.70
Closed 15/9–28/9;
20/2–4/3; Sun.
p.m.; Wed. o.o.s.
V.

How pleased we used to be to tie up the boat at the end of a long
sail, at the safe anchorage in the river at Lézardrieux, knowing
that we had only to puff up the hill into the village to find a real
French meal at **Le Trieux**. The old creeper-coloured restaurant,
miraculously, hasn't changed much. It hasn't smartened itself
and its prices up, it hasn't gone all *noove*, it still offers
remarkable value, and, unlike most nostalgia, is every bit as
good as I remembered it. Super fishy menus at 50f.

Relais Brenner
(HR)L
(96) 20.11.05
Closed 3/11–23/3
AE, DC, V.

About as different as could be. A modern, very smart
establishment, named after its owners, offering luxury
accommodation at luxury prices. Much better inside than first
impressions indicate, with wonderful views down upon the
estuary. The rooms are exceptionally comfortable, the dining
room extremely attractive, the service most efficient. Rooms
cost 270–450f, meals start at 120f. Relais et Châteaux.

Map 1C	**LOCQUIREC** (Finistère) 22 km W of Lannion

*Mkt: Wed in
season*

Super little port and lively seaside resort. The tide recedes for
miles, leaving three wide sandy beaches. On the south-facing
one I saw more 'topless' than anywhere else on this coast,
which I attribute more to the shelter of the harbour wall than to
any particular laxness of local morals. A substantial stream
trickles through the east-facing beach, making serious paddling
possible at all states of the tide; Les Sables Blancs, facing north
out to sea, has fine sand, lots of rocks, fewer bodies, so there's
something for everyone here.

Overlooking the port is:

🏆 🏆

Hôtel du Port
(HR)S
(98) 67.42.10
*Closed Sept.–
Easter*

Simple friendly family pension with downstairs bar; all the
rooms have views of the sea, and some have terraces from
which to check up on all the harbour comings and goings. Good
basic rooms from 97–150f, *pension* 180f, menus from 70f.

**Grand Hotel des
Bains** 🛉
(HR)S
(98) 67.41.62

Closed Sept.–Apr.

Prime position, surrounded by sea views; large old fashioned
family hotel, obviously extremely popular and extremely full of
regulars who meet up here every year. They were draped all
over the extensive cliff-edge gardens in recliners and on
benches, playing tennis, chatting and socialising, making a very
lively atmosphere.

All rooms were taken so I could not check, but they are
certainly cheap enough at 120–140f a double, with bath or

shower, many of them having balconies from which to admire the fabulous view over the peninsula. Full pension insisted on for July-September, at 120–130f, which represents amazing value.

Map 3B **LOCRONAN** (Finistère) 22 km NW of Quimper on the D63

Mkt: 1st Tues

A living musuem of a town, almost too picturesque to be true. The large paved square, featuring an old well, is surrounded by a stage setting of grey Renaissance houses, built at a time when the canvas industry brought prosperity to the town. Nowadays the textile tradition has been revived in the shape of weaving and knitting; nearly all the old buildings house craft centres.

The town took its name from a 9th-century Irish monk, Ronan, after whom is named the imposing church on the square. Take in the best view of it from the cemetery, with a calvary in which St.-Ronan and the Virgin flank the crucified Christ, before going inside to see the stone vaulted roof, rare in Brittany, added in the 16th-century to the 1420 origins. The ten medallions round the pulpit relate the story of St.-Ronan's adventures. The saint's tomb is in the adjoining chapel, Le Pénity, which, sadly, is increasingly being eroded by the underground springs.

If you happen to be around Locronon in 1989 you might be lucky enough to witness an almost unique cermony, the Grand Troménie, an eight-mile procession through the countryside, following St.-Ronan's supposed route. It takes place on the third Sunday in July every six years, to the solemn sound of drums, stopping at 44 resting places where arched branches shelter statues from the local parishes. The faithful process up the mountain to a block of granite known as St.-Ronan's chair, which the locals have no doubt is the boat in which the saint sailed from Ireland to Armorica. In other years, on the same day, is the Minor Tronénie, a mere three miles long.

Locronan has more than its share of tourists to feed and water and caters for them with several bars, a *crêperie* and two restaurants. Right in the square is:

Au Fer à Cheval
(R)M
(98) 91.70.74
Closed 11/11–15/12
AE, DC, V.

Well-known and popular restaurant; if you bag a window seat on the first-floor dining room you get an elevated view of that stunning square. Don't be put off by the noisy bar down below. Menus from 50f.

The management runs a hotel by the same name, a kilometre or so outside the village signposted off the D63, but the best I can say for it is that it is certainly functional and (excruciatingly) modern. 35 plastic rooms cost from 160–270f.

Much more to my taste is:

Le Prieuré
(HR)S
(98) 91.70.89
Closed 1/10–2/11;
Mon. o.o.s.

A pretty old granite *Logis* at the entrance to the village, with a nice dining room and attractive country-style bedrooms. Mme Jézéquel told me that the new ones in the annex were even better, but they weren't functioning as early as Easter, when I was there. Good value at 125f for a double with bath. Menus are not exciting, but par for the course at 60f.

►**Manoir de Moëllien**
(HR)M
(98) 92.50.40
Closed 4/1–15/3;
15/11–5/12; Rest.
closed Wed. o.o.s.
P.
DC, V.

3 km N on the C10, well signposted. The grey 17th-century manor house was the home of Chateaubriand's lover, Thérèse de Moëllien. Very impressive is the approach down a tree-lined drive to carved stone gateway guarded by two lions, as is the manor itself, and particularly appealing in the summer when banks of hydrangeas soften the harshness.

The present owners, M. and Mme Le Corré, found it in ruins and lovingly restored it as a restaurant. Chef Bruno Garet gives excellent value for money in what could easily be a tourist trap, since the manoir features in many guidebooks and is a Château Hotel and a Relais du Silence. The dining room is lovely — beamed, log fire, elegant *couverts*.

So far so good, but on our last visit the service let the side down badly. Having obeyed the instruction to be in our seats by 8 p.m., the 1½ hour wait for first courses seemed unreasonable and as the delay became more and more evident the atmosphere in the dining room grew tenser. Conversation hesitated and almost died, as appetites remained unsatisfied. Dirty looks were exchanged to make sure that precedence of arrival was strictly observed. When the food did come, it was excellent but we fell upon it (marinaded salmon) with such indecent haste I don't remember much about it. We ate on the 100f menu (could have been 65f) and apart from the numb bum situation, it was one of the best meals of that particular tour. My scallops were superbly fresh and generous. Lightly poached, it can't have been them that took the time in the kitchen.

Husband's straightforward tastes were very happy with *carré d'agneau à l'ail et au thym* — four little loin chops, perfectly pink and gently herbed. Vegetables were unusually good and so

Manoir de Moëllien

were cheeses and desserts, but the occasion had been spoiled irrevocably and we were relieved to eat out the second night of our stay.

The bedrooms are very quiet and comfortable, in an annex contrived from the old stables. French windows are the only ventilation, which might prove a hazard in summer for stiff-upper-lip Englishmen like us who like to sleep with some air around. As it was blowing a south-westerly straight from America when we were there, that particular problem didn't arise, but I felt extremely sorry for the poor girl who had to brave the weather to carry out our breakfast trays, under an umbrella. Good breakfast, good bathroom, good value at 240f a double, just meriting an arrow for acccommodation and the hope that the poor restaurant service was an isolated experience.

Map 4B	**LOCTUDY** (Finistère) 6 km SE of Pont-l'Abbé

Mkt: Tues

A fishing port, most interesting because it has the best-preserved Romanesque church in Brittany, whose first prior was St.-Tudy who landed on the coast of Armorica in the 5th century from Britain. There are those who will make the journey specially to look at the barrel-vaulted chancel and there are those who will seek out the rather rude carvings on the base of the capitals!

Another reason for visiting Locturdy is the splendid view from the port towards Ile Tudy, (see p. 74) no distance at all away across the water but a fair drive round the soft and gentle river Odet, lined to waters' edge with pine trees.

 There is a good bar and grill by the port, **Le Rafiot**, and a recommended *crêperie* in the village.

Map 3E	**LOUDÉAC** (C. du N.) 85 km W of Rennes

Mkt: Sat

Included only as a useful stopping place on the axis of several roads, including St.-Brieuc-Vannes, and Rennes-Morlaix.

Auberge du Cheval Blanc
(R)S
pl. Église
(96) 28.00.31
Closed Mon.

Good, cheap, central, menu at 45f.

If an overnight stop were required, the **Hotel France**, 1 r. Cadélai, (96) 28.00.15, is modern and functional, with rooms from 60–200f.

Map 2H	**LOUVIGNÉ-DU-DÉSERT** (I. et V.) 16 km N of Fougères on the D177, 159 km from Cherbourg – *Mkt: Thurs*

Hôtel du Manoir
(HR)M
1 pl. Général de Gaulle
(99) 98.02.40
Closed 15/11–1/12;
1/2–1/3; Sun. p.m.;
Mon.

A nice old grey stone house, white-shuttered, slate-roofed, only a step from the main road but set well back in a quiet square, and surrounded by a peaceful garden. A useful stop in fact on the way south.

The bedrooms are pleasant and comfortable — 140f for a double with bath in the main house and slightly more in the annex. M. Saffray is chef–patron and his menus, from 68f, looked good.

Map 1F	**MATIGNON** (C. du N.) 6 km SW of St.-Cast

La Musardière
(R)S
(96) 41.12.43
Closed 30/1–15/3;
Tue.

Signposted off the St.-Cast road. The cheapest menu I found in the area; for 38f you get five courses, of the pâté, pork chop, chicken, etc. variety. Greater elaborations come to 61f, 72f, 89f or 140f.

The setting is the distinctive feature. *Very* rural. An old stone and slate farmhouse down a country lane, with only the scuttering of bantams and the swishing of cows' tails to disturb the deep calm. Pleasantly rustic inside — beams and log fire — and a few tables with umbrellas outside, from which to keep an eye on the kids working hard at their '*amusements*' — swings etc. Not at all smart, but locals recommend it.

Map 3F	**MAURON** (Morbihan) 49 km W of Rennes

Nothing special about this little town, with Friday market, and I note it only because it lies at the hub of six roads, between Dinan and Vannes, on the D766, and it might be appropriate for a traveller's rest.

Brambily
(R)S
pl. Mairie
(97) 22.61.67
Closed 15/9–15/10;
Sun. p.m.; Mon.

Central, noisy, but cheap, with a good 40f menu popular with the locals.

Map 5F	**MISSILAC** (Loire-Atl.) Half-way between Nantes and Vannes, 1 km off the N165

Make the détour anyway, even if you have no intention of staying, just for the experience of seeing:

Hôtel du Golf de la Bretesche
(40) 88.30.05
DC, V.

A stunning castle reflected, fairytale-wise, in the water of the immense lake on whose very edge it stands. The 14th-century original was successively burned and pillaged over the centuries, but the 19th-century restoration has been a clever one, and now the Renaissance towers, sharply pinnacled, set in mellow grey stone, cannot fail to impress.

The setting is truly magnificent; 500 acres of surrounding parkland include an 18-hole championship golf course, and package holiday golfers ensure that even out of season this hotel is never dead. Old stables round a flowery courtyard have been harmoniously converted into self-catering accommodation (details from hotel) and the 25 bedrooms in the hotel proper are all extremely comfortable, light and cheerful; an overnight stop here (250–300f a double) would be a luxurious one.

If you can stand the golfing chat, make full use of the spacious lounges and terraces, enjoy the calm of the outstandingly beautiful surrounds, then plan to eat out – the menus looked expensive and boring.

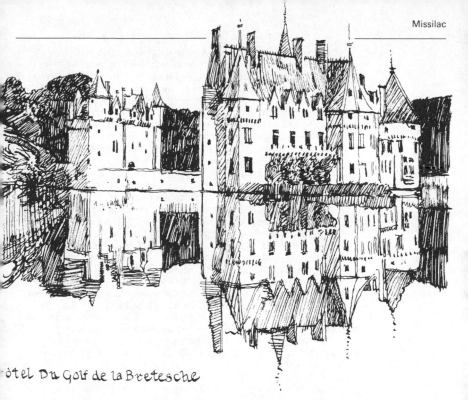

ôtel Du Golf de la Bretesche

MORBIHAN (the Gulf)

Morbihan means 'little sea' in Breton, and the gulf is just that —
an inland sea almost landlocked by the two arms of Quiberon
and the Presqu'île du Rhuys. With 58 km of water and 200 km of
coastline, there is a very special, enclosed, world-apart feeling
to this most magic seascape.

They say there are as many islands in the gulf as days of the
year, some inhabited, some mere reefs, but the two biggest are
Ile d'Arz and **Ile aux Moines**; both are connected to the mainland
by ferries, a cheap way of getting a view of the gulf.

The Ile d'Arz has the best restaurant, **l'Escale**, open from April to
October, at the landing stage. Lunch there on a fine day is a very
good idea. The food is excellent and not as expensive as one
would expect in a short-season, tourist-orientated spot. You can
stay at **l'Escale** too I believe.

The Ile aux Moines is the most beautiful island of them all.
Three miles long, with Mediterranean vegetation, mimosas,
eucalyptus, palm trees, and even a few fig trees. There are
beaches and cliffs, woods with romantic names like Forêt
d'Amour, heaths and pines, and a steep path up to the old
village from whose terrace you can identify bearings. Several
nothing-special restaurants, bars, *crêperies* to deal with hunger/
thirst pangs.

The best way to enjoy the panorama, of course, is by boat and the possibilities and permutations of excursions are many. Vannes is the main departure point for the *Vedettes Vertes* — vast plate-glass palaces of pleasure steamers with excellent vision from within but not much aesthetic appeal from the shore. You can pick one up from Locmariaquer, Port-Navalo or Auray, combine a bus-trip one way, have dinner on board, or lunch, and so on. The schedule is drastically depleted after the high season and it is best to make enquiries at the depot on the Promenade de la Rabine (Vannes 66.10.78) at the port in Auray, on the jetty in Port Navalo or at the *tabac* in Locmariaquer.

The round trip to and from Vannes takes several hours and is quite expensive. Our recipe for a perfect day was to drive to Port Blanc to catch the ferry across to the Ile aux Moines, picnic there under the pines before a swim from the sandy beach, and then to pick up the round-the-islands boat for the last 1½ hours of its tour. This called in at Port Navalo and Locmariaquer and returned us, gratifyingly tanned, to the island. A highly recommended tourist treat.

Forty of the islands are inhabited, many are pleasantly wooded, some have beaches and landing stages for dinghies to land picnickers. There are few prettier sights than the bay on a sunny day, water glittering, little boats bobbing, yachts burgeoning, windsurfers queening. Take any turning south off the N101, which loops along the bay between Auray and Vannes, and it will end in a little harbour with a few houses, often a simple hotel, and a different aspect of island and water.

The two main towns take their names from the rivers on whose estuaries they stand — the Auray and the Vannes. Both are charmers (see p. 31 and p. 171). In fact the whole area is one delight after another, especially given a particularly good climate — the flora is similar to that in the South of France.

Map 2G	**MORDREUC** (C. du N.) 16 km NE of Dinan

2 km W off the D29 at Pleudihen-sur-Rance

No doubt about which hotel in the 'S' category has the best position. A site on a bend of the beautiful river Rance, range of vision filled with little boats, suspension bridge, green trees dipping into water's edge, stone jetties, grey flowery cottages, takes some beating. All this at Mordreuc and more.

►**L'Abri des Flots**
(HR)S
(96) 83.20.43

All things to all men — *épicerie*, bar, restaurant, hotel, petrol station, central meeting place. A double room, with stunning river view, costs 70f.

No, Madam, there is no bathroom *en suite*, and I'm sorry about the cold floor, and you can't read very well in bed because there's only one central light, and you may even be disturbed by the village young playing the wretched pinball machine in the bar. Your dinner will be five courses of little choice — vegetable soup, tureen left on table, a melon or *crudités* or pâté, pork chop and *frites*, cheeseboard and simple dessert. As it will cost 35f, please think carefully before you grumble. Bear in mind the view from your bedroom window and forget that there are no curtains, consider how much the constant hot water costs and forgive the missing light bulb above the basin, note the shine on the humble lino when you have to pad down the corridor in the night. Have two bowlsful of soup, lots of fesh bread and unlimited butter, weigh up the cost of a Charantais melon at home and overlook a certain toughness in the pork. Forego the commercial ice cream, eat several nectarines and grapes instead and congratulate yourself on a very good deal indeed. Arrowed for excellent value, superb position. Runner up for S Hotel of the Year.

| Map 3A | **MORGAT** (Finistère) 37 km W of Chateaulin |

The trident of the Crozon Peninsula jutting out into the Atlantic, next stop America, bounded by the Rade de Brest to the north and the Baie de Douarnenez to the south, encompasses a whole secret world of spectacular seascapes, coves, creeks, rocks, cliffs and pounding waves. Impressive, sometimes awesome, this is no gentle green country but rather an expression of nature at its most untamed.

Best taken at a leisurely pace, with time to explore whatever lane looks promising, invariably ending by the water's edge. Particularly stunning sea views are to the south-west between the Pointe de Dinan and the Cap de la Chèvre; between these points lie a succession of little rocky coves, headlands, indented with caves and beaches.

Don't miss the 68m (227ft) high Pointe de Pen-Hir, a bird sanctuary with fantastic views of a panorama of headlands and islands, or the Pointe des Espagnols to the north, whose telescope, pointing eastward, will reveal a totally different aspect — the whole of the Plougastel peninsula from the harbour of Brest, with the bridge across the estuary of the Élorn.

This is no area to explore unaided though — its treasures are revealed reluctantly; buy a local guide if you intend to penetrate the Fairy Grotto — *les Grottes des Korrigans* — whose colours are as remarkable as their lofty roofs, and don't even try to explore the secrets of the Ile Longue — the finger pointing towards Brest — it's a nuclear submarine base!

Better look elsewhere for undemanding family holiday resorts — this is not carricot country. Even harbours are few — **Camaret**, a little lobster and crayfish port, and **le Fret**, a popular day excursion away from Brest. The only resort is **Morgat**, to the south, curving round a bay sheltered from the prevailing westerlies. You can take a boat trip from here to the caves, Les Grandes Grottes, lie on the sandy beach or watch the fishing boats unload their catch, and that's about it.

I found the hotel and restaurant scene disappointing, with never a sign of the little fishy bistro I had hoped to discover near the port. Plenty of bars and *crêperies*. The main hotels, overlooking the water, are unremarkable, but tucked away behind the town, alas with no seaview but still no distance from the beach, I found one nice little hotel:

Hotel Julia
(HR)M
43 r. du Trèfle
(98) 27.05.89
Closed 15/11–30/
12; Rest. closed
Fri.
V.

Good value bedrooms, all full of regulars at Easter-time when I called, are from 100–150f for a well furnished double with bath. The dining room is super — surprisingly elegant. Menus from 60.50–104f offer safe but dull choices, with lurid desserts, but you can always stick to the seafood, which is irreproachable, and the grilled lobster is a treat.

Map 2C

MORLAIX (Finistère) 85 km W of St.-Brieuc

Mkt: Sat

Set in a steep-sided valley, where the rivers Jarlot and Queffleut join, and dominated by a giant viaduct, built in 1864 for the Paris–Brest railway – the object of an unsuccessful British air raid in 1943.

The English had also unsuccessfully attacked Morlaix in 1552 when the massacre of the would-be invaders led to the strange town motto: 'If they bite you, bite back'! (*S'ils te mordent, mords-les*).

Best approached from the north, via the D76 which follows the river past the many yachts tied up at the entrance to the town. Some of the river has been covered in and many of the old houses demolished but traces of antiquity remain in steep cobbled streets, now pedestrianised, like the Grand' rue. Duchesse Anne's house, a tall 16th-century mansion, is one of the town's showpieces. It was built in 1505 when Queen Anne made a pilgrimage to all the saints of her duchy, to give thanks for the recovery of the King from a serious illness. The façade is decorated with statues of the saints.

I find Morlaix a pleasant colourful town, which would make a good base, but I didn't have much luck with the hotels. The **Hôtel de l'Europe** is central, not too expensive and has a good restaurant, but it is too big and impersonal for my taste. I believe the rooms vary enormously, but the one I saw was incongruously decorated in ultra-modern style, and very dark. Better to consider **Plouigneau** (see p. 112) or **Ste.-Antoine** (p. 142) if an inland stay is preferred.

La Marée Bleue
(R)M
3 rampe Ste.-
Mélanie
(98) 63.24.21
Closed 15/9–1/10;
15/2–1/3; Sat.
lunch; Mon.
V.

An old stone house, up an alleyway that leads to the Flamboyant Gothic church of Ste.-Mélanie.

Pretty and smart inside, with a nice atmosphere generated by friendly patrons M. and Mme Coquart. They make a speciality of traditional cooking, so this is the place to make for if you're sick of *noove*, but the locals say the standard varies. Can be expensive if you don't stick to the very good menus at 50f, 75f and 100f, with a superior wine list.

Auberge des Gourmets
(R)S
90 r. Gambetta
(98) 88.06.06
Closed 15/10–15/
11; Mon.

In a far less attractive part of the town, up by the station, but much more frequented by locals. Unpretentious good cooking on menus from 45f.

Map 3D

MUR-DE-BRETAGNE (C. du N.) on the N164, 45 km S of St.-Brieuc, 100 km W of Rennes

Mur is one of inland Brittany's busiest tourist centres, thanks mainly to the proximity, to the west, of the artificial Guerlédan Lake, and the forest of Quénécan, both offering peaceful countryside diversions. The barrage is a fearsome ugly grey sprawl and I wouldn't bother to take the signposted D18 to it, but you can do a tour right round the lake, catching glimpses from different viewpoints of the water far below in the Blavet Gorges.

Auberge Grand'
Maison
(R)M
1 r. Léon le Cerf
(96) 28.51.10
Closed 25/9–25/10;
25/6–30/6; Sun.
p.m.; Mon.

Perhaps we were expecting too much of this well-known, rosetted, be-toqued, restaurant; perhaps our hopeful dash through torrential rain to find well-laid tables in the comfortable dining room, Mme Guillo's welcome and reassurance that indeed she could accommodate two unreserved *couverts*, and the interesting menus at very reasonable prices, all led us to sit down gratefully, rubbing hands and looking forward with undue enthusiasm to our late lunch. Be that as it may, it seemed to me that the acclaimed cooking of M. Guillo promised more than it produced. I can be a fervent admirer of *nouvelle cuisine* tenets, but here I found justification for all the usual carpings against it. The portions were distressingly small, the old clichés — raw magrets, babyfood purées, kiwifruit rampant — were all in evidence and the effusive chi-chiness of the menu descriptions — *les tendres filets mignons du canard et la réduction d'échalotte au Bourgueil*, followed by *gratin de fruits de la passion au sirop de fruits rouges et la glace de gousses de vanille en coroles* took longer to read than to swallow. The *carte* would work out about 200f.

That said, the restaurant is classy, the service accomplished and the 90f three course, no-choice *menu promotionel* (*pâté de colin, civet de porc, charlotte aux poires* on our visit) good value if you pick a day when you fancy the items on offer.

The rooms were another disappointment — small and too expensive at 275f on a noisy site.

Map 6G

NANTES (Loire-Atl.) 107 km from Rennes

Mkt: Every day,
principally Sat

'S'blood,' cried Henri IV, on seeing Nantes castle for the first time, 'the Dukes of Brittany do not do things by halves.' They certainly didn't — the castle's impressive bulk dominates the centre of this fascinating city. The residence of the Dukes since the time of François II and his daughter, the famous Duchesse Anne, it has provided throughout the years the setting for numerous historic treaties and marriages. Two mighty towers, the Doe's Foot and the Baker, flank its main entrance in the r. d'Etats, and two more, the giant Horseshoe Tower and the River Tower overlook the Pl. Duchesse Anne.

Once the river Loire flowed past its walls but now the moat is laid out in flowerbeds and all is a green and peaceful contrast to the city bustle. Inside the courtyard, more contrasts. Like Josselin, here the massive gives way to the delicate, the military to the domestic, with Renaissance patterned brickwork, intricate wrought iron on Italianate loggias and a well topped with a once-gilded ducal crown. Seven sides to the well, seven pulleys, seven gargoyles refer to the number held most sacred.

Don't miss the courtyard — it's open every day, but the castle interior is closed on Tuesdays (other days 10 a.m.– 12 noon, 2–6 p.m. in summer and 2–5 p.m. from October–April, free on Saturdays and Sundays). Three museums here too — Decorative arts, Naval, and Traditional Arts and Crafts.

But the castle is only part of what I must confess is my favourite Breton city. I think Nantes has everything – good shops, good restaurants, interesting architecture, rivers, cathedral, good climate. It would be my first choice for a winter break, especially since I have found two very different central hotels that should cater for most tastes.

Little Paris is one description and it's true that here is an elegant city. Perhaps this is the influence of the Loire, along whose banks the nobility were prone to build their country homes, bringing Paris to Nantes. To find the expensive labels, walk down the r. Crébillon, diverting to gape at the Passage Pommeraie, a fantasy arcade, three-tiered, glazed, embellished with curvaceous ironwork and curvaceous caryatids.

The backbone of the city is the Cours des Cinquante Otages, harking back to the execution of fifty hostages in 1941. Battered though the city was by air raids, with thousands of houses destroyed and damaged, the restoration has been unobtrusive and convincing. The pl. Royale, with its spectacular fountain, had to be almost entirely re-built.

A pleasant place to picnic is the formal gardens of the Cours Cambronne. From there you can stroll along the quai de la Fosse, which runs along the banks of the Loire, admiring the 18th-century shipbuilders' houses with their ornate balconies, especially no. 70, the former East India Company's offices.

The Cours St.-Pierre and the Cours St.-André, shady promenades lined with 18th-century houses, run from the river Erdre to the castle. Their regularity is broken by the elgant pl. du Marechal Foch, and here is a good place to park before a visit to the cathedral.

St.-Pierre is a very beautiful Gothic building in the Flamboyant style, with some interesting tombs inside, particularly that of François II and his wife Margarette de Foix; if you are as intrigued as I am at the ubiquitous Duchesse Anne, their daughter, here is a chance to see what she looked like — *Justice*, one of the four allegorical statues at the corners of the tomb is said to be modelled on that popular lady.

▶**Hôtel du Château**
(H)S
5 pl. de la
Duchesse-Anne
(40) 74.17.16
Open all year
P. in square
opposite

An unprecedented piece of luck. I mistook the entrance for that of **l'Hôtel** (see below) two doors away. Encouraged to proceed past the seedy passage only by the false assumption that both the correct Michelin and the upmarket Gault-Millau had commended it, I climbed up the narrow stairs to make a real find — the charming young Mme Le-Riguer, who showed me over the dozen rooms of her little hotel, each costing an incredible 66f for a double, mostly with shower.

They are simply but perfectly adequately furnished and irreproachably clean. Those at the rear are quieter, those on the front have a splendid view of castle and gardens (and as the building is tall and narrow, the higher you go, the more distant becomes the traffic noise).

There is a pleasant, parlourish *salon* on the first floor, with riveting outlook; breakfast here can be a very friendly chatty affair if that's what you want. Otherwise it can be served in bed.

There is no connection with the **Restaurant du Château** next door (good but expensive) but Mme Le-Riguer has plenty of suggestions for good cheap eating places for her clients, all within easy walking distance.

I consider £3 a head for a good room, in this perfect central position, combined with the friendliness of the patronne, unbeatable value, and a dead-cert arrow. I shall sit back and wait for compliments.

▶ **L'Hôtel**
(H)M-L
6 pl. de la Duchesse-Anne
(40) 29.30.31
Open all year
AE, V.

Confusingly named, almost next door to the **Hôtel du Château**. Very different, but equally good in its class. All new in 1983, classy modern décor, black velvety carpets. Super bedrooms and luxury bathrooms, with same view as the **Château**, but the extra money buys sound-proofing. The largest room is 260f, the smallest 180f, but in this case I think the latter is better value, since they are all extremely comfortable. Helpful management, garage, and that ideal situation, with a restaurant next door if it's raining, all go to make up another arrow for a luxury hotel at a non-luxury price.

L'Esquinade
(R)M
7 r. St.-Denis
(40) 48.17.22
Closed 10/7–31/7;
Sun. p.m.; Mon.
AE, DC, V.

An elegant little restaurant close to the cathedral, with warm, friendly atmosphere and not as expensive as it looks if you eat (very well, with lots of choice) on the 95f menu.

Le Change
(R)S
11 r. Juiverie
(40) 48.02.28
Closed 17/7–17/8;
Sun. p.m.; Mon.
V.

There are many restaurants to choose from in the pedestrianised area behind the château, but this is one of the steadies. Nothing exciting, but a reliable 42f menu.

Les Voyageurs
(R)M
16 allée Cdt.–
Charcot
Closed 2/1–7/1;
Sat. o.o.s.
V.

Very near the two recommended hotels and with a red R in Michelin for a specially good value menu at 52f. Usefully open on Sundays too.

Le Mangeoire
(R)S
*16 r. des Petites
Écuries
(40) 48.70.83
Closed Mon. p.m.
o.o.s.; Sat. lunch;
Sun.*

A most attractive little restaurant in the pedestrianised area, with copious menus at 43f and 72f, recommended home-made desserts. Good wine list.

Les Maraîchers
(R)L
*21 r. Fouré
(40) 47.06.51
Closed Aug.; Sun;
Mon.*

Nantes' smartest restaurant, boasting Michelin star, G-M toques, and a chef from Boyer at Reims. If you eat à la carte you will pay heavily for all these goodies, but at lunch-time there is a wonderful 135f menu, inclusive of everything from apéritif to coffee (even wine) which allows the opportunity to try a master chef's version of dishes like: *saumon au gingembre*, or *volaille farcie à la fondue de poireaux*. In the evening there is another menu at 195f. Here is *the* place to sample that Nantais speciality — the delectable *sauce beurre blanc*.

Relais St.-Yves
(R)M
*buffet de la Gare
(40) 74.79.60
Closed Sat. p.m.;
Sun.
AE, DC.*

When in doubt, head for the station buffet holds good generally, but this is the supremo of all station buffet menus. For 68f you get a sublime meal which you can relish all over again next time your lot is a sticky bun at Crewe. Imagine a British station buffet admitting to having a chef with a name! Here M. Le Bris dishes up *terrine de pigeonne a l'ail, salade de coquilles St.-Jacques et d'huitres pochées*, and *caneton rôti au miel et aux pommes*. Full of businessmen at lunchtime — always a good sign. Recommended for marvellous value in the most unlikely surroundings.

La Cigale
(R)S
*4 pl. Graslin
(40) 89.34.84*

An amazing *Belle Époque brasserie*, vivid with enamelled tiles, panelled ceilings, gilding and mirrors. Sit at a marble table to take in all this phantasmagoria or on the pavement in the square in fine weather, sip a coffee or beer and watch the Nantais world go by. A good place for lunch too, with salads at around 25f, or perhaps *moules à la crème* for 30f, and at any time of day a splendid array of pastries and desserts.

Map 6G

NORT-SUR-ERDRE (Loire-Atl.) 29 km N of Nantes, 82 km from Rennes

---

A rather disappointing little town considering its position on canal and river Erdre. Eight roads converge, to make it an unpleasantly dusty and traffic-ridden thoroughfare.

Seen from the *bassin*, however, it is another story. All is delightfully serene and photogenic, with swans and boats obligingly deployed and old ladies knitting in the shade of the surrounding chestnut trees. Nowhere here, alas, to eat or drink. For this you must struggle up the main street to:

Hôtel de Bretagne (HR)S *41 r. A. Briand* *(40) 72.21.95* *Rest. closed 1/10–* *7/10; 1/3–15/3;* *Sun. p.m.; Mon.*	More impressive inside than out and the dining room was full of French on an o.o.s. mid-week evening. Menus start at 39f but we were in the mood for an *assiette de fruits de mer* (as opposed to a *plateau* which was even more substantial). At 50f, it was excellent value, incorporating expensive components like oysters, *langoustines* and half a crab. The rooms are pretty dull, but clean, and at 50f a double (or 75f with bath) would make a cheap over-nighter.

NOTRE DAME de Guildo – See St. Caste-le-Guildo, p. 144

Map 3G	**NOYAL-SUR-VILAINE** (I. et V.) 12 km E of Rennes, N off the N157 – *Mkt: Tues*

Les Forges (HR)M *(99) 00.51.08* *Closed 6/8–27/8;* *15/2–28/2; Sun.* *p.m.*	A little modern building, with fairly ordinary rooms at 140–160f, but a pleasant dining room wtih excellent cooking on the 60f menus by chef patron M. André Pilard, warranting a red R in Michelin, particularly strong on fish, cooked often in seaweed — *à la vapeur d'algues*. Useful perhaps as a peaceful, hassle-free base from which to explore Rennes.

Map 6G	**ORVAULT** (Lore Atl.) 7 km N of Nantes

La Domaine **d'Orvault** (HR)L *(40) 76.84.02* *Closed Feb.; Mon.* *lunch. P.* *AE, DC, V.*	Hellishly difficult to track down, and definitely not, as Michelin says, on the D42, unless you're arriving on foot (and I doubt if many of the **Domaine**'s guests are). Better turn off the N137 heading towards Rennes, on to the r. d'Arbois and left again down a little road, le Chemin des Marais de Cens. I didn't really think it was worth the trouble. For a Relais et Châteaux member, the vaguely-Spanish style suburban villa is not exciting and the décor is downright mean. Aiming at the modern, the wood is placcy, as are the flowers, and the hectic carpet soon degenerates into felt along the economically-lit corridors. An unfortunate penchant for orange dominates. The bedrooms are too ordinary to merit their price of 360f, especially as the bedside light didn't work and the water in the mock marble bathroom was cold. But the food — ah that's another story. Well worth driving out from Nantes to relish M. Bernard's cooking, particularly when the four-course menu costs a mere 120f, and includes superb free *amuses-gueules* and *petits fours*. Others at 170f, 190f, 260f and 350f would please all tastes. No skimping on the cheaper menu though — we started with a *parfait de foies de canard aux raisins* which tasted as expensive as it looked, followed by a perfect turbot swathed in a fresh *sauce tomate* incorporating clams, then roast goat's cheese and a wickedly delicious iced chocolate mousse. So a bouquet for unusually good cooking, worthy of more than one rosette I would have thought, but a boo for the disappointing hotel.

Map 3G	**PACÉ** (I. et V.) 7 km NW of Rennes

Turn off the N12 very conveniently before getting embroiled in the Rennes agglomeration, to find a haven of non-motorway calm, where the Pont de Pacy crosses the river Flume. No less than four restaurants and a hotel to choose from:

►La Griotte
(R)M
42 r. du Dr Léon
(99) 60.62.48
Closed Mon.; Tue.
p.m.

Q. What is the most reliable guide to a good restaurant ? – *Michelin? Gault-Millau? French Entrée?*
A. None of them. Look for a car park overflowing with French cars.

A not-to-be ignored crowd of parked cars outside **La Griotte** diverted my lunch intention from the Michelin-recommended **Hôtel du Pont**, and I could not have wished for a better guide.

Inside the din was prodigious, both in the large bar area, cherry-red as the restaurant's namesake, and in the light garden extension. Regulars arrived, were greated warmly by Mme Morand and with much chat on the way escorted to their tables; the telephone rang with insistent bookings, the rattle of a busy lunchtime's cutlery and plattery necessitated an even higher decibel count for animated conversation throughout, and it was all very bright, cheerful, efficient and exactly what was needed to enliven a grey November day.

Not hard to see why **La Griotte** is so popular — the 50f menu was a comfortable three courses of excellent value choices — *soupe d'etrilles* or *pâté de foie maison* or perhaps six oysters, then *brochettes* of pork, rumpsteak, etc; but there was even more interest on the next one up at 69.50f, like *pâté de brochet aux crevettes, fricassé de gesiers d'oie*, with walnuts, *brochettes de poissons*. With four veg, an excellent cheese board and super desserts, including a good range of interesting home-made sorbets, I find this one hard to beat in the area for value and atmosphere. Arrowed too for its strategic position.

Hôtel du Pont
(H)S(R)M
Pont de Pace
(99) 60.61.06
Closed Mon.

A useful cheap stop, just off the main road, well situated for Rennes. Bedrooms extremely simple, but adequate, 70–85f for a double, but with no bathroom or shower choices.

I got the impression that perhaps the hotel and restaurant were past their prime, but M. and Mme Delabrosse are welcoming hosts and their traditional-style food is well-presented in a comfortable dining room, altogether more tranquil than at the **Griotte**. The *gratin* of turbot with *sauce Cardinale* and the fresh salmon with sorrel were both praiseworthy, but the desserts were dismal, so here is a case where it might be provident to eat *à la carte* and avoid the mistakes on the 75f or 105f menus. And of course, there are alternative eateries within a step or two.

La Flume
(R)S
Pont de Pacé
(99) 60.61.10
Open every day

Forgive the somewhat flowery presentation of the menu in this little restaurant popular for local weddings and knees-ups. At 45f it offers splendid value. I quote:
1. *Premier Regard: la terrine de lapin aux pruneaux â la crème de ciboulette.* 2. *Second Caprice: les langoustines flambées au cognac.* 3. *Le Summum du Chef: le confit d'oie aux pommes rissolées* 4. *Les Joies du Palais: La coupe Klavia.*
Not bad for four quid!

Le Relais du Vieux Pont
(R)S
Pont de Pacé
(99) 60.61.83

Good grills of hefty steaks, chops etc. or substantial country dishes like a *cassoulet au confit de canard*. Menu at 50f.

Map 1D

PAIMPOL (Côtes–du–Nord) 45 km NW of St- Brieuc

The harbour is not as appealing as are many along this stretch, but the little town behind, with pedestrianised shopping area, is attractive enough, with a few bars in the main square that catch the evening sun better than those on the quay.

Repaire de Kerroc'h
(HR)L
quai Moraud
(96) 20.50.13
Closed Jan.
AE, DC, V.

Difficult to be fair, since, on the evening we dined here, husband and I were having words. My view is that *nouvelle cuisine* is all right in its place; he will have no truck with it whatsoever, so mine were about his being inflexible and his were about me being plain stupid. He had just said: 'If I have any more baby food my teeth will fall out, redundant', when his first course on the 130f menu arrived. *Flan de petits poireaux* we had carelessly assumed would be leeks in a pastry case, but of course a flan can also be a kind of mousse and here yet again was a khaki mush. I thought it was delicate and delicious; he sighed heavily and lit a cigarette.

It was then that the American next door, who had obviously suffered in the same way, let fly. Poking his cube of carefully arranged monkfish he spat,' I thought fish was meant to be cheap in Brittany – is this all you can afford here?'

The audience fell silent in delighted horror at this The-King-is-in-the-Altogether daring. I admired his courage but not his tastes, until he added, 'I hope we're gonna get better fish 'n' chips than this in England', and suddenly a vision of crisp golden batter encasing fat juicy common fish, wicked chips accompanying, salt and vinegar unflavoured with raspberries, greaseproof paper garni, flashed before my eyes and, somehow the umpteenth portion of steamed fish in front of me, fanned with two potato olives and three steamed courgette slices, didn't seem worth eating any more.

So you see, all I can tell you is that the dining room is of stone, elegant, the service is willing and efficient, the Brits and Americans (mostly) love it, the food is *noove* without concessions (and I think imagination — all the old clichés), the oysters are very good and the desserts very disappointing, the bill can be as little as 90f, up to 130f, 150f, 180f or sky-high *carte*, the wines are prestigious and expensive, and neither the American nor husband could get out fast enough.

The rooms incidentally are like the food — elegant, very small, and expensive.

La Cotriade
(R)S
16 quai Armand Dargot
(96) 20.81.08
Open all year

The antidote perhaps for the chi-chis. Simple fish restaurant on opposite side of the quay, serving straightforward fish and grills, in a pleasant jovial atmosphere, on menus from 55–90f.

Vieille Tour
(R)M
13 r. Église
(96) 20.83.18
Closed 15/11–10/
12; Tue. p.m.;
Wed.

Climb up the steep cobbled main street towards the church to find this most attractive old stone restaurant, meriting its red R in Michelin for a 68f menu, predominantly fishy but with some interesting alternatives. Stray from the menus and the *à la carte* could be expensive, but altogether good value in pleasant surroundings.

The only hotel alternative I could find is at the other end of the scale from the Relais et Châteaux Repaire de Kerroc'h:

Hotel de la Marne
(HR)S
30 r. de la Marne
(96) 20.82.16
Closed 31/10–1/1

A little Logis de France, attractive enough but possibly with noise problems for the rooms on the front. Rooms from 90–170f, menus from 60f.

Map 3F

THE FOREST OF PAIMPONT (I. et V.) 40 km SW of Rennes on the N24 and D38

Centre of Arthurian legends and still, I wouldn't be at all surprised, capable of practising all manner of magic on those who seek to discover its secrets. Many give up trying to make map references tie up with road signs, and although locals readily hand over brochures describing the charms of Brocéliande, they never seem at all upset to see you back again after a frustrating hour's abortive circuit. Are these the natural heirs to Merlin's wizardry, conniving to keep their prisoners inside the ancient forest's bounds?

I never did find Merlin's tomb, criss-cross though I might through the shaded tracks of the eastern side of the forest where it purports to lie. The largest of the fourteen lakes is here, the Pas du Houx, 212 acres of silent water, presided over by Brocéliande Manor. A good place to park the car, abandon a set plan of campaign, get out the picnic basket and let the faery kingdom weave its spell.

To the west, near the village of **Tréhorenteuc**, the forest paths lead to the Val Sans Retour, which features in many a legend. Here, Morgane La Fée, King Arthur's sister, in a fine piece of mediaeval womens' lib (her morals were distinctly flexible), lured all the lovers who had been unfaithful to her into the enchanted valley from which there was no escape. Go inside the church to see an odd juxtaposition of symbols pagan (a voluptuous Morgane) and Christian (the 9th station of the Cross) or King Arthur's knights experiencing a vision of the Holy Grail, in a strange set of paintings (1946-ish).

Take the D141 a few km north of here to stop at the hamlet of Folle-Pensée, and walk down to the Barenton Fountain, a rather insignificant trickle whose medicinal properties nevertheless are said to have rid Merlin of some of his more disturbing fantasies. They say if you pour water from the fountain on to Merlin Steps you can conjure up a storm, but someone had been there before me — it was already blowing, raining, howling.

The Arthurian ladies were a wily bunch. Poor Merlin himself fell victim to the lovely fairy Viviane, when she practised one of his own spells on him — how to charm men. By this very fountain he fell asleep one day and Viviane recited the words he had taught her, imprisoning him forever in an enchanted castle. A shame really. Half devil, half Christian, he sounds a far more interesting character than any of those goody goody knights.

Comper Castle lies 3 km E of **Concoret**, in the middle of a bleak moorland, overlooking another lake. Only the ramparts and moat remain of the original castle, where Viviane is said to have been born, but another Comper Castle built by Merlin lies submerged beneath the waters of the lake, or so they say.

Les Forges de Paimpont is one of the most attractive sections of the forest and since it is easily accessible, via the N24 and D773, make for this spot if time is limited and map-reading doubtful. Iron was smelted here in Renaissance times until about the last century. Now the ancient cottages, mills and fountains lie silently in a picturesque huddle beside a gorgeous lake.

Paimpont

This little market town attracts most tourists, with invariably a coach pulled up outside the intriguing abbey church, restored from the 13th-century original. Well worth going inside to see the 17th-century wooden statue of Our Lady of Paimpont, jauntily painted.

The setting is most attractive out of season, when footsteps echo in the single street of the *bourg,* approached through a stone archway, and the anachronistic *crêperie* and souvenir shops are unobtrusive. The lake is vast, altogether a delightful spot at any season, lively with pedalos and windsurfers in summer, always good for walking round or sitting by. Refreshment is at hand.

Relais de Brocéliande 🏠
(HR)S
(99) 07.81.07
Closed Mon. o.o.s.
AE, V.

Stone-walled, slate-roofed, geraniumed, with surprisingly comfy and spacious bedrooms in the adjoining annexe, where a large well-furnished room with bath costs 170f and the cheapest, 85f. The well-patronised bar is decorated with stuffed creatures of the forest and has a log fire to comfort chilled fishermen. Good value simple meals from 55f.

An inexpensive base in a most attractive area, strategically placed as an overnight staging post, near Rennes, and well on the way to coastal destinations, particularly combined with a meal at:

►**Le Manoir du Tertre** 👍
(H)S(R)M
(99) 07.81.02
Closed 1/10–15/10;
5/2–21/2; Tue.

Take the D71 Beignon road out of Paimpont and the **Manoir** is well signed off to the right, 4 km from the village. It's a pleasant old stone farmhouse set on a hill above utterly peaceful countryside. Inside are the kind of antiques that are there to be used not looked at, with an ancient carved staircase, treads precariously sloping, leading to dim upper regions. Big fires, fresh flowers, delightful dining room. Mme Alix opened her restaurant there only a few years ago but is already attracting a discerning clientèle to her tucked-away eyrie, as word of the fine cooking and good value spreads.

In April, when the restaurant was full of French, we ate the best meal of the week here. My 55f menu was remarkable value — *poële de foies au thym* (could have been a generous plateful of expensive *jambon cru*), with slices of chicken livers, cooked *à point*, delicately scented with thyme, on a bed of lambs lettuce and endive; then a *mousseline de poissons au confit d'oignons* (could have been *steak poëlé a l'ail*), with a perfectly balanced fish *mousseline* sharpened with the onion preserve and served with *sauce au beurre.* That very rare treat on modestly priced menus — interesting vegetables — was thrown in in the form of celeriac *purée* and potato *gratin*, then a good cheeseboard, or full choice of *à la carte* desserts.

I plumped for two perfectly poached fresh pears in a sharp redcurrant sauce, accompanied by the delicious eggy cream that the French call *anglaise* but bears no resemblance to our yellow-peril custard. Husband's 72f version supplied him with a very satisfactory *feuilleté de coquillage à l'oseille*, followed by a *filet de rascasse au saffran.* All interesting and well thought out.

A chat with the talented young chef, Joel Hévin, revealed that he likes particularly to use game from the surrounding forest, in season, but always goes for local produce, topped up with lots of fish. All the *pâtisserie* is of his own making.

About the rooms at the **Manoir** I have reservations. I personally enjoyed my stay there but, without very specific clarification, I am sure to get another letter from the hapless reader who wrote: 'My wife, who has very keen eyesight, found some fluff under the bed and thinks I ought to tell you so.' Mrs Hapless would undoubtedly find not only a spot of fluff at the Manoir but, were she to stand on a chair, might well come across the odd cobweb or two in the rafters. This is no hotel for sterilised cube-fanciers.

Mme Alix told me quite frankly that it is not for the elderly (stairs too rickety) or the incontinent (long lanes of lino to get to the distant loo) but, she said, the young love to stay here, and the English, who go for character not conformity (but not Mrs Hapless).

Our room had its eccentricities – hangings on the magnificent carved four-poster were droopily pinned, like the chintz curtains at the long windows; only two of the chandelier's arms had functioning bulbs (but in France that's often due to deliberate economy rather than carelessness), the bath was the kind on legs, and the plumbing rumbled a bit, but the water was hot, the heating switched on, the room was spacious and gracious, an excellent breakfast arrived spot on requested time, and our bill for 140f convinced me at least that here again was good value for them that like it. The arrow, however, must be for the restaurant alone.

Map 3H	**LA PEINIÈRE** (I. et V.) 26 km E of Rennes

A hamlet lying between the N157 and the autoroute, 5 km E of Chateaubourg.

Pen 'Roc
(HR)M
(99) 00.33.02
Closed 1/11–24/11;
Rest. closed Sun.
p.m. P.
AE, DC, EC.

An attractive little Logis, stone-built, modernised sympathetically, set in very peaceful countryside near the village of St.-Didier. M. Froc is patron-chef, offering interesting dishes contrived from local ingredients, some from his own garden. Try his fresh salmon with chive sauce, or turbot with sweet peppers, duck with honey, on menus starting at 65f; reasonable wine list too. The rooms are deliberately *rustique*, comfortable and warm out of season, from 147.50–220f.

Facilities for conferences made me fear the usual impersonality that goes with catering for numbers not people, but I found the staff friendly and helpful, and I suppose in the country the only way to stay open in winter is to rely on group bookings.

Map 5E	**PEN-LAN** (Morbihan) 4.5 km S of Muzillac, 37 km SW of Redon

The coastline north of the Vilaine estuary is imposingly wild and rocky. A thin neck of sand straggles out from Billiers to bulge into the granite headland of the Pointe de Pen-Lan, with a stunning bay on either side, and dominated by:

Château de Rochevilaine
(HR)L
(97) 41.69.27
Closed 1/11–1/4
AE, DC, V.

To hell with the expense — 'twas our wedding anniversary and I'd always fancied staying at the **Domaine de Rochevilaine**, one of the few Relais et Châteaux outposts literally at the edge of the sea. Very impressive approach, a sprawl of white, more village than hotel, built out on to the Atlantic rocks.

'*Non,*' said the unsmiling reception, '*Complet.*' 'Not even a little room?' '*Non*' (and only the French can make that word quite so definitive). 'What about tomorrow?' we asked, clutching at straws. 'Possibly' — and if we would take the same room for two nights, miraculously it had become immediately free. Weakly, we agreed (we were due to join a canal boat soon and this might be a last taste of *luxe*); gulping slightly, we accepted the mind-blowing price of 650f, and guiltily we inspected the *domaine* we had just bought.

But all was not well in our patch of Eden. The service (40 mins. for two thick white cups of tea to be plonked down ungraciously with no milk, no lemon, no sugars) working out at £1.20 a teabag!), and the ambiance (sour receptionist increasingly bolshie). We were not pleased to hear latecomers getting cheaper rooms. The menu for dinner in that gorgeous dining room looked a pretty dull 160f worth and the wine list mortgage-worthy. Who wants to eat in France surrounded by Americans any way?

Craven husband sent me to tell Po-face that we weren't staying, and like thieves in the night (how *very* British for *us* to feel guilty) we humped our luggage out to the car and drove down the road to:

Le Celtic
(HR)M
Billiers
(97) 41.64.11
Closed 1/11–3/3;
Sat. Sun. o.o.s. P.
EC.

An altogether different story, making us consider ourselves better off in every sense. A warm welcome for a start, a simple bedroom for 170f, and a loo with a view. I used to think the height of luxury was watching TV from the bath, but that doesn't compare with watching the evening sun on the water from the bathroom of no. 10 at **Le Celtic**. Its position on the neck of the peninsula, overlooking a choice of sandy bays, is quite perfect. Walk round behind the hotel (having first put some clothes on) to the little fishing harbour and an alternative range of beaches, near and far, presents itself.

Good fishy comprehensive menus from 65f. This is primarily a family hotel, I suppose, and full pension works out at 200f per person.

Map 1C

PERROS GUIREC (C. du N.) 12 km N of Lannion

Mkt: Fri

The largest resort along the pink granite coast and used to be the smartest but has lately succumbed to the souvenir and ice cream stalls. The town is a lively modern one, with a good Friday market.

Several beautiful bays edge the point, fringed with pines. Trestraou, the biggest, has the harbour from which the *Vedettes Blanches* chug away on an excursion to the **Sept Îles** off the coast, thrice daily in season but book ahead — very popular.

And deservedly so — the memorable trip starts with a visit to the **Ile des Oiseaux**, white with seagulls, the haunt of little penguins and guillemots. I thought our boat would sink with the weight of the expensive and expansive equipment its passengers required to photo and observe the wild life. Then on to the **Ile aux Moines** for a hour's visit ashore — not a minute too long to climb to the summit for the most remarkable panorama of the coastline as far as Roscoff and the Ile de Batz. One would have thought the formidable surrounding reefs would have deterred invaders, but the island was fortified by Vauban, and his fort remains, with the odd canon still in position. Flat warm grass, closely cropped by the rabbit population, makes for ideal picnicking in a unique site.

The boat's homeward route follows the coast from **Ploumanach**, a little fishing village facing south in the lee of a hook of land, with the commentator pointing out the extraordinary rocks along the way. Sure enough, if you try hard enough, you too can make out the turtle, the scallop shell, the old man, the elephant, formed by the creasing and crumpling of these strange phenomena, more like Spitting Image puppets than real rocks or real anything else.

The grassy cliff edge is dotted with walkers, following the Douaniers' path — another wonderful (and cheaper) way to view the coastline.

In the centre of Trestraou is:

L'Homard Bleu
(R)M
(96) 23.24.55
Closed Sun. p.m;
Mon.

For fish of course, upmarket ones, served in a smartish restaurant, big glass windows catching the view. No harm done at all to stick to the cheapest menu, at 80f, if that's what you fancy, or perhaps go mad on a lobster treat.

Les Feux des Îles
(HR)M
rte. de la Corniche
(96) 23.22.94
Closed 10/1–30/1;
14/10–12/11; Sun.
p.m.; Mon. o.o.s.

It says in the brochure *Mme Le Roux pour votre accueil*. On the day I was there Mme Le Roux knew she had all her rooms fully booked and wasn't worrying too much about the '*accueil*', but it was July and rare is the French hotel bird who smiles much then.

When I did extract a key from her for a nosey, I found the rooms were smallish but very pleasant, some with a view of the sea beyond the large sloping garden and not expensive, at 160f with bath.

So, in spite of its *patronne*, I include this one for good value in a quiet position near the town and beaches, and particularly for its restaurant. I did not meet M. Le Roux but no doubt he was busy preparing lunch for the *pensionnaires*. I'm told the food is very good indeed and in fact this is more a restaurant with rooms than vice versa. All of which is good news, since demi-pension is compulsory in season at 130–230f. Non-residents would also do very well in the pleasant dining room whose bay windows take in the view, and excellent menus start at 70f.

Printania
(HR)M
12 r. des Bons
Enfants
(96) 23.21.00
Closed 15/12–10/1;
Sun. o.o.s.
V.

The smartest hotel nowadays in Perros, whose era of grandeur between the wars has been left far behind. A lot of charm in this large white balconied house, with a superb position overlooking the bay and Les Sept Îles. Well-tended garden and tennis court.

Most of the rooms overlook the sea and are comfortable enough; everything is a bit plastic, but expensive plastic, for 254–315f. Demi-pension obligatory in season from 293f but I know nothing about the restaurant.

Map 2F

PLANCOËT (C. du N.) 17 km NW Dinan on the D794

Mkt: Sat

The river Arguegnon rushes surprisingly through the centre of this little town, with a bridge just opposite:

Chez Crouzil
(HR)M
les Quais
(96) 84.10.24
Closed 15/10–30/
10; 15/1–30/1; Sun.
p.m.; Mon.
AE, DC, V.

A little restaurant in front of the station but not at all the English concept of a station caff. Named after its *patron* of the past 36 years, Jean-Pierre Crouzil, here is an attractive comfortable stop, well worth making a considerable détour, by road or railcard. Jean-Pierre believes, however, (how wise) that the less travelling his ingredients do the better, so his refreshingly regional menus feature fish from Erquy, oysters from Cancale, strawberries from Jugon. Traditional cooking, but never heavy, unlike the *carte* which is too ponderous by half. The line of least resistance is to settle for the menus and the 65f one is no hardship whatsoever, 130f a splendid alternative. Good, reasonable wine list, a terrace, and fourteen rooms from 85–250f, uninspected by me so far but said to be as comfortable as the restaurant.

'We give high marks to Chez Crouzil — *an unprepossessing situation but a welcoming and comfortable hotel, with an excellent restaurant' — John Richards.*

Restaurant de la Source
(R)S
(96) 84.10.11
Closed Mon.

Unpromising exterior on main road compensated for by way-above-average cooking at way-below-average prices.

On the 50f menu came six oysters, *poulet au Whisky,* salad and cheeses; on the 75f, 100f and 130f alternatives were a range of straightforward but well-cooked and substantial dishes — *terrine de brochet, turbot hollandaise, gigôt à l'ail.* Good honest value.

Map 1D

PLÉHEDEL (C. du. N.) 10 km S of Paimpol

Château de Coatguélen
(HR)L
(96) 22.31.24
Closed 1/11–1/4;
Wed. lunch; Tue.
o.o.s. P.
AE, DC.

On the D7 between Lanvallon and Paimpol. An imposing 1850 mansion looking down through its 100 hectares over the nine hole golf course towards an extensive lake.

The rooms vary enormously – if you can afford it, this is no time for economy. Ours, in the former attics, was poor value at 375f, dark and not spacious, though attractively furnished and comfy enough. For 490f we could have had no. 5, a really superb turret room, exceptionally elegant, with lovely views of the lake, a canopied double bed and luxury bathroom. Breakfast a let-down: half-toasted bread and not enough coffee.

The best news is that the public rooms are delightful, warmly panelled, cleverly curtained, grand piano in salon ready for occasional recitals; and the dining room is pure delight, all golden linen, and sunlight streaming through long windows

Château Hôtel de Coatguélen

that open onto swimming pool on one side and lake on t'other. Lovely on a summer's day.

The chef is Louis LeRoy, who runs cookery courses at the **Château**. We split a 130f and 170f menu between us and both were excellent value, incorporating some house specialities, like hot oysters with chives, and honey-coated duck served pink, with legs grilled as a separate course. Delectable desserts, especially *pâtisserie*.

Recommended for a no-expense-spared stopover.

Map 4F	**PLÉLAN LE GRAND** (I. et V.) 39 km SW of Rennes on the D24

A boring little main-road town, with a Tuesday market, but the site of an unsually good restaurant, most useful to know for a lunch stop in this gastronomic desert.

Relais des Diligences
(R)S
2 pl. de l'Église
(99) 06.81.44
Closed Oct.;
evenings except
Sats.; Wed.

Equally boring from the outside, but enlivened inside by M. Launay's light touch with fresh salmon salad *feuilleté d'escargots au Saumur, bar aux ciboulettes*, all featuring on menus starting at 40f. Good grills and desserts too. Excellent value.

Map 2D	**PLÉLO** (C. du N.) 15 km E of Guingamp, 3 km NE of Châtelaudren, N of the N12, or *via* the D4, south of the D6

Signposted from the village

►Au Char à Bancs
(R)S
Moulin de la Ville
Geffroy
(96) 74.13.63
Closed Tue.;
Mon.–Thur. o.o.s.

'The' *crêperie*. The setting is an old mill, raftered dining room overlooking millstream, tables contrived from rugged millstones or long polished oak boards, huge log fire on which simmers continuously their famous *potée,* a thick stew, made from home-grown vegs. They also grow much of the cereal, to make the flour, to make the pancakes and galettes.

Run by a charming enthusiast family, Papa Lamour cooking *crêpes* and mingling with his guests (150 covers, very popular, so book at weekends), two pretty Lamourettes serving and Lamour fils attending to the ponies, whose rides are just one of the attractions of this idyllic spot. Do go.

Arrowed as no. 1 crêperie.

Map 2G	**PLEUDIHEN-SUR-RANCE** (C. du N.) 15 km NE of Dinan on the D29

La Brochetterie
(HR)S
(96) 83.31.10
Closed 1/10–15/10;
Wed.

The village is nothing special and the hotel's situation plumb on the road doesn't instantly allure, but inside all is calm, pristine and warm, (which makes it worth considering for an off-season situation). A comfy double room with shower costs 160f. Mme Soulard, the patronne, lives up to the Logis de France requirement that welcome is important too.

Good honest regional cooking on a 49f menu makes this an economical stop near a busy tourist-orientated area, where many hotels only open for the summer.

| Map 2G | **PLEUGUENEUC** (I. et V.) 12 km SE of Dinan 14 km W of Combourg on the N137 |

►Château de la Motte Beaumanoir
(HR)L
(99) 45.26.37
Open all year

One of a recent breed of châteaux opening their doors to paying guests. Charles Bernard offers four stunning rooms in his beautiful 15th–18th-century home. They all look over the vast lake, where the trout leap, into the 2,400 hectares of surrounding woodland.

The decorations have been achieved with a good deal of taste as well as expense and I would find it hard to choose between them. Maybe the one with the little tower sitting room. They all have luxurious bathrooms and would certainly make a wonderful sybaritic retreat, for 400f a double. Honeymoon perhaps?

You should telephone ahead, especially in winter, and if you want an evening meal, for 150f, it has to be pre-ordered, (but I know nothing about its quality). Otherwise there are plenty of alternatives at Dinan, St.-Malo, Combourg and Cancale.

Arrowed as a memorable and outstandingly beautiful stop.

| Map 2F | **PLÉVEN** (C. du. N.) 24 km NW of Dinan, *via* the D794 and the D28 from Plancoët |

Here a bridge crosses the reservoir, 17 km long, created by the damming of the Arguenon. Lovely walking and picnicking country around the wooded water's edge. Nearby, is the ruined château of Hunandaie, built in the 13th century, damaged, rebuilt, partly demolished in the Revolution, on the edge of the lovely Forêt de la Hunandaie. Buried in deepest calm on the edge of the forest stands another interesting building:

Le Manoir de Vaumadeuc
(HR)L
(96) 84.46.17
Closed 15/2–20/3

How the Americans must love it! Personally I found the ambiance of mediaeval manor part-intimidating, part-comic, and altogether over the top. The sheer scale of everything – the cavernous bedrooms, looming four-posters, fireplaces for roasting oxen in, platforms to climb, baronial halls, acres of tapestry, menacing suits of armour, mammoth stuffed heads on panelling, massive iron chandeliers — does not lead to a rollicking holiday stopover. Not sure I could live up to it, but for amateurs of the fantastical with 500f to spare for a double room, (20th-century plumbing), it could be a memorable experience.

Even less to my liking is the compulsion to eat in during the season, at a starting price of 140f. Gault-Millau says shortly *'prix sévères'*, which is my sentiment exactly.

Map 4B	**PLOBANNALEC** (Finistère) 5 km S of Pont l'Abbé on D102

Auberge du Petit Kéroulé
(R)M–L
Kéroulé-Bihan
(98) 81.22.55
Closed 1/10–24/10;
Mon. p.m.; Tue.
 New chef

In the heart of the **Bigouden** area, an old granite farmhouse elegantly restored and under a young chef, Jean-Pierre Stephan, who learned his trade under the doyen chef of the region, Adolphe Bosser from Le Goyen at Audierne. Plobannalec is only a few kilometres from the fishing fleet at Lesconil, and the best of their catch features on his menu. I recommend the 105f version as both interesting and good value, including *coquilles st.-Jacques* et *soles bigouden* and a wonderful crab *feuilleté*, that contrives to be both light and rich.

The décor is warm and attractive, as is the welcome from Mme. Bovo, and altogether this is one of the best bets in the area. A future arrow I suspect.

Map 4E	**PLOËRMEL** (Morbihan) 46 km NE of Vannes, 68 km SW of Dinan, 60 km SW of Rennes

A useful stop at the hub of several main roads.

Named after St. Armel, who arrived from Britain in the 6th century and promptly took on the local dragons. In this church you can see him leading away a very subdued specimen and making practical use of his stole as a halter. The 1944 air raids damaged nearly all the Renaissance stained glass in the church, but there remains one 16th-century window, featuring the Rod of Jesse.

Otherwise, apart from its ruined 12th-century ramparts, not a particularly interesting town. I would probably drive on for a picnic 2 km NW on the Loudéac road to the huge lake, the Étang du Duc, but if more substantial refreshment were required, try:

Commerce-Reberminard
(HR)S
70 r. de la Gare
(97) 74.05.32
Closed 2/1–22/1;
Sun. p.m.; Mon.
o.o.s.

The brothers Reberminard run this unspectacular, very French restaurant in the centre. The red R in Michelin for its 50f menu indicates the excellent value that regularly fills up its dining rooms.

There are rooms at 70–130f but the staff were far too busy at Sunday lunchtime for me to ask to see them.

Map 4B	**PLOGASTEL-ST.-GERMAIN** (Finistère) 8 km W of Quimper

Make for Plugaffen, and it's just off the Poldreuzic road.

Rôtisserie Ty Pin
(R)S
Pen Allée
(98) 94.00.56
Closed Mon.

The favourite of some local friends, who reckon it offers the best value around for charcoal grills and roasts, in a pleasant rural setting. Their menu sounds music to my poor tired-of-*noove-cuis.* ears — *pot au feu, ragoûts, pigeon, poularde au riz,* spit-roasted chicken, farm vegs. I look forward to this one.

| Map 4A | **PLOGOFF** (Finistère) 4 km E of the Pointe du Raz, on the D784 |

Kermoor
(HR)S
(98) 70.62.06

On the Plage du Loch, a simple family hotel, with just a road between it and the gorgeous sandy beach. Very basic but everywhere clean, friendly and cheap at 75f for a double room overlooking the sea. Menus from 78f and lobsters always available from the wicker pots manufactured by M. Curzon, the patron. The cheapest base I found from which to explore this area of Finistère.

| Map 4A | **PLOMEUR** (Finistère) 5 km SW of Pont-l'Abbé |

I find the south coast of the **Bigouden peninsula** disappointing, **Lesconil** and **Lechigat** lack the usual charm of little fishing ports, and **Guilvinec** and **St.-Guénolé** are plain grim; but still very near the delights of the rest of the area is:

Ferme du Relais Bigouden
(HR)M
rte. de Guilvinec
(98) 58.01.32
Closed 10/12–10/1

A new smart Logis, Breton-style farmhouse, grey stone, slate roof. The combination of the appeal of the rustic with the practicalities of the modern should please many people. Friendly proprietor, anxious to please and get established, which I'm sure will be very soon.

Bright cheerful well-equipped bedrooms cost 185f; there are bar, lounge, garden, terrace and tennis court. It has its own dining-room but there is a sister establishment, **Le Relais Bigouden**, in the town of Plomeur itself for alternative eating, on menus from 46f. As both establishments are open o.o.s., there's a good deal going for them.

| Map 3B | **PLOMODIERNE** (Finistère) 20 km N of Douarnenez |

Turn off the D65, 3 km E of the village on the C4, well-signposted.

Ferme de Pors Morvan
(H)M
(98) 81.53.23
V.

An old stone farmhouse restored to provide eight motel-style rooms in the utterly peaceful depths of the rolling countryside. The bedrooms, unfortunately orange vinyled, are uncomfortable only to the eye, being well equipped, with excellent bathrooms apiece, at 170f, which includes, unusually, breakfast.

No restaurant, apart from a *crêperie*, open in summer only, and a pleasant terrace on which to sit in the sun and have a tea-break.

With the sea only 6 km away and a tennis court available, I think this could make a convenient and agreeable stop in the winter when seaside hotels are closed and in summer when they're full and expensive.

| Map 4A | **PLONEOUR-LANVERN** (Finistère) 8 km NW of Pont-l'Abbé, 18 km from Quimper on the D2 |

In the heart of the **Bigouden** area, an unremarkable village. In its centre:

La Mairie 🔼
(HR)S
3 r. Jules Ferry
(98) 87.61.34
Closed 20/12–10/1
V.

A spic and span little Logis, comfortable, friendly and inexpensive. The bedrooms are pretty and cheerful, and good value at 86–162f, and nice Mme Dilosquer aims to please.

Her husband is chef and his cooking of local produce (the kitchen was seething with *langoustes* when I was there) has made his restaurant popular with tourists and Bretons alike. Good menus from 55f.

A possible future arrow I feel.

From a local resident: *"An excellent establishment . . . I have known the patron, who does the cooking, and Madame for twenty years. Lots of our friends use it, to their complete satisfaction."* Hervé Coatalen.

Map 2F | **PLOUASNE** (C du N) 28 km NW of Rennes, 22 km S of Dinan, 1 km N off the D220

Here's one I would never have found without local guidance:

La Petite
Hôtellerine
(96) 86.48.18

NEW
OWNERS

It was recommended by M. Quintin of the **d'Avaugour** in Dinan, when I told him I was looking for friendly inexpensive hotels of character, preferably undiscovered by other guides. Tucked away in deep countryside, well placed for through routes to west or south, for a cheap overnight stop it has a lot to offer. The young Mme Heard speaks good English and will go to any trouble to make her guests at home — like organising picnics for them or hiring out bicycles.

She is doing up all the bedrooms in different colours — *Bleue* is 75f, *Rose*, *Verte* and *Caramel*, with showers, are 100f. There are two dining rooms, a little one, quite smart with a big fire and menus at 45f, 60f and 80f, and a bigger one at the rear where she serves the *menu du jour* — no-choice, 31f, for *rapide* eaters.

Map 1B | **PLOUESCAT** (Finistère) 15 km W of St.-Pol-de-Leon

Westwards and northwards the coast lies low, sand-duney, windswept. Plouescat, inside the bay of Kernic, is a fishing and market garden centre, with a 16th-century covered market.

L'Azou 🔼 🔼
(HR)S
r. Gen Leclere
(98) 69.60.16
d. 25/9–25/10,
23/2–3/3,
Wed. lunch & Tue.
o.o.s.
AE, DC, V.

A simple hotel with a rear courtyard, popular locally for its surprisingly smart restaurant, presided over by patron–chef M. Azou. His cheapest menu at 45f, with lots of seafood, is recommended, but you can go up to 230f if you want lobster.

Eight simple rooms for 80–110f, all taken when I tried to look.

Map 1C | **PLOUGASNOU** (Finistère) 17 km N of Morlaix, 2 km inland from the Pointe de Primel

A pleasant little town facing round a green and leafy square and old church.

Hôtel de France
(HR)S
pl. de l'Église
(98) 67.30.15
Closed Oct.

Very much the centre of the town, year round, with a much appreciated restaurant offering far better value than you would find on the coast itself. For 49.50f you get four excellent courses, which include crab and *langoustines*, and the house wine is a mere 12f. But understand that this is very much a family pension hotel and you are required to sit down to dinner by 7.15 p.m., so that the staff can get off home.

The 12 simple rooms in the old house are only 95f a double. Those in the new annexe are a very pleasant surprise, being particularly spacious, very comfortable, well furnished, all with baths, at 170f.

Demi-pension at least would be required in the summer but with such good food that shouldn't be too hard to bear.

Map 5D   **PLOUHARNEL** (Morbihan) 3 km NW of Carnac

Auberge de Kerank
(R)M
(97) 52.35.36
rte. de Quiberon
Closed Mon. in
Dec.–Jan.

Anyone driving along the coast road is bound to be lured by this attractive old building right on the waters' edge. Inside is quite lovely, with shining copper antiques, but when you get down to the real business of the day — eating — it's a bit of a let-down. *Andouillettes* may be a house speciality but they should never feature on a no-choice 119f menu in mid-June. À la carte is OK but not cheap. Perhaps on a beautiful day it might be worthwhile having a meal on the terrace, say with just one fish dish or charcoal grilled *brochettes*, and it is usefully open every day, so might serve as a desperation resort in this area of few good eateries, but otherwise — drive on.

Map 2C   **PLOUIGNEAU** (Finistère) 10 km E of Morlaix on the N12

Auberge de Pen-ar-C'hra
(R)M
29 rte. Nationale
(98) 67.70.02
Closed Nov.; Mon.

An example to us all. Short menu, proposing only what is freshest and best in the market that day, unfussy rustic décor, irreproachable *couverts*, efficient service, warm welcome from *patronne*, Mme Penil; superb food from chef M. Penil, basically traditional but making good use of new ideas. Unusually good value — perfectly good menus at 49f (not w/e), or 90f or 135f. You couldn't hope to find a better main road stop. I forecast an arrow.

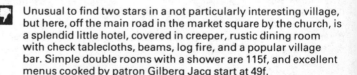

An Ty Korn
(HR)S
(98) 67.72.72.
Closed Sun.

Unusual to find two stars in a not particularly interesting village, but here, off the main road in the market square by the church, is a splendid little hotel, covered in creeper, rustic dining room with check tablecloths, beams, log fire, and a popular village bar. Simple double rooms with a shower are 115f, and excellent menus cooked by patron Gilberg Jacq start at 49f.

What with a quiet garden, no compulsion to eat in (thereby warranting an agreeable visit up the road) and those prices, I believe this is a better bet than anywhere in Morlaix itself and, with some confirmation, that another arrow will be merited for Plouigneau.

Map 2C	**PLOUNÉRIN** (C. du N.) 30 km W of Guincamp. Take the old RN12

Le Bon Voyage
(R)M
(96) 38.61.04
Closed 8/1–31/1;
Jan.; Tue. p.m.
o.o.s.; Wed.

An example of an important restaurant, Michelin star, well-known chef – patron Patrick Fer, where it is possible to get a bargain menu. The 85f version gives the savour of *haute cuisine* without the *haute* check.

No one could complain at the value of *salade de lotte*, grilled duckling, cheese and dessert prepared by a chef who trained with the great Fernand Point, but if one ventured onto the *carte*, which would involve a bill of more than double, there might be a few reservations. The welcome and service aren't that hot.

The restaurant is far more agreeable inside than out, at the rear of the building well away from the traffic thunder (rather less nowadays, since the *Route Express* bypasses the village).

A convenient stop for far better than average food.

Map 2F	**PLUDUNO** (C. du N.) 18 km W of Dinan on the D794

Just a hamlet, 2 km from Plancoët.

Le Petit Bignon
(HR)S
(96) 84.15.37
Open all year
except Sun. lunch;
Mon.
V.

An old grey stone farmhouse converted into a rustic Logis de France hotel, restaurant and *crêperie*. Bedrooms, in a wing round a courtyard, have sloping ceilings, dormer windows, all very simple, very clean, at 75–110f. You eat at one long table in the farmhouse bit, with log fire in winter, complete with satisfied cat on rug, and the nice Mme Frostin cooks good simple fare for 55f. A cheaper summer alternative is the *crêperie* in another wing, for variations on the *crêpe* theme and good for modest lunchtimes.

A useful inland budget stop, with all the beaches of the Côte Emeraude within easy reach.

Map 6D	**LE PÔ** (Morbihan) 15 km SW of Amay

Follow the coast road west of Carnac for a couple of kilometres to find the strange little village of Le Pô, entirely dedicated to the raising and selling of molluscs and crustaceans, with primitive flat-bottomed boats pulled up all along the shore. If you're self-catering, this is the place to buy a lobster or oysters or mussels.

Here is that rare Carnac breed — a genuine little restaurant — with the inappropriate name of:

Le Calypso
(R)M
(97) 52.06.14
Closed 3/11–20/12;
20/2–28/2; Tue.
p.m. o.o.s., Wed.
lunch o.o.s.

Very different from the conventional hotel meals and tourist menus of the town. This offers simple *fruits de mer*, prime grilled fish and meat, and very good too. Menus from 63f.

Map 4C

PONT-AVEN (Finistère) 15 km W of Concarneau
Mkt: Tues

The wide tidal estuary of the river Aven probes deep inland to this little town, where it becomes narrow enough for a bridge to cross it.

Here was the meeting place for the followers of Paul Gauguin at the end of the last century. 'I love Brittany,' he wrote. 'I find wildness and primitiveness there; when my wooden shoes ring on the gravel, I hear the muffled dull powerful tone I seek in my painting.' He often stayed and painted in the town and along the river banks and was a founder member of the Pont–Aven school. One of his favourite themes was the simple faith and apparently trouble-free life of the Breton peasants and he used the Pont–Aven ladies in their distinctive *coiffes* to illustrate his point. 'Jacob Wrestling with the Angel' is one of the best-known, painted in the town in 1888.

The town is still full of art galleries but I found no works of genius there. I did find a splendid winery though, where a free *dégustation* of Loire specialities cheered up the morning no end. **Au Cellier de l'Aven** 5 r. Louis Lourenech (near the town hall) is a good place to stock up on duty-frees. The Muscadet-sur-Lie, Crémant de Loire and Bourgueil we chose there all proved excellent buys, but if there are enough allowances in the party to make up 15 litres you could buy the wine *en vrac*, which is an ingenious plastic box, collapsible interior to keep out the air, working out at 50p a litre for some perfectly acceptable *vins de table*.

The bridge is the centre of the town but don't omit to follow the river to the 'port', an extremely pretty walk or drive along the banks, by water dotted with sailing boats, with green parks providing perfect picnicking space.

A hundred years ago they claimed that Port Aven had fourteen mills and fifteen houses. One of the mills has been converted into:

Moulin Rosmaduc
(R)L
*(98) 06.00.02
Closed 15/10–15/11; Sun. p.m. o.o.s.; Wed.*

One of the prettiest imaginable settings, on a loop of the river, set in a garden full of roses. The old beamed dining room is bright with flowers and pink cloths, place settings are elegant, the service and welcome exemplary. Pierre Sebillau's reputation and Michelin star are of long standing and this is a very well known Breton restaurant.

It appeared from the menu that this would be one of the rare places to eat simple food — grilled fish, plain beef, duck – in luxury surroundings (so far so good) but I fear the reality was an expensive let-down. The *nouvelle cuisine* vogue has obviously at last caught up and this chef's attempts to tag along just don't succeed. The meat and fish swam in uncalled-for sauces, too much, too thin. On a beautiful June night there should have been more appropriate veg. on offer than cliché *purées* of swede and celeriac. And where were the seasonal dishes inspired by the cornucopias currently in the markets. No asparagus? No strawberries?

Starters were particularly dull and unimaginative at 60–80f;

main courses at 80f and expensive wine (though impressive) pushed up the bill sky high. Perhaps we should have stuck to the non-choice menu, which at 85f sounded good value, but on our night it seemed a bit dull – trout, spiced chicken, sorbet.

If you are lucky enough to light upon a menu you fancy, this would probably be a very pleasant and rewarding occasion, but otherwise I cannot urge a visit.

Auberge La Taupinière
(R)L
(98) 06.03.12
Closed 15/9–10/10;
Mon. p.m. o.o.s.;
Tue.
AE, DC.

4 km on the Concarneau road. This is the one the locals recommend for a real gastro-treat. Chef Guy Guilloux takes the usual prime regional ingredients and conjures up his own-style miracles, without relying slavishly on either traditional or *noove cuis*. No-one does giant grilled *langoustines* as well as he, and his *soupe de moules en croute* at the other end of the price range is a different and delicious variation on an old theme. Good lamb and Breton ham too if fish palls.

Elegant décor, with big fireplace put to good effect for winter grills, and super efficient service. No menus, but expect a bill of around 150f, which is good value for such quality.

Map 4D

PONTIVY (Morbihan) 107 km W of Rennes – *Mkt: Mon p.m.*

The main market town in central Brittany, bustling and lively, Pontivy straddles the river Blavet. One look at the map will show how today it is the hub of a wheel of roads, river and canal. Napoleon recognised its strategic importance and laid out a formal town plan, with barracks, town hall, law courts; he made it a junction of the Nantes–Brest canal, with the intention of setting up his administrative centre for the whole area. It was actually called Napoléonville three times: 1802–14, during his One Hundred Days in 1815, and again during the Second Empire.

But the origins of the town's current name hark back to a Welsh monk, St. Ivy, who built the first mediaeval bridge over the river, and in the 15th century it became the seat of the powerful Rohan family, who built the mighty castle there.

Its history gives the town two distinct characters — the imperial to the south and the medieval to the north huddling round the picturesque pl. du Martray, with the Rohans' old hunting lodge still there.

The **Bar Central** here is the central meeting place for the townsfolk, always full, always lively. There we met Graham Willis, over with a party from Taunton on a twinning expedition, a valuable source of local information since he knows the town inside out. He confirmed my choice of hotel/restaurant:

Hotel Robic
(H)S
r. Jean-Jaurès
(97) 25.11.80
Closed Sun. p.m.
in winter
V.

The *patron* is mayor of Pontivy, so this is a local favourite. Good value menus from 42f and rooms from 60–120f.

PONT-L'ABBÉ (Finistère) 20 km Sw of Quimper

The monks of Loctudy (see p. 87) built the original bridge that gave the town its name. Capital of the **Bigouden** area, formed by a chunky peninsula, Pont-l'Abbé centres on a vast market square, taken over on Thursdays by a real French country market. Here, and indeed on other days and especially on fêtes, you can see the black-dressed old ladies going unselfconsciously about their business in their amazing *coiffes*. Hard not to stare. The Pont-l'Abbé version used to be small and neat, but within the present century it has shot skywards and now, tall and narrow with streamers behind, it is probably the

La Bretagne

most spectacular in Brittany. If you don't hit lucky in the streets, you can always see a fine array of local *coiffes* in the Bigouden museum, housed in the 13th and 18th-century Town Hall.

In 1857 Flaubert described Pont-l'Abbé as a quiet little town and, market days apart, it still is, with a peaceful walks along the river bank. The best reason of all for a visit is:

►**Hotel Bretagne**
(HR)M
24 pl. de la
République
(98) 87.17.22
Closed 15/10–30/
10; 15/1–31/1;
Rest. closed Mon.
o.o.s.
'M' Hotel of the
Year

Unbeatable value. Marcel Cossec, once a fisherman, is a natural cook. Recognising a fellow foodie, he proudly produced, at the end of a memorable meal, a plastic bucket, inelegant true, but full of the most wonderful fish *fumet*, reduced and jellied, ready to enrich tomorrow's fish dishes. In this area of abundant fresh seafood, it is all too easy to get a reputation as a good chef simply by poaching or grilling the stuff and dishing it up to tolerant customers. Nothing wrong with that, but here is the little extra that sorts out the stars.

His *langoustines grillées à la crème* are the best I have ever tasted. His poached turbot is not only pearly fresh, generously sized, but comes accompanied with a perfect *sauce au beurre blanc*, served instinctively, without any *nouvelle cuisine* dicta, underneath the fish, so as to enhance not disguise.

And what value! The *langoustine* evening was hardly a test; we had eaten there with local friends and advisers, the Coatalens, who had no hesitation in directing us to the **Bretagne** as simply 'the best'; we sat down very late, in high spirits induced by several glasses and much chat with the fishermen in the bar on Île Tudy, and we ate just those (providently ordered ahead *NB*) washed down with several more glasses, declared it was the perfect meal and remembered very little else next day. So several months later we arrived alone and ate on the menus.

For 60f there was a *gratin de coquilles St.-Jacques* — must have been six of 'em — in fat juicy cubes, poached just *à point*, coated in a sauce that owed a lot to the famous *fumet*, and gratinéed. Then a wing of skate (how much more interesting than the trendy monkfish) covered the dinner plate. Around it, *beurre noisette*, browned to a nutty turn, tangy with lemon and capers, *pommes vapeur* accompanying. Dessert nothing special, except that the chocolate mousse and crème caramel were home-made and that the fruit basket included expensive nectarines (Mme Cossec pressed me to have several).

Husband's 97F treat was no less good value. A dozen oysters preceded the generous hunk of fresh *turbot*, delicately garnished with fresh asparagus, surrounded with *beurre blanc*. Elsewhere we had been eating half as well for twice as much.

Super professional service, unfussy but attentive, in a charming dining room that looks out onto a little terrace full of flowers and with an old well, all very romantic for summer eating. Fresh flowers everywhere and all the little touches that show the owners care.

I certainly care for their bedrooms, which are among the most comfortable and attractive encountered in Brittany. Bargains all the way, from the simple 147f to the worth-every-penny 194f with twin beds and super bathroom, or 335f for four.

Marcel and Marie-José Cossec are the friendliest of hosts and are obviously proud of what they have achieved from what could have been an everyday tale of country folk. Their individual style of retaining the best of the old (the **Bretagne** lives up to its name and is no tourist pub; on Thursdays it is full of stallholders from the market and local shoppers) with willingness to add the best of the new is totally admirable. No doubt that English guests will be delighted with my Hotel of the Year, in the *M* bracket.

La Tour d'Auvergne 👍👍
(H)M
galerie Marchande
(98) 87.00.47

The **Bretagne** is a hard act to follow, but just in case it shold be full or closed, there is a new alternative. A nice young couple, M. and Mme Babault, have recently taken over this strange hotel, above the shops in a covered arcade. Off the long corridors to the right lead most unusual bedrooms, loo and bathroom downstairs, bed above, up a pine staircase. All fresh and Laura-Ashley-esque. On the left are more traditional rooms, all good value at 160f. Bar but no restaurant.

When I inspected they had only been open three weeks, and no closing dates had been decided. Further reports welcome.

I also found an unusually good and popular patisserie/tea shop **Auclert**, 4 r. du Château. M. Auclert calls himself *Maître du Thé*; certainly he sells a great variety of real tea, along with good ices and pastries, in a most pleasant and lively atmosphere.

Map 5D

PONT-LOROIS (Morbihan) 16 km S of Hennebont

The D781 crosses the wide river Étel and on the Plouhinic side, tucked away almost in the lee of the bridge, is:

Les Roches Brunes
(R)S
(97) 36.76.95
Closed Tue. p.m.;
Wed. lunch o.o.s.

Don't be put off by the seedy exterior and lack of paint. You come here for the view over the river and the very freshest of fish, prepared in interesting ways like *turbot á la crème de betteraves,* or *salade tiède de coquilles St.-Jacques aux pointes d'asperges.* Meat is good too — try *rôti de boeuf au coulis de tomates.*

Short on chi-chi means short on the bill. Menus start at 59f, and the wine list is equally good value.

Map 2E

LES PONTS-NEUFS (C. du N.) 12 km NW of Lamballe

A hamlet just off the D786.

Lorand-Barre
(R)L
(96) 32.78.71
Closed 15/12–1/3;
Mon.

Little clue from the creeper-covered exterior of this old house in a hamlet just off the D786 that it claims one of only three double-Michelin-stars in the whole of Brittany. It seems that nowadays it is so rare to find well-executed traditional cuisine that chef M. Damour can charge upwards from 350f for his simply grilled lobster, *ris de veau au porto, poulet sauté a l'estragon,* and still fill his little restaurant every night. Three times I have tried to book; sometimes weeks ahead from England; twice I've failed and the third time foul weather conditions slowed me down still some kilometres away so that I had to telephone and cancel. They weren't too upset, but I was.

| Map 1D | **PORT BLANC** (C. du N.) 17 km E of Perros-Guirec |

A little fishing port which gets its name for the white(ish) pebbles on its beach; to be sure there's not a lot of sand there but nearby are some relatively unknown stretches of coastline, with practically untenanted beaches and plenty of sands to choose from, backed by pine trees for picnickers.

To the right of the little harbour is a statue of the Virgin in a rock top shelter and before the village is a well-known and much photographed chapel, whose pitched roof reaches down to the grass; Gothic nave, with wooden rafters.

Hotel des Îles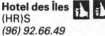
(HR)S
(96) 92.66.49
Closed Oct-Easter

Nothing special about this little Logis, not even on the beach, but it does offer good value for a family holiday, with simple rooms at 75f, or a good sized one with bath at 160f. And the food is good and copious on menus from 55f.

| Map 1D | **PORS EVEN** (C. du N.) 5 km NE of Paimpol |

A typically Breton little fishing port, all lobster pots and oyster trays, with no concessions to tourists except the **Café du Port** for drinks, *dégustations* and a good view, and:

Pension Bocher
(HR)S
(96) 55.84.16
Closed 5/11–1/4
AE.

A charming low grey stone house, covered in creeper, set sideways onto the road leading down to the port. More a restaurant with rooms, which is always a good sign, although here there are in fact surprisingly 23 bedrooms, all spic and span, four with sea views, from 63–184f, and a lounge to relax in with log fire after a **Bocher**-style substantial meal. Predictably, seafood is the house speciality, and for 67f you get expensive varieties like *langoustines* and *lotte* on your menu. Unpretentious good value.

| Map 3B | **PORT LAUNAY** (Finistère) 2 km NE of Chateaulin on the D770 |

An attractive road following the river leads to a few houses strung out along its banks; barges tie up here on the flower-lined jetty and little boats bob appealingly on their moorings.

Au Bon Accueil
(HR)M
(98) 86.15.77
Closed 20/11–30/
11; Jan.; Rest.
closed Sun. p.m.;
Mon. o.o.s.
Garage.
AE, DC, V.

The road runs between hotel and river but you can still get a good view of boats and water from the dining room. Menus from 50f. The rooms are modern, clean and not expensive at 80–172f, but you have to decide between a bath and a river view.

The hotel will organise fishing, pedalos, canoes and swimming and as there are 59 rooms availabe, I see it as a distinct possibility for a family base, from which to explore the coast at busy holiday times when beach hotels are full and expensive. Special facilities for the handicapped and good too for the elderly or indolent, with lifts, sauna and solarium all at hand.

Map 5C	**PORT-LOUIS** (Morbihan) 145 km SE of Rennes

At the mouth of the river Blavet, opposite Lorient. Nowadays a small fishing port and beach resort, once an important fortress. A trading centre from mediaeval times but developed in the time of Louis XIII, from whom the town took its name. Richelieu completed its fortification in 1636; his sea-pounded granite citadel still stands guard on the entrance to Lorient which has long since superseded Port Louis as a port. Even the sardine fishing industry has declined but the fishing fleet in the harbour inside the headland still brings in the giant tunny.

Pass through a gap in the ramparts to find the gorgeous beach – fine sand and lots going on, with a view across the estuary to Larmor Plage and the Ile de Groix lying a pleasureboat-trip away. All very seasonal though; on a beautiful early September day the beach cafés were shuttered.

The little town lies between port and beach, preoccupied on Saturday with its market which straggles along the main street and fills the market place, completely surrounding:

Hotel du Commerce
(HR)S
pl. Marché (98)
82.46.06
Closed Sun. p.m.;
Mon. o.o.s. P.

Nothing special – just a cheap base from which to explore the area; good for the kids, with a pleasant green garden and only 200 metres from that beach. A double is from 74–181f and good fishy menus start at 45f. Popularity with locals augurs well.

Map 4A	**POULDREUZIC** (Finistère) 16 km N of Pont-l'Abbé

Take the D2 NW of the village of Lababan, to find:

Ker Ansquer
(HR)M
(98) 54.41.83
Closed 1/10–1/5;
open for Easter

A solidly comfortable stone-walled, slate-roofed hotel of eleven rooms, 186f with bath. Modern, but very Breton in flavour. Mme Ansquer greeted me in *sabots* and the end wall of the charming dining room (meals *sur commande*) is elaborately carved and painted in traditional designs by local craftsmen. Near the beach of Penhors but probably more suitable for those in search of a rural rest than for young families.

►**Moulin de Brenizenec**
(H)M
(98) 58.30.33
Closed 15/9–Easter

On the main road to Audierne, between Pouldreuzic and Plozevet. A lovely old stone mill set back in its utterly delightful shady gardens, stream running through small lake, lots of flowers. Ten most attractive bedrooms have been contrived, all individually furnished with 'real' furniture at 270f a double, including breakfast. No restaurant but a nice *salon* to relax in when the garden's too damp.

Peaceful situation, helpful owner, anxious to make his guests comfortable. Would make a most agreeable base from which to explore the area and be free to try the local restaurants. An arrow for style and convenience.

Hôtel Ker Ansquer

Breiz-Armor
(HR)M
plage de Penhors
(98) 54.40.41
Closed mid-Oct–1/
4; Mon. o.o.s

A modern motel-type Logis in the middle of the bay of Audierne, right on the vast windswept beach of Penhors. Good views from the bedroom balconies of the spectacular rollers.

It's all a bit plastic and predictable, but the beach is good, the swimming under surveillance, and best of all it has an unusually good restaurant. At Easter it was solid with locals, who know a good *plateau de fruits de mer* when they see one. Menus from 68 to 200f with a huge *langouste*. All rooms with bath at 180f.

Map 5C

LE POULDU (Finistère) 14 km S of Quimperlé

In 1890 Gauguin painted the stunning 'Farm at Pouldu' here in the village he came to prefer to Pont Aven. His lodging is now the **Hôtel de la Plage.**

Pouldu is a seaside resort with two distinct faces. The one with the beaches looking out to sea has big hotels, with names like **Les Bains**, **Les Dunes**, all with superb views over the water; the port, which I prefer, looking in the opposite direction over the river Laïta, has a nice old-fashioned hotel, **Le Pouldu**, with balconied bedrooms, a seafood restaurant and a bar with terrace from which to contemplate the odd small fishing boat. Here I made what I think may well be a find:

►**Ster Laïta**
(HR)M
(98) 39.94.98

A nice old stone house with lots of character in its beamy dining-room, summer terrace and delightful bedrooms. Only three functioning in 1985, but soon there will be seven. The ones I saw were quite charming — spacious, elegantly furnished, views of the water, and good value at 140f.

The menus start at 57f. On the 73f we ate oysters, *langoustines*, monkfish and sea trout, cheese and dessert, all well cooked and served. There's a very pleasant faintly amateur feel about the place, as though you were staying in a home not a hotel, and maybe if standardised professionalism is top priority, this might not work, but I give it an arrow for individuality, position, charming rooms, good food and welcome.

Map 5E | **QUESTEMBERT** (Morbihan) 88 km from Rennes

Kistin is the Breton name for the chestnuts from which 'Questembert' derives and which feature on its coat of arms. A splendid 17th-century covered market hall dominates and gives a lot of character to the little town, and there is a carved calvary to inspect in the cemetery of St. Michael's chapel.

Bretagne
(R)L
r. St.-Michel
(97) 26.11.12
P.

Interesting. I dined at this famous restaurant, a *Relais de Campagne*, with high hopes and a *nouvelle cuisine* antagonist (OK, so it was my husband). Generally in domestic discussion (!) I tend to support the concept (though heartily sick of the subject at the same time – never has a culinary fashion attracted so much rubbish written and declared). I love the new freshness, colour, delicacy, inventiveness – but here in one meal I met all the cons and few pros. It left husband, fully vindicated, looking smug, and me convincingly left-footed, admitting that in the wrong hands the idea can be a disaster.

At first sight the 140f menu looked as if it were on my side. Here was the inventiveness — *raviole de grenouille*. How could one resist that experience? But in reality a pretty silly idea — frogs don't taste of much at the best of times and when you make 'em into a mousse and stuff 'em into pasta, their own mothers wouldn't acknowledge them. Then *suprême de poulinette, mousse de poireaux*. Much of the same. And accompanied, would you believe, with more pasta — noodle-shaped this time. The clichéd fan of vegetables proved to be potatoes, so already we have pale pasta, pale stuffing, pale chicken, pale stuffing, pale pasta again, pale veg. and two pale sauces. I longed for some green crunchiness. Worse to come — the satisfying-sounding, very un-*noove-cuis. tarte canelle* (blackcurrant tart) was unapologetically 'off' (with only four other tables taken?) and its substitute proved to be a *fromage blanc* and apple mousse (same texture, same colour as first two courses.)

Nothing *nouvelle* about the petits fours, and we gobbled them greedily, since truth to tell the other *n. c.* malaise — hunger pangs — were troubling.

Gault-Millau continues to rave about George Paneau's cooking, awarding him a rare three red toques. Bully for Michelin in this case, who sorted out the pretentious from the truly talented and reduced their rating to one star.

The restaurant, incidentally, is very grand, panelled and gracious, and the five bedrooms are attractive too, as well they might be at a cost of between 328 and 656f a double.

Map 6D   **QUIBERON** (Morbihan) 46 km SW of Vannes

Once an island, now joined to the mainland by a narrow strip of land, the Quiberon peninsula is fairly boring centrally, but has great variety of coastal interest. The Côte Sauvage to the west is the more interesting, with wild rollers crashing into little coves. Good walking, with spectacular views, along the stretch between **Pontivy** and **Port Maria**. For safe bathing it must be the sheltered bay facing eastwards.

You can take the ferry from Quiberon to the well-named **Belle Île**. I long to go and explore and in fact got as far as making a hotel booking, but the mainland proved so rich in discoveries that it had to take precedence. I believe there are several good hotels and restaurants in the island — **La Forge** is the name that cropped up most often — and one day I'll get there for what I'm sure will be a delightful visit.

The town of Quiberon is a busy seaside resort with dozens of hotels. Personally if a beach holliday were indicated I would prefer Carnac — even better sands, quieter and more accessible — and I found the Quiberon hoteliers too over-confident to want to please much, but here are one or two ideas:

Le Gulf Stream
(HR)M
bvd. Chanard
(97) 50.16.96
Closed 15/11–1/3
currently (but
check)

An unusually attractive little hotel on the front, beach just below. Lots of character in the shady terrace, the interior patio bright with flowers as are the bedrooms. No. 1 is super. Stone walls retained and washed white, balcony, good furnishings.

Unfortunately there are plans for contracting the season still further and insisting on demi-pension throughout. This will be 456f per day for two. It would certainly be little hardship to eat in the pretty dining room opening on to the garden and the no-choice menu, which changes daily, looked more interesting than in many hotels — avocados with *langoustines, magret de canard* and desserts.

The rest of the hotels all looked the same to me — **Ker Noyal, Bellevue, Ty Breiz** probably the best, all perfectly adequate but all insisting on demi-pension, which means that you need to know a lot more about the chef than I can tell you before deciding where to stay.

My hunch would be to make for: **St. Julien**, 2 km N.

Au Vieux Logis
(HR)S
(97) 50.12.20
Hotel closed 16/
10–15/3; Rest.
closed 1/10–1/5

In the centre of the village, an enchantingly pretty old stone house covered in roses, with green views from its windows. Flowery terrace, shady garden, all very different from the razzamatazz down the road.

The bedrooms are simple country-style at 95–195f. Dinner (menus from 60f) tends to end up round the piano or sitting round the big log fire, so it's all very sociable.

Another alternative is at **St.-Pierre Quiberon**, 4.5 km N. St.-Pierre is a friendly little village with a fine sandy beach, ideal for family holidays.

Hotel de la Plage
(HR)M
(97) 30.92.10
Closed 1/10–1/5

A modern hotel on the front, with good sea views from the balconies of its 41 bedrooms, and friendly management (I tested their sympathy by walking into a plate glass window). Comfortable rooms 200–310f menus from 75.

Back in Quiberon. . .

Ancienne Forge
(R)M
20 r. Verdun
(97) 50.18.64
Closed 7/1–31/1;
Wed. o.o.s.

This would be my first choice restaurant. Tucked away in a cul de sac off the main road it is unexpectedly tranquil and pretty. Interesting but no-choice menus start at 70f. Probably at its best in the evening.

Up the same alley is nice little tea place, **Ty Cup**, for a range of teas and home ices.

Les Pêcheurs
(R)S
Port Maria
(97) 50.12.75
Closed Jan., Mon.
o.o.s.

A no-frills modern building on the seafront by the port, with the best of fish. Get there early or book because it's small and justly popular. Take the 50f menu, whose three courses includes the fish of the day.

La Goursen
(R)M
10 quai de l'Océan
(97) 50.07.91
Closed 31/3–I1/11;
Tue.

A newish and attractive *fin de siècle*-style bistro overlooking the sea, with above average food and some interesting variations on the fishy theme. From 55f.

The two *crêperies* voted by local friends as easily the best are the **crêperie du Vieux Port** just past Port Haliguen on the east side of the peninsula and **Ty Briez Izel** at St.-Pierre Quiberon.

Map 4B · **QUIMPER** (Finistère) 204 km from Rennes

Mkt: Tues, Sat

The capital of **Cornouaille** is a delightful place to spend more than a few hours. Its natural blessings include the wide river Odet, that flows through its centre to meet the river Steir, and its setting, encircled by gentle hills and dales. Man has added his enhancements – the fascinating old streets around the cathedral, like the rue Keréon (the shoemakers' street), the squares with intriguing names like pl. au Beurre, the quays where strolling under the chestnuts can be very soothing, the r. du Salle with what must be the most elegantly housed *crêperie* anywhere, with beams and corbels and carved fireplaces, and the Terre au duc, all alleyways and timbered houses.

The Gothic cathedral was started in the 13th century and took five more to complete. It takes its name from St.-Corentin, first bishop of Quimper. On the west side stands an equestrian statue of the king of Cornouaille, Gradlon, who retreated to Quimper when his daughter Dahud succumbed to the Devil and opened the sluice gates to drown his kingdom of Ys (see Douarnenez, p. 63).

The old Bishop's palace overlooking the river is a good place to spend a grey day. (My previous memories of Quimper were solely of rain-swept streets, since we used to use it as a wet weather refuge from the dampness of camping at the splendid

Orangerie site nearby). Here is the Breton museum of pottery, costumes and furniture.

For a fine day, a tour of the river Odet down to its enchanting estuary is a good idea.

A more modern attraction is the new market, not far from the cathedral, a splendid conception of a vast wooden hall, ceiling-lighted, with all the treasures of a traditional marketplace under cover. Every day, year round.

The faïence of Quimper is charming, well-known, and unfortunately quite expensive. However, a brightly coloured plate, lively with the little stylised Breton figures, makes the perfect holiday souvenir and this is the place to buy it. Wherever you wander, through the pedestrianised shopping area or along the quays, you will find enticing pottery shops. The other take-home trophy from Quimper is its teatime speciality, whose name — *dentelles* — describes the laciness of these crisp little sweet pancakes, rolled like cigars and packed into painted tin boxes.

For such an obviously attractive town, ideally placed for the tourist geographically, particularly out of season when the coastal hotels are shut, I find it strange that Quimper has so few hotels. The old **Tour d'Argent** (13 r. Réguaires, 95.08.70) has lost most of its old charm for me and is now more of a businessmens' hotel than a discerning traveller's; the **Griffon** (rte. Bénodet, 90.33.33) is a vast modern pile outside the town, expensive and boring, and I personally didn't like the atmosphere of **La Sapinière** (rte. Bénodet, 90.39.63) which was full of smoke and commercial travellers when I was there (but I am told I was unlucky).

I am still looking for a hotel to do the town justice (and would very much like to hear of one such) but meanwhile I would stay outside and come in for shopping, especially on Wednesday and Saturday, when the square outside the cathedral is full of peasant ladies sitting engulfed in bunchy black skirts and shawls, occasionally coiffed, selling a bunch of wild daffodils or a dozen speckled eggs.

Restaurants too are oddly thin on the ground, but there are always the *crêperies*. The best I can offer:

Le Capucin Gourmand
(R)M
29 r. des Réguaires
(98) 95.43.12
Closed 16/8–1/9;
Sun. p.m.; Mon.
DC, AE.

In a rather grim street not far from the cathedral and, truth to tell, a bit bleak looking itself in its uncompromising granite shell, but inside it perks up a bit and serves food in the 'correct' French way. Good value for serious eaters on the 100f menu, which offers that ideal combination of quality and quantity. Prime fresh ingredients, particularly fish, are served in generous portions. I remember a salad of *langoustines* with great affection.

Les Tritons
(R)S
allées de Locmaria
(98) 90.61.78
Closed 27/8–24/9;
Mon.

Open only for dinner and then it stays open very late indeed – at least 1 a.m. — so obviously useful in special circumstances if you don't mind the smoke. The food is not as sophisticated as the hours and owes more to the peasant — *daubes* and *potées* — than to the townee. No bad thing. Not expensive, with menus from 65f, and cheap wines.

125

Café de Bretagne
(R)S
Les Quais

This is where I think I should end up eating in Quimper, becuase it can be all things to all men. You can take a coffee or a drink on the terrace, watching the river (and a lot of traffic) go by, take an inexpensive snack at the bar, like the *plat du jour* which was an excellent *rognons de veau* for us, at 35f, or penetrate further to the more sophisticated tables for a full scale meal to suit all tastes and pockets. Always lively and good value and you can usually park nearby on the quayside.

Map 4C

QUIMPERLÉ (Finistère) 34 km E of Concarneau

Mkt: Fri

Kemper Ellé = confluence of the Ellé, and here that river joins the Isole to form the Laïta, with the town set in its narrow valley. The old part in the lower town centres on the curiously shaped Ste.-Croix, modelled on the Church of the Holy Sepulchre in Jerusalem; the lovely apse and crypt are Romanesque but the rest of the church had to be rebuilt 100 years ago after the belfy collapsed. Across the river climb up the rue Savéry to reach the beautiful Gothic church of St.-Michel.

The road from **Le Pouldu**, the D49, cuts through the cool and peaceful forest of Carnouet. 3 km south of Quimperlé is:

Auberge de Toulfoën
(H)S(R)M
(98) 96.00.29
Hotel closed 25/9–31/10; Mon. o.o.s.;
Rest. closed 25/9–1/4; Mon.
AE, DC, V.

Just a simple erstwhile coaching-inn but with a high standard of country cooking — the 68f menu kicks off with eight oysters and for 94f you get five courses. Nine rooms at 87.50f for one with a shower or 200f with bath.

Manoir de Kerroch
(H)M
(98) 96.04.66
Closed 31/10–1/4

A km further on towards Quimperlé is this pleasant manorhouse standing high with a good view of its own grounds and swimming pool.

The rooms are in different buildings and vary accordingly. All are excellent value from 150–250f, but the more expensive ones are particularly attractive and well-furnished.

Now run by a nice family and no longer with any connection with the **Relais du Roch**, the restaurant at the foot of the drive.

Map 5C

RAGUENÈS PLAGE (Finistère) 12 km SW of Pont Aven

Raguenès in argoat means 'opposite the island'. Here the islet is joined to the mainland, except at high water, by a causeway of fine sand, which curves out from the little harbour, bolstered by rocks, making the kind of picturebook combination that has the photographers readily clicking.

Magnificent is the only word for the main beach just below the hotel **Men Du**. It sweeps around the bay, firm sands inviting walkers. Even on a cold blustery day there is usually the odd stalwart bent against the wind but enjoying the kilometre or so of splendid scenery. You can walk along the cliff edge too in either direction, fields, poppies, nightingales to one side, breakers, seaweed and gulls to the other.

The **Nevez Peninsula** of which Raguenès forms the tip, is remarkably unspoiled. **Kerascoët** is a tiny village said to be 'typically' Breton but rare in its attractiveness. All its small granite cottages have thatched roofs, flowers tumble, chickens cluck, dogs doze.

Drive through it, down green honeysuckled lanes, to **Rospico**, a deep sheltered inlet with fine sands and a bar/*crêpérie*, and then on to **Port Manec'h**, a popular little seaside resort set in the pines on the estuary of the Aven — sands, beach huts, fishing harbour. I didn't care much for any of the hotels but there is a very attractive bar, in a large old stone house covered in wisteria, with a good terrace overlooking the sandy bay, so an excursion and light lunch should be no problem.

If it's peak season and you hanker for solitude you could find it by following the signs to Kerantré and bumping down a spectacular drive of chestnuts to a little inlet called **Poulguin**, with a small shingly beach and a few boats, all completely sheltered from the west. Then on to **Kerdruc**, whose little harbour is full of yachts and fishing boats, with a bar and picnic seats overlooking the water. From here the old road crosses an ancient narrow bridge and leads to Pont Aven.

But there's no doubt that the star of the peninsula is Raguenès, with two hotels to choose from:

▶**Men Du**
(H)M
r. des Îles
(98) 06.84.22
Closed 1/10–31/3

A lonely little white building standing solitarily above the beach. It looked so windswept that we were somewhat dejected that our stay there should have coincided with bad weather, but there is a large glassed-in bar/terrace from which to catch the view in inclement times, and a cosy bar. No restaurant but the place is always animated with locals and tourists. M. Ollivier, the

en -Du at Raguénès Plage.

patron, finds nothing too much trouble to serve his customers and Mme Ollivier ditto, with lots of excellent ideas for excursions and local restaurants.

The rooms all claim to have views of the sea but it has to be said that the windows are small and set high, so a splendid opportunity to lie in bed and enjoy the fabulous surroundings has been lost. They're on the small side too but immaculately presented, extremely comfortable and well furnished with a good bathroom, at 200f.

Everything about the hotel is on a small scale but of a high quality, the management is particularly friendly, the site supreme and no restaurant means freedom to eat out. One of my favourites.

Chez Pierre 👍 👍
(HR)M
(98) 06.81.06
Closed 1/10–1/5

In the village but still no great distance from the sea; very popular with the Brits, who congregate happily in the pleasant bar and garden and greet old friends from previous years. They come primarily for the food, which used to be outstandingly good; recently there have been grumbles that chef, patron Xavier Guillou, is perhaps cashing in on his popularity, and certainly the waiting time is appalling. Menus at 70f. Rooms are very pleasant, at 199f with bath.

Map 4A

POINTE DU RAZ (Finistère)

There's something alluring about extremities. Land's End and Raz attract the tourists not only because they are spectacular but because they are ultimates. The vast car parks at Raz testify to the numbers expected in summer, from whom the *crêperies* and souvenir shops will no doubt exact a second toll (parking 8f).

But forget the matazz and concentrate on the Raz; there's a lot of it to go round and it's hard not to be impressed with the power of the wind, the waves and the knowledge that the race below the dizzying cliffs is one of the most dangerous in the world. Beyond the lighthouse of the Old Lady, 10 km offshore, is the Island of Sein, reef encircled. The druids were rowed out to their burial ground here from the Baie des Trépassés, or so they say. Another theory is that the bay derived its name (a *trépassé* is a dead man) from the bodies of shipwrecked mariners washed ashore here. All stirring stuff, imbuing a certain thoughtfulness in those, vertigo-free, who walk over the scattered rocks to the edge of France and ponder for a moment on the fury of the forces unleashed below.

Serious climbers can take a guide for a 1½ hour tour of the point round l'Enfer de Plogoff (the Plogoff Inferno) where a sheer chasm and the untiring waves meet like battering rams; their clash is deafening, orchestrated by an odd moaning, said to be the souls of the dead!

For more relaxed appreciation there is still plenty to see and wonder at; Notre-Dame des Naufragés (Our Lady of the Shipwrecked) stands a comfortable distance away from the precipice, reassuringly calm and untroubled; walk past her to one of the less adventurous paths and you will still enjoy a memorable panorma.

I wouldn't suggest eating seriously at any of the tourist restaurants up here, but recommend doubling back, *via* the D784 and V0 to:

►Hôtel de la Baie des Trépassés
(HR)M
(98) 70.61.34.
Closed 15/11–1/3

Standing centrally, solitarily, in the wide sweep of the bay, with its marvellous sands and treacherous tides, is the large white hotel. Here on Easter Monday I ate the best Bank Holiday lunch I remember — a Gargantua of a crab.

It so happened that the previous week I'd ordered 'fresh crab salad' at an English seaside town. Poking dubiously at the cotton wool blob dumped on the vinegary beetroot that bled on to the hothouse lettuce limpness, and avoiding the dreaded word 'freezer' I commented that the specimen was very — er — cold? 'Oh *yes* Madam', came the righteous reply, 'we keep all our shellfish in a cold cabinet.' *Keep*? The *Trépassé* monster had been kept only as long as it took to heave him off the boat into the pan and was still steaming from his immolatory immersion.

No genteel English 'dressing' for him, with breadcrumbs and colouring and chemical mayonnaise. Cleavered in half was all his presentation. Not even the unreasonable doubt that the customer couldn't work out for himself which bits tasted good — you just heaved out the dead mens' fingers and enjoyed the rest. (Query — another theory for the name of the bay — did the poisoned ones never come back?) The wicked pincers alone yielded several frozen packs worth of delectable, juicy, pearly flesh. Along with a bowl of home made mayonnaise, quantities of *baguette* and fresh butter, all washed down with Muscadet sur Lie, I could not ask for better. The cost — £5.

Had smaller portions of more courses been the mood, there is an excellent and sensible 52f menu — crab mayonnaise, six oysters, mussels etc., followed by three kinds of fish with a choice of three kinds of sauces (or chicken or pork) and a splendid *tarte aux myrtilles*. Lobster, bass and sole feature on the 78f, 105f or 160f menus, but no doubt that the general favourite was the *plâteau de fruits de mer*. All round it was heads-down, with a cracking, and a spitting, and a mopping, and every table a battlefield of débris, from *langoustines*, oysters, mussels, clams and whelks. Not much conversation until the coffee stage, and then what a patting of stomachs and loosening of napkins!

Some very attractive new rooms have been built on recently, making full use of the view over the bay. At 180–210f for a double with bath, they are as good value as the food and the combination gets an undoubted arrow.

Map 5F   **REDON** (I. et V.) 65 kms SW of Rennes on the D177

The Nantes-Brest canal crosses the river Vilaine here, making the town a natural centre for the Brittany water network. It is a very agreeable exercise to stroll along the quays, expecially the quay St-Jacques, with its fine 18th-century houses, and peer down inquisitively on the canal boats invariably tied up there.

Their occupants have only a short walk up the delightful Grand'rue to the market place, brimming over with outside stalls on Mondays, but always a good place to stock up the boats with fresh vegetables, cheeses, terrines and fish from the excellent covered market hall.

The largest romanesque tower in Brittany looms over the square, seven centuries old, detached from St.-Sauveur, the old abbey. Some of the frescoes being restored inside are just as old.

One wet and windy night it was only a scamper from our little boat tied up by the lock to:

►La Bogue
(R)M
3 r. des États
(99) 71.12.95
Closed 2/1–1/2;
Tue. p.m.; Wed. P.
V.

We could not have chanced upon better. A delightful little restaurant, warm and welcoming, with Mme Hatté ditto. The four course 81.30f. menu was not only a bargain but at least as good as those of some of the starred and vaunted restaurants sampled on the same holiday. The twelve oysters alone for a first course made my husband's evening when he reflected what they would have cost back home. I ate *rillette de saumon* — tiny almond-shaped moulds of a flavoursome salmon pâté, sitting in a delicate cream and chive sauce. The *steak marchand du vin*, generous and well sauced, and the *côte de veau fermière* — tender veal garnished with lardons of bacon, mushrooms and buttery potatoes, were both prime, but for me the most interesting dish was a *râgout* of snails, beautifully presented out of their shells, artichoke heart slices fanned around, in a memorable cream and basil sauce.

An enterprising use of the local speciality — chestnuts — is made in a *gâteau de châtaignes*, but if you wish to try my favourite — the hot *feuilleté de pommes* — you must remember to order it at the beginning of your meal. Its crisp flakiness, caramelised apples, dollops of *crème frâiche* really should not be missed. An arrow for good value, imaginative cooking, pleasant ambiance.

Gare Relais du Gastronome
(H)S(R)M
10 r. Gare
(99) 71.02.04
Closed 15/6–30/6;
15/2–28/2; Sat.
lunch o.o.s.

Described as a restaurant with rooms, and indeed they are very simple, but clean and adequate at 90f. Not a lot of atmosphere to the restaurant but good food on the 65f menu, and a more ambitious choice up to 220f.

Map 3G

RENNES (I. et V.) *Mkt: Every day in Les Halles*

The administrative and cultural capital of Brittany, lacking the immediate charm of its long-term rival, Nantes, but, thanks to its two universities, a lively city, always animated by a population of chattering students. Parking is diabolical; best make for the section of the Vilaine now covered over and used as a car park. Ask for Le Parking Nouvelles Galeries and you will be within walking distance of all the action.

Until the early 18th century here was a city of mediaeval black-and-white timbered houses, separated by narrow winding streets, but a fire that blazed for six days in 1720 changed all that. Most of the centre was razed and nowadays only the 'Vieux Rennes' area round the cathedral gives any feeling of an old Breton town. Here there are cobbled streets, narrow crooked houses, over-hanging gables, beams galore, to activate the sentimental tourist's Kodak, but of the Rennais in this quarter there are few — for them the heart of their city is a few blocks eastwards, the spacious pl. de la Mairie, where the students and the pigeons foregather and the flowers festoon the baroque town hall, designed by the architect Gabriel, appointed by Louis XV to build a new city.

But the most noteworthy building of all (pity about the lumpish cathedral) is undoubtedly the former Breton Houses of Parliament, now the law courts, which dominate the pl. du Palais with their elegant 17th-century ensemble, designed by the Palais de Luxembourg's architect. You can visit its Hall of the Great Pillars, *via* a series of impressively decorated rooms culminating in the panelled Grand' Chambre, which used to be the parliamentary debating chamber.

A short walk from here, in a north-eastern direction, leads to the Thabor Gardens, an unusually calm retreat in the heart of a city, good for a picnic or restorative. It used to be the garden of the Benedictine abbey and some of the cloistered serenity seems to have endured in its 1,080 hectares of park, flower beds and shrubberies.

Most of the hotels are in the newer area, south of the river, centering on the pl. de la Gare. The old **Du Guesclin** is here, but alas, the colourful façade is more interesting than the interior, now distressingly plasticised under its Minimote owners. However the new Salad Bar might be useful for a cheap light lunch — 36f menu, open every day.

Le Président
(H)M
27 av. Janvier
(99) 65.42.22
Garage
AE, DC, V.

Undoubtedly my first choice. Central, quiet, thanks to sound-proofing, no parking problems, efficient friendly staff and most attractively furnished and well-equipped rooms and bathrooms. No plastic here. Worth every penny of 187.50–245.40f for a double.

Le Sévigné
(H)M
47 av. Janvier
(99) 67.27.55
AE, EC, V.

Nothing like as stylish as **Le Président** but cheaper, equally central, and useful as a fall-back. It also has the advantage of a restaurant next door with the same name but different management, which specialises in Alsation food, and very good too. Allow around 70f for the *à la carte* consumption of *choucroute*, or excellent beef steaks, followed by splendid desserts, but note that the restaurant is closed on Saturday lunch and Sunday. The hotel rooms are modern and efficient and cost from 140–195f.

Anne de Bretagne
(H)L
4 r. Tronjolly
V.

A large insistently modern hotel in a new section of the city, south of the river, but still within walking distance of the centre. 210–240f.
'New, clean and comfortable. Twin bedded rooms excellently furnished with modern bathrooms; staff courteous and friendly. Would certainly stay there again.' — C. Comley.

Assessing the number of Michelin stars and Gault-Millau toques gives a useful idea of the character of the city. In Rennes single stars and toques are liberally dotted about, but no more than that. This I take to mean that here is no great gastronomic centre but no shortage of reasonably affluent residents and businessmen. The students are beginning to make their presence felt, encouraging the opening of several new bistros, *crêperies*, pizza parlours, but generally eating here is a reliable, but unexciting and expensive experience.

To start with two Michelin stars:

Le Corsaire
(R)M
52 r. d'Antrain
(99) 36.33.69
Closed Sun. p.m.;
Sun. all day in July
and Aug.
AE, DC, EC.

The r. d'Antrain runs north of the pl. Ste.-Anne, in a straight line from the pl. de la Mairie. A smart little navy-blue lacquered restaurant, whose chef has recently also become patron. As he was Grand Véfour-trained, I had high hopes. Perhaps it was these that led to a vague disappointment, especially with the items chosen from the *carte*. My *mousse St.-Jacques*, encased in a cabbage leaf, sounded more exciting than it looked, with more than a suspicion of cabbage leakage into the *sauce langoustines*. All a bit flabby and colourless. *Magret de canard* undistinguised. My companion, who loyally tackled the menu, fared distinctly better. Her choice of *coquillages, sauce cressonière, filets de lieu*, followed by a sensational *dégustation* of seven excellent desserts which I unashamedly shared, pointed out the message here — stick to the 75f menu and you can't grumble at the value. Good wine list, with Touraine wines especially recommendable.

Le Palais
(H)M
7 pl. du Parlement
(99) 30.21.19
Closed Sun. p.m.;
Mon; Aug. and
Feb. school hols.
AE, DC.

The same tactics didn't work here. The 70f menu, recited with such aplomb by Bernard Anffray, had us enthusiastic about the prospects of a *mousse* of scallops, *coulis de tomate*, until we tasted the india-rubber reality, unredeemed by the suspiciously vermilion blob of tomato sauce. All three main choices were sampled and all three found wanting. *Poulette à la crème* was a disgrace in presentation, quantity and flavour — an elderly grey chicken leg, scales 'n all, sitting uneasily in a puddle of thin white sauce. My fish of the day was unmitigated cod and the presentation of the over cooked *longe de boeuf* failed to disguise the fact that this is a cheap and unflavoursome cut of meat that needs skilful handling and saucing to make it palatable. The *tarte aux poires* would have disgraced a *relais routiers* in its thin limp pastiness.

The restaurant is smart, middle-aged, middle-class. Perhaps the accolades refer to the *carte* rather than to the set menu, but I shan't be going back to find out.

Chouin
(R)M
12 r. d'Isly
(99) 30.87.86
Closed Aug.; two
weeks in Dec./Jan.;
Sun.; Mon. Book.

I would have been far cleverer to have listened to the locals and eaten here. **Chouin** is a splendid fish shop, proffering all manner of marine creatures, in glistening colourful heaps, on marble slabs. Next door is a little navy blue restaurant, with portholes and lifebelts in case you hadn't got the message. But high quality fish doesn't come cheap anywhere, and if you take, say, a dozen prime oysters and a helping of perfectly grilled pearly white turbot, expect a bill of around 120f. Mercifully the white wines here are not expensive, and there is a lunchtime menu of three courses for 88f. Or, of course, you could settle, as I did, for just a steaming bowl of *moules à la crème*, with bread mopper-up, for 30f. In any case you will get value for money.

Ti-Koz
(R)M–L
3 r. St.-Guillaume
(99) 79.33.89
Closed Aug.; Sun.
DC, EC.

Du Guesclin was a local lad who made good six centuries ago and whose name keeps cropping up all over France and is far from forgotten in his home territory. Dinan was his home but it was at Rennes that he first won fame in the jousting lists and at Rennes that he was subsequently knighted for his successes in a series of military campaigns against France's enemies. particularly the English. He ended up High Constable of France. They say **Ti-Koz** was his home, as well it might have been, in all its crooked, dark beaminess. Americans love it, of course, but it doesn't rely entirely on its antiquity to bring in the customers. The 120f menu is the one I recommend — marinaded raw salmon and haddock surprisingly delicious, then a hot fish terrine, *magret* of duck with blackcurrants, cheese and *pâtisserie*. Wines are splendid but pricey and service leisurely, so pick the right occasion.

La Cotriade
(R)M
40 r. St.-Georges
(99) 33.34.76
Closed Sat. lunch;
Sun. lunch; Mon.
EC.

The r. St.-Georges is one of the most picturesque in Rennes. It runs eastwards from the pl. du Palais, is cobbled, bordered with immensely old buildings, and newly blessed with a selection of small restaurants; something for everyone, from *crêperies* to Italian, and half a dozen bistros, the best of which is *La Cotriade*, new in 1984 but already one of Rennes' most popular restaurants. Not hard to see why — small, beamed, very pretty indeed, original cooking — leave room for their *feuillantine de poires caramélisées et son coulis de fruits rouges* — and a warm welcome from the moustachioed *patron*. Lunch menu is only 48f for something simple, or 85f for the *menu gastronomique*. In the evenings it's *à la carte* — allow 100f. Good house wine — Muscadet, Bordeaux or Burgundy — *en carafe*.

Le Baron
(R)M
26. r. St.-Georges
(99) 38.87.56
Closed Aug.
EC, AE.

A few doors away from the (preferred) **Cotriade**, older-established, less enticing ambiance, but usefully open every day. Food is more traditional, like a *tournedos de charolais, sauce bearnaise*, well cooked and presented, except for the desserts which are disappointing. Menus from 61.50f.

Le Moutardier
(R)M
38 r. St.-Georges
(99) 38.79.43
Closed Sun.
EC

Opposite **La Cotriade**, and similarly small old, beamy, atmospheric. Painted appropriately mustard-colour. Good menus at 69.70f or 99.50f for an interesting *gastronomique*.

La Chope
(R)S
3 r. de la Chalotais
(99) 79.34.54
Closed Sun.
AE, EC, DC.

The best-known brasserie in Rennes, near the pl. de la République, and popular with the students, since it doesn't throw them out until midnight. Straightforward brasserie staples like *choucroute* or *cassoulet*, all well done but some more individual items too, like *rouelles de coquilles St.-Jacques*. Good value at 45.70f.

South of the river down the r. de Nemours to the pl. H.
Commeurec are the central markets, open every day except
Sundays and fêtes. After a stroll around, sniffing, admiring,
envying, some light refreshment might be in order. Make for:

La Pâtisserie
(R)S
34 bd. de la Liberté
Closed Sun.

Not only a pâtisserie, good for elevenses or tea, but a good
choice for a light lunch. So good in fact that the queues start to
form, so get there early or late to get a table, and enjoy a set
lunch for 30f, which includes not only service but wine too.

Le Piano Blanc
(R)M
Sainte-Foix
(99) 67.37.74
Closed 1/1–7/1;
Sun; Sat. lunch

A very unusual restaurant indeed, and especially useful if you
do not wish to get embroiled in the centre of the city. Take the
Route de la Prévalaye off the western ring road (next after the
Vannes exit) to find an unprepossessing exterior disguising one
of the most attractive, and certainly the most original,
restaurants around. It gets its name from the white grand piano
which dominates one of the dining rooms – all *fin de siècle*,
lacquered walls, potted palms. In summer it is particularly
popular because of the courtyard area where it is most
agreeable to sit by the fountain and sip and sup, but the value of
the lunch menu — 45f for three interesting courses — draws
businessmen from the city all year round, and it is wise to book.

In the evenings there is sometimes music, centering round
that piano and then the *à la carte* will cost around 120f. The food
is as attractive as the surroundings, leaning towards *nouvelle
cuisine*, with dishes like *coussin de loup à la mousseline de
persil*, and *terrine de fruits en crème d'amandes au sirop de
framboise*.

Well worth discovering. Coming from the centre of the city,
the rte. de la Prévalaye is the extension of the bd. Voltaire.

Map 1F

LA RICHARDAIS (I. et V.) 3 km S of Dinard on the D114

If approaching from St.-Malo don't follow the signs to la
Richardais after the barrage, but turn right towards Dinard to
find:

Le Petit Robinson
(R)M
(99) 46.14.82
Closed 15/11–15/
12; Tue. p.m.
o.o.s.; Wed.

Much smarter than its roadside appearance might suggest. A
well-known *restaurant gastronomique* with hefty portions of
traditional cooking, with, of course, good shellfish. Menus at
55f, 80f and 150f.

Map 4C

RIEC-SUR-BÉLON (Finistère) 4.5 km SE of Pont Aven

Chez Mélanie
(HR)M
pl. de l'Église
(98) 06.91.05
Closed 2 weeks in
Jan.; Tue.
DC

A deliciously old-fashioned restaurant/hotel in the centre of this
little market town, all dark varnish, walls almost covered with
paintings of Breton ladies in coiffes and pinafores by Pont-Aven
artists. One shows the great chef Curnonsky cracking oysters
with the legendary Mélanie from whom the hostelry takes its
name.

Lots of Bélon oysters of course, the celebrated speciality
homard Mélanie and other seafood on menus from 86f.

The bedrooms are charming too, at 159–178f but some of them could be noisy.

4 km away on the right bank of the river Bélon, via the D24, well signed:

Chez Jacky
(R)M
(98) 06.90.32
Open from
Whitsun–end Sept.
except Mon.

An oyster-cultivator *patron*, who sells oysters direct from the trays behind his restaurant or serves them in the charming dining-room built out over this, to my mind, most beautiful stretch of river (see p. 34)

A dozen of the best *belons* will cost 50f, smaller *creuzes* 40f. Or you can eat all manner of crustaceans, from lobster *bisque* at 30f or *langoustines* at 40f, to his justly famous platter of assorted seafood.

Well-known, so book if possible, but even if there is no occasion to eat here, the area is so pretty that a visit to the oyster beds would be an agreeable excursion.

▶**Auberge de Kerland** 🔒
(R)M
(98) 06.42.98
Closed 3/1–10/3

3 km S, well signposted off the D24. The restaurant with the most beautiful site in the book. High in the pine trees above the valley of the Bélon, it has to be seen to be appreciated. A drink on the terrace above the wide winding water, deep mysterious green banks and pine perfumes is as good a way as I know to . start an evening.

Inside is pretty nice too — an elegant Louis XV dining room, a log fire when it's chilly, and everything calm and ordered. Very good news to hear that there will soon be ten new bedrooms, and I look forward to visiting them for an *FE5* update.

The food is almost as good as the view. Chef–patron M. Chatelain cooks his fish with interesting variations of his own — *langoustines* come with the lightest touch of curry, lobster is gently perfumed with ginger, but my *panaché de poissons au beurre d'ail* was as good as fresh prime ingredients, simply cooked, could make it. No need to spend a fortune — the 85f menu is usually very good news. Arrowed for idyllic site, interesting food.

Map 5F

LA ROCHE-BERNARD (Morbihan) 40 km SE of Vannes, 95 km SW of Rennes

---

A perfect anchorage, with old and new harbours, on the river Vilaine, upriver of the *barrage*. The river is particularly attractive just here, wide and tree-lined; two ancient cannons defend the entrance, many masts swim in the early morning mists beneath the great new bridge.

The main street is dull, but the old quarter leading down from the pl. du Bouffay to the creek is picturesquely cobbled and geraniumed.

Market day is Thursday, in the square flanked by:

Auberge des Deux Magots
(HR)M
pl. du Bouffay
(99) 90.60.75
Closed 6/10–22/10;
15/12–15/1; Sun.
p.m. o.o.s.; Mon.
P.

Large comfortable bedrooms, well furnished, with lots of character. One luxurious double with bath and loo costs 177.70f and the cheapest with bath is 137.60f. M. Joel Morice is patron–chef and prepares copious and good menus from 40f. Recommended and potential arrow.

Hôtel de Bretagne
(HR)S
15 Crespel de
Latouche
(99) 90.60.65
Closed Mon.

At the other end of the town, near the new bridge. Without the character of the Deux Magots perhaps, but the rooms are spotlessly clean, good-sized, well-equipped with excellent bathrooms and cheap. A *'simple'* is 80f and one with a private bathroom is 139.50f. Nice dining room, with panoramic view, on the first floor and menus from 60f cooked by the owner M. Le Bot.

L'Auberge Bretonne
(HR)M
(99) 90.60.28
Closed 15/11–15/
12; Fri. lunch;
Thur.
AE, DC, V.

Gault-Millau's got it all wrong — *not* small, *not* bistroesque, *not* near the big bridge. In fact this is a very elegant restaurant at the top of the main street in a small square. One large stone-walled room aims at the rustic but is unable to resist the expensive tapestried chairs so favoured by the upmarket French restaurateur; the overflow room is like a little jewel box, red velvet walled.

Swift deft service, a smiling efficient Madame, and an amazing wine list (but with house wine at 40f).

No *carte* but most interesting menus, whose permutations take some unravelling. The cheapest, no-choice, at 40f, suited me very well, with delicious thick *soupe d'étrilles* (baby crabs), *charlotte d'agneau* (an aubergine-lined mould of casseroled spicy lamb) and *pouding caramel* (a rare steamed pudding). Excellent imaginative value.

My companions ate more ambitiously on the 110f menu (others at 77f, 95f, 145f and a *dégustation* at 250f) with a lobster and mango salad, followed by *aiguillette* of beef — little rounds of thinly sliced fillet fanned out around a peperonata mound, all in a thick rich winey sauce.

Their puddings too were interesting — hot apple *chausson* with rhubarb mousse and fresh pear slices with chocolate sauce, but we all felt somehow that the parts were greater than the whole — each dish lacked the flair that distinguishes the adequate from the inspired. This unpredictable factor can never be determined until the food is actually consumed — a lot can be read from a menu but far from all, and just as the interesting-sounding ones can prove let-downs, sometimes the obvious and dull menus provide pleasant surprises in extra unrecorded touches. Full marks here for trying though!

They do have seven rooms, which I have not seen.

Map 5F	**ROCHEFORT-EN-TERRE** (Morbihan) 25 km NW of Redon

Clinging to a spur overlooking the deep valleys of the Arz and Gueuzon rivers, this is one of the prettiest villages in Brittany. The main street is lined with 17th-century granite houses, whose owners vie with one another for the Best-Kept-Windowbox. Flowers tumble everywhere, their geranium-reds and hydrangea-blues enlivening the greyness of mediaeval fortress ruins, old gateway, horseshoe covered market, and Our Lady of Tronchaye's Church. A *tronchaye* is the bole of a tree, where a statue of the Virgin was found by a shepherd a thousand years ago; the church was built on that spot.

It's a favourite excursion for tourists and to cater for their needs is:

Lion d'Or
(R)M
(97) 43.32.80
Closed 15/11–31/
11; 25/2–15/3;
Mon. p.m.; Tue.

A 16th-century coaching inn, as flower-bedecked as the rest of the village. Menus from 85f.

Auberge Moulin Neuf
(R)M
(97) 43.32.19

A converted windmill in an exceptional site at the edge of a lake, with good regional cooking lightened to suit modern tastes. Menus from 80f.

Map 2B	**ROCHE MAURICE** (Finistère) 4 km NE of Landerneau

Rearing high on a rock outcrop above the river Élorn and dominated by the ruins of the mediaeval castle built to protect Landerneau. The church of St.-Yves has a Renaissance rood screen with finely carved grotesque figures and a beautiful 16th-century Passion Window; its *enclos paroissiale* (see pp. 18, 79 & 159) includes an ossuary with a macabre skeleton issuing a warning to those who gape: 'I'll get you all.' Make hastily for

Le Vieux Château
(R)S
4 Grand' Place
(98) 20.40.52
Closed 1/11–20/11;
6/3–27/3

Lunch only, fresh, simple, copious. For 58f you could have six oysters, *Langoustines armoricaines*, *gigôt* with *flageolets* and *tarte maison*, but this menu is for weekdays only. Otherwise it's 85f, 95f and 160f.

Milin an Élorn
(R)S
Ancienne rte. de Landivisiau
(98) 20.41.46

A picturesque old watermill on the river Élorn, converted into a good *crêperie* and modest grill.

Map 1B	**ROSCOFF** (Finistère) 5 km N of St.-Pol-de-Léon

Roscoff is foremost a port, or rather a series of ports — the old harbour, the ferry terminal and the new harbour with the gangway into the deep water for the **Ile de Batz** boats at low tide (see p. 31).

137

This island is the biggest of many, some mere reefs, that lie off the coast, a panorama of unfailing interest. Little coves and beaches surround the headland — you pick the one to suit the weather conditions and your mood.

Most of the animation centres around the quays, where the cafès and bars are always full and the families parade in the early evening sunshine. Or not, as was the case on my last visit, blighted with fog and drizzle. Still the stalwarts battled out to the end of the jetty, more in search of exercise than a view, but when the weather fails — and that is bad luck because the climate is unusually gentle — the town comes into its own and the shops selling souvenirs and fishermens' sweaters do good trade. Even the old 16th-century church gets visited and the plaque commemorating Mary Stuart's landing in 1584 noted.

I looked at all the hotels — no easy feat in August when the *complet* signs were up. The **Bains** is a vast easy-going old-fashioned concern, overlooking the new harbour, rooms from 100–200f. The best food in town is said to be at the modern **Gulf Stream**, with smaller rooms at 180f, or 220f for a sea view, but some distance from the town and with a cheapest menu of 90f. The **Bellevue** at the other end of of town overlooking the old harbour also has a reputation for good food, but the rooms are even smaller at 132–239f. I stayed at the **Regina**; (a) because it has no restaurant and (b) because it was the only one I could get into. At 200f the room was adequate, the management friendly and helpful. My choice would undoubtedly be:

Les Alizés
(H)M
quai d'Auxerre
(98) 69.72.22
Closed 1/10–1/3

A really nice little hotel in a good position overlooking the old port, with a terrace from which to observe all the activity. Well-furnished bedrooms with seaviews and bathroom cost 145–155f, and a family room 175f. Friendly management adds to the good deal.

Le Brittany
(H)M–L
bd. Ste.-Barbe
(98) 69.70.78

An unexpectedly luxurious hotel overlooking the old harbour. Lovely galleried entrance hall, elegant lounges, stone-walled panelled breakfast room with seaviews framed in its arched windows. Lovely bedrooms from 230–367f and a swimming pool make it worth every penny if you can run to it.

They have recently opened a crypt restaurant, whose appearance (17th-century stone walls, candlelit) is infinitely better than its food (tourist orientated). Early days though and the potential is there. Meanwhile no compulsion to eat in.

Restaurants are not easy in Roscoff — lots of *crêperies* but nothing outstanding. Those who don't eat in their hotels make for St.-Pol-de-Léon. The best I could find was:

Chez Gaston
(R)S
r. J. Bara.
(98) 69.75.65

A *familial*, with straightforward cooking on menus from 45f. Popular with locals and tourists, as offering good value in pleasant bistro atmosphere.

Map 1G	**ROTHÉNEUF** (I. et V.) 6 km N of St.-Malo

The Rothéneufs were pirates and smugglers who lived here in the 16th-century, a powerful and much respected family. On a rocky headland nearby a priest, Father Foure (who died in 1910) sculptured their legend. His gigantic granite fresco depicting 300 characters makes a unique memorial.

Follow the coast road further west towards Cancale and by turning down an unmarked lane to the left discover an almost landlocked sea, fringed with pines, sheltered, ideal for water sports at high tide and with a lovely beach at low water. Perfect for kids, so a family hotel nearby must be good news:

Hôtel Centre et du Canada
(HR)S
(99) 56.96.16
Closed Oct.; 15/12–
1/2; Mon. o.o.s.

The friendly son of M. Boudevant has now taken over this favourite old family hotel but only the name seems to have changed, with *Canada* being added as a tribute to many transatlantic connections. Otherwise it is as delightfully old-fashioned, caring and cheap as I remembered it from bucket and spade days. In the centre of the village, but behind is a large garden which leads on to the beach.

The rooms are simple but fine at 72–139f, the meals are lavish, enough to cope with growing appetites and particularly inspired with local fish.

Reports on some more recent visits than mine could easily lead to an arrow, I believe.

Map 2G	**LE ROUVRE** (I. et V.) 9 km NW of Combourg. Well signposted off the D10

I set off to find an old farmhouse recommended by a reader, *Le Clos du Rouvre*, but got hopelessly lost in the maze of country lanes between St. Pierre de Plesguen and Lanhelin. Apologies for not having located what sounded a most interesting possibility, with eight bedrooms and friendly owners. If any readers have better luck, I should like to know. Instead I stumbled upon:

Le Petit Moulin du Rouvre
(HR)S
St.-Pierre de Prescuen
(99) 73.85.84
Open all year

The borderline between a gîte, b and b, and a *pension* gets very blurred. Here is an old 17th-century watermill restored so that Mme Annie Michel can provide accommodation for three families on any of these bases. They cost 200f for two or 360f for three including breakfast, and a three-course evening meal using home-grown, home-made ingredients can be requested for another 68f.

The rooms are simple but comfortable and downstairs is a beamed salon with log fire, and a dining room where it would be very easy to chat to your fellow guests if so inclined.

The setting is lovely, with a lake in front (fishing available) trees all round the house, and a terrace. I thought it a haven of quiet for an overnight stop after a long haul, and so did the young French couple on their honeymoon I met there.

Map 1F	**SABLES-D'OR-LES-PINS** (C. du N.) 44 km NW of Dinan

Well-named indeed. Golden sands and pine trees are what this little resort is all about. The beaches must be a strong candidate for being the finest in Britany. On a blustery May day, when the sand yachts had the main north-facing beach all to themselves, I found, by climbing over the sand dunes, through the pine woods, another splendid beach, facing due south, so sheltered that sweaters and trousers soon gave way to bikinis. I could easily have spent all day there (and will another time) but a picnic in the pines' shade and wonderful walk following the twists and turns of the river through the sands, round the headland, right over to the little harbour, did very well indeed.

The 'town' is virtually one street, often dusted with fine flying sand when the wind is strong. Not very exciting — all new buildings, custom-built to make the most of the natural advantages of the town's name.

Diane
(H)M
(96) 41.42.07
Closed 16/9–26/5

Some sea views if you crane a little, no restaurant, with a wide choice of rooms to suit all tastes and pockets, from 90f to 250f.

Morgane
(H)M
(96) 41.46.90
Closed 20/9–25/5

Smaller, pristine new, no restaurant, simple rooms at 160–260f.

Les Pins
(HR)M
(96) 41.42.20
Closed 30/9–25/3
EC, V.

Nice terrace, lots of balconies, 22 rooms at 90–120f. Restaurant 62–110f.

Au Bon Accueil
(HR)M
(96) 41.42.19
Closed Oct.–Easter

Run by the same family for fifty years. All the 45 rooms have recently been modernised and now most have their own bathrooms, for 250f. Regional cooking and a nice garden.

Le Manoir St.-Michel
(H)M
(96) 41.48.87
Closed Nov.–20/3

At **Le Carquois**, 1.5 km NE on the Fréhel road. A converted 16th-century manorhouse — a bit over-converted perhaps, to give a brand new look. The rooms are a bit stereotyped and small for the 260f price tag, but they are spotlessly clean and well equipped and there's an expensive air about the terrace furniture. Comfortable, guaranteed quiet, with no obligation to eat in — for those who want a dead safe bet this could be the answer.

Map 5D

STE.-ANNE-D'AURAY (Morbihan) 16 km W of Vannes on the D779

The largest *pardon* in Britany is on July 25 and 26 when pilgrims come here from all over France and beyond to pray to the mother of the Virgin Mary. The legend is that Anne was born in Armorica, was married, widowed, travelled to Palestine and re-married producing a daughter, Mary; when she came back to Armorica, she was visited by Jesus.

There are other smaller *pardons* throughout the year and if you are lucky enough to witness one, the costumes and colour are unforgettable. Michelin says severely 'visitors to the pilgrimage closes must respect local traditions and be circumspectly dressed.'

The present elephantine basilica was built in the last century.

►**L'Auberge** 👍 👍
(HR)S
56 r. Vannes
(97) 57.61.55
Closed Tue. p.m.;
Wed. o.o.s. P.
V.

👍

Worth making a pilgrimage. A surprising interior of red striped awning tent-roof, copper pans, Breton lace, with a huge log fire gently smouldering and welcoming on a chill autumn evening. All very bright and cheerful.

Allow plenty of time for decisions. Michelin gives a red R to the 47f menu, as well they might, but every one of the four alternatives had particularly interesting components. As it was the last night of the holiday, I pushed the boat out on the most expensive, at 130f, and relished every mouthful of a terrine of three different mushrooms, chunks of tender *cêpes* contrasting with the puréed *champignons* and *chanterelles*, then superb baby *coquilles St.-Jacques* — lots of 'em swimming (*à la nage*) in a sea of *beurre blanc*, then *magret de canard* sharpened with raspberry vinegar. Unusually, lots of good vegs, including an excellent potato *gâteau*, a hot *crottin* (goats cheese, just melting) with expensive salad, and then a wicked assortment of desserts — six *dégustations* of hot *tarte normande, marquise au chocolate, sorbet d'orange, charlotte aux fraises* and fresh strawberries (o.o.s.).

A note from the chef on the menu, craving clients' patience over the fact that everything depended on the market and was freshly cooked to order, proved unnecessary — the first was quite obvious and the waits not excessive (and in my case welcome between so many courses).

Husband was more than happy on the cheapest menu, with perfect *oeufs pochés*, a shoulder of lamb braised with fennel and a good cheese board. With house wine at 22f, or the alternative of a well-chosen wine list, this all adds up to an unusually good stop, especially since the value of the nine rooms upstairs is as good as the food. A spacious and comfortable double costs 125f and a more modest version is 80f. Aim for one at the rear.

Friendly and helpful owners, the best food I found for miles around at reasonable prices, and excellent bedrooms make this a certain arrow.

But here is another discovery, in the little town:

👍

I would like to recommend most highly: **Hotel de la Boule d'Or**, *run by M. Alain Prieur. Clean and comfortable, nice airy bedrooms with showers and washbasin. The food was excellent, all local dishes, with beautiful sauces. We were so pleased that we stayed six days and had a different menu each evening. We chose the four course simple menu: sorrel soup, fish, guineafowl, vegetables and choice of sweret, like Rhum Baba with plenty of genuine rum and cream, and we were always being asked if we would like things like fresh salmon and fresh melon that were not on the menu. At breakfast we had lovely small dishes of beautiful butter. This was the cheapest* *place we found and we cannot speak too highly of it, or of the excellent staff and service.'* — Mrs L. A. Bonner.

Here's one I shall certainly investigate.

Map 3B

STE.-ANNE-LA-PALUD (Finistère) 16 km N of Douarnenez

Turn west off the D63 towards the Bay of Douarnenez. In the midst of the rather desolate undulations stands Ste.-Anne's chapel, the destination for the great *pardon*, one of the most spectacular in Brittany, that takes place on the last weekend in August, when thousands of pilgrims, stallholders, sightseers flock to this lonely site.

Carry on to the coast for wonderful walks in all directions, along the spectacular sandy beach or above it amongst the dunes. Solitarily stands:

La Plage
(HR)L
(98) 92.50.12
Closed 6/10–31/3
AE, DC.

Supposing that absolute peace and tranquillity, allied with supreme comfort, along with superb food, in an outstandingly beautiful natural setting, and supposing again that around 450f for a double room were no object, make for **La Plage**. I have yet to hear of a visitor who did not love it and wish to return.

The building is ugly, modern, white, right on the beach. Inside all is spaciousness, light and luxury, taking full advantage of the marine aspect by having the dining room overlooking the sea. This is the territory of a combination of talented young local chef, Jean Pierre Glouanec, the patron M. Le Coz, and his son and daughter-in-law. Between them they prepare and serve a remarkable menu at 130f (not Sundays) which has clients queueing up to book. The emphasis, predictably, is on seafood — *Salade de rougets à l'huile de noix, bar grillé au beurre blanc, pânaché de poissons,* all faultless, with sauces enhancing not disguising their immaculate freshness. The dessert course is also star quality, particularly the *pâtisserie*. I find it exactly the right combination of traditional ingredients in their prime, with exciting inventiveness not just for inventiveness sake, all totally professional but not pompous.

All the rooms, as you would expect from a Relais et Château hotel, are comfortable and well equipped, but this is a case for pushing the boat out and going for one on the front. The hotel faces due west and to catch that most spectacular sunset from your own balcony is worth a lot. The best rooms cost 618f and the cheapest 400f. Demi-pension, at 480–980f, is obligatory in high season.

There is a swimming pool, sauna and games-room, but the biggest attraction of all is the silence.

The rooms have been fully-booked, so I cannot confer a personal arrow, but I look forward to doing so soon.

Map 1C

ST.-ANTOINE-PLOUEZOC'H (Finistère) 6 km N of Morlaix on the D46

The most attractive way to arrive is *via* the D76 from Morlaix, following the valley of the Dourdouff ('Black Water' in Breton).

Hotel Menez
(H)M
(98) 67.28.85
Closed 15/9–29/10;
Sun. p.m.; Mon.
o.o.s.

A substantial granite house standing at a cross roads in the middle of nowhere. Well tended hydrangea garden and immaculate inside too. Ten comfortable well-furnished rooms from 100f to 170f with bath. No restaurant makes life easier for those who like to eat out. Just opposite is:

Auberge St.-
Antoine
(R)S
(98) 67.27.05

The best value and some of the best food in Finistère. If you have been hankering for a lobster, take it here on the 135f menu. You warm up with *langoustines* (15 giants) or 12 oysters, proceed to the half-lobster, simply grilled, butterly deliciously fresh, press on to sea bass or sole or steak, and fill in the odd corner with salad and cheese and dessert.

Viande du jour and *poisson du jour* turned out to be *rôti de veau* and monkfish respectively, and these featured on the 40f, 50f and 90f menus, preceded in appropriate variety, by *crudités* oysters and *soupe de poissons*. Daughter, with a shellfish allergy, took the 50f version and was well pleased with her choice of three pâtés and raw ham for starters, then tender skate dripping in *beurre noir*. House wine is an eminently affordable 11f.

I would arrow the **St.-Antoine** for quite exceptional value, but it falls down sadly on just one requirement — the all-important *accueil*. The young Mme Le Godec is much more interested in chatting to her friends and coping with fractious toddler than in making her visitors welcome; the service is atrocious — not only slow but totally disinterested, to the point of incivility. The dining-room is not an attractive place at the best of times but the dismal ambiance can be attributed directly to the personnel. Go in a party and make your own evening.

Such a pity because M. Le Godec's bite is much better than his bark.

Map 1F

ST.-BRIAC-SUR-MER (I. et V.) 16 km W of St.-Malo

I could wax lyrical about St.-Briac. Dammit, I will wax lyrical about S.B. After all it's not often you find two perfect horseshoe bays, facing west and south, fringed with pines, fine sand shelving down to water clearer, bluer than the Aegean (if perhaps not quite so warm), blessed with a vista of islands, other bays, other beaches.

Follow the signs to Les Plages and choose between them, taking a stroll round the headland with the funny château to get bearings, confused by such a plethora of inlets and no glimpse of the way the Channel lies.

The village of St.-Briac, mercifully, slumbers away with only a passing nod at the tourists. Its signposts seem intent on evasion and a wrong turn will lead down narrow streets of little granite houses and cottage gardens. Only one modest hotel and that nowhere near the beach or I might take up residence in it. It's the **Hôtel de la Houle** in the main street, but as it was shuttered on the day I wanted to check the bedrooms, I cannot vouch for them. They cost from 90–130f, and the menus start at 60f. Phone (99) 88.32.17 and please report to me.

Map 2E	**ST.-BRIEUC** (C. du N.) 58 km W of Dinan

A rapidly growing town — the largest in the area, with a busy Saturday market. I don't think I would choose to stay here in summer, but if the coastal weather were drear I suppose it might make sense to look inland. I found one hotel that would certainly make an attractive town base:

Ker Izel
(H)M
20 r. Gouet
(96) 33.46.29
AE, DC, EC, V.

In a quiet side street not far from the cathedral, with all the rooms recently and most attractively redecorated. A double with bath costs 220f.

Le Covec
(H)M
pl. Poste-et-
Théâtre
(98) 33.23.18
Closed Sun.
AE, DC, EC, V.

Facing on to the colourful market square, a little modern hotel, well furnished and efficiently run. A double with bath costs 160f.

La Vieille Tour
(R)M–L
Port de St. Brieuc
75 r. de la Tour, Le
Légué
(96) 33.10.30
Closed 15/6–1/7;
23/12–14/1; Sun.,
but see below.

Follow the river on the north bank along the D24 for 3 unprepossessing km to find the best restaurant in the area. The *vieille tour* in question is the Cesson tower, now in ruins.

The *patron*, Michel Hellio, has won a Michelin star for his inspired seafood cooking, duck with homemade pasta, and inventive desserts, all served in a first floor restaurant overlooking the bay of St.-Brieuc, but when we took our keenly anticipating tastebuds there on a Saturday lunchtime, it was closed for no good reason that we could discern, so I cannot report personally. Perhaps some reader had better luck?

Menus start at 90f, but it was the 170f version that we were most miserable to have missed.

Map 1F	**ST.-CAST-LE-GUILDO** (C. du N.) 36 km NW of Dinan.

Mkt: Tues, Fri

St.-Cast and Le-Guildo together cover the narrow peninsula pointing to St.-Malo at the Pointe de St.-Cast. All round the promontory are scattered beaches of fine sands and rocks and some spectacular views, making it a popular resort.

The most promising hotel, unfortunately, is in the little town, only a step or two from the beach admittedly, but lacking those sea views:

Hotel des Dunes
(HR)M
r. Primauguet
(96) 41.80.31
Closed 5/11–20/3

Modern, bright, cheerful, efficient, nice patron, M. Fecet, and above-average food, much appreciated by the regular *pensionnaires*, who tuck in appreciatively to grilled scallops, *gigôt de lotte à l'ail*, extra good desserts: their demi-pension costs from 200–440f. O.o.s rooms are 105–200f, some with balconies. The menu at 77f is a bargain, as is the 95f. alternative.

On the beach of Pen Guen to the east of the promontory is:

Le Biniou
(R)M
(96) 41.94.53
Closed 21/9–20/3;
Wed. o.o.s.

A trim little restaurant, well recommended locally, with a terrace above the beautiful beach, which judging by the size of the parking must be pretty busy. Rustic but quite smart — not the place for a damp bathing suit. Fishy menus from 70f.

At **Notre Dame de Guildo**, 10 km south, a bridge crosses the river Arguenon and shortly afterwards a sign announces:

Château du Val d'Arguenon
(H)M
(96) 41.07.03

M. and Mme de la Blanchardière have adapted their stately old family home into a guest house, with some rooms in the main château and some in the stable wing. They are not luxurious in the way that those in the **Château de la Motte Beaumanoir** (see p. 108) are, but comfortable and roomy and the price is very different. Here it is from 180–260f including breakfast, or 360f for a four-bedder. No restaurant but helpful Mme de la Blanchardière has a list of good local restaurants to suit all tastes and pockets.

The grounds are extensive and slope down to the estuary, so that you can bathe without getting out the car, and there is a tennis court.

I met some English ladies staying there for the second time, who were well pleased with the set-up and I should think this would make a good unfettered base of more than usual interest.

Notre · Dame · de · Guildo

Map 4B	**ST.-EVARZEC** (Finistère) 17 km SE of Quimper

Not in the village of St.-Evarzec at all, but 2 km away on the busy D783.

La Fontaine des Chapons
(R)M
(98) 94.80.03
Closed Tue. p.m.;
Wed.
AE, V.

Useful in both its situation and its Sunday p.m. and Monday opening, when it is nigh impossible in this area to eat out.

A pretty little restaurant, approached from the rear, with good parking. Chic dining-room where chef–patron Jean-Yves Herlédant serves *moules poulette, brochette de boeuf*, etc. on a 70f menu, or 12 oysters, *fricassée de lotte*, on the 99f, or superb lobsters *à la carte*. A local business-man recommended this one to me highly, and I think he could be right.

Map 1F	**ST.-JACUT** (C. du N.) 8 km SW of Dinard

Set on a long spit of land between two deep bays, with an unsurpassed panorama of wild rocks, sands and neighbouring headlands. Boasts eleven beaches, so there should always be one out of the wind.

Le Vieux Moulin
(HR)M
(96) 27.71.62
Closed 1/110–15/3
V.

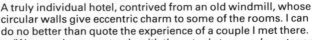

A truly individual hotel, contrived from an old windmill, whose circular walls give eccentric charm to some of the rooms. I can do no better than quote the experience of a couple I met there.

'We were happy not only with the actual stone and mortar and the character of the building itself, but with much more — the very peaceful and convenient situation away from the main roads, our lovely room with antique furniture and circular bathroom in one of the turrets, and of course with the food. What food! Naturally seafood featured predominately on the five-course menu, (the cheapest menu was an incredible 51.50f), but all the other dishes were just as delicious and all served in that lovely dining-room with the attention to detail that makes such a difference. We were very impressed that the soupière, platter or whatever was always left on the table for extra helpings.

Knowing your quite proper requirement for a good Continental breakfast, you will be pleased to hear that here butter came from the dish and conserve from the pot, not the packet. We will go back!' — Michael Madgwick

This does sound a foolproof recommendation, but Madame did mention that she was not well and was handing over to her daughter, so anything could happen. Meanwhile demi-pension is from 148–206f per person.

Le Terrier
(R)M
r. des Sciaux
(96) 27.71.46

Down the road from the **Moulin**, a charming old fashioned restaurant, with two small rooms looking out on to a garden and terrace. Nice, friendly *patronne* adds to the appeal. Excellent, unusual menus, with lots of fresh fish dishes, like *turbot safran, barbue au basilic, St.-Jacques sur lit d'épinards* for 70f, and a 45f lunch menu except Sundays.

Recommended as a definite cut above other local possibilities, and particularly valuable in winter (but phone first) when dinner is served by candlelight in that most romantic dining-room.

| Map 1C | **ST.-JEAN-DU-DOIGT** (Finistère) 17 km NE of Morlaix |

This village, nestling in the shelter of a deep valley which later widens out to the sea, derives its curious name from the story that 500 years ago a young man from the neighbouring parish of Plougasnou chanced upon the finger of St. John the Baptist, no less, and bequeathed it to the village. By so doing he ensured that every year on St. John's Day those who bathe their eyes in 'the water of the finger' that flows from the gorgeous Italianate fountain in the parish close will have perfect eyesight. The villagers must have got tired of the sceptics, for a tetchy notice pinned upon the church says 'contrary to what is written in many guidebooks, the finger of St. John is not on public display.'

Le Ty Pont H
(HR)S
(98) 67.34.06 R
Closed 15/10–
Easter; Tue; Wed.
o.o.s.

A modest little pub in the village centre, popular with the locals, and offering some of the cheapest accommodation I found in the area. A double room — and they are all perfectly adequate — costs from 71–148f and the menus start at 45f. A *sole meunière*, which I always take as my price guide, is a mere 35f here.

| Map 1F | **ST.-MALO** (I. et V.) 65 km from Avranches |

Mkt: Thurs, Fri

For the British, probably the best-known of all Breton towns, and deservedly so. But far from typically Breton.

The Malouins have always been a breed apart, noted for their independence, with a motto 'Malouin first and foremost, Breton perhaps, French if there is anything left.' This distinctive character really does still exist, deriving from centuries of sea and land battles, and the fact that until the 18th-century the rock on which the town is built was linked to the mainland only by a sandbank, tide-covered for most of the day. Follow the signs to *Intra Muros* (Within the Walls) and you step into another world, which certainly accounts for some of the towns's appeal.

The rebel Malouins fiercely resisted the idea of being linked to either Brittany or France, refusing to recognise Jean de Montfort as Duke of Brittany and defending the town under the leadership of privateers like Du Guesclin and Morfouace, still local heroes. Jean IV had to blockade the town, building the Solidor Tower in St.-Servan in the process, before the inhabitants finally submitted, but at the first opportunity they broke away to become French subjects. Their reluctant allegiance to either side swung to and fro as Charles VI gave the troublesome town back to Brittany in 1415, reverting again to France when Duchesse Anne of Brittany married Charles VIII. It was she who had engraved on the castle tower 'Quic en groigne, ainsi sera, c'est mon plaisir' — 'Grumble as you may, it will be thus because I wish it so', but the loyalty of the citizens was to remain to St.-Malo first and foremost.

The Quic-en-Groigne museum is now installed in this tower, with waxwork figures of local historic scenes. The Musée d'Histoire contains relics of some of the unsually large number of famous sons of the town, like Jacques Cartier, who almost by accident (he was looking for a northern passage to India)

Saint-Malo

discovered Newfoundland in 1534. The subsequent opening up of the St. Lawrence seaway and of Canada brought great prosperity to St.-Malo, based on cod-fishing off Newfoundland and the fur trade. In the 17th century it was France's largest port.

The obstinate Malouin character produced a number of privateers (licensed pirates), like Surcouf, the last and greatest of them all, who, after legendary feats of dering-do, like capturing the treasure-laden *Kent* from the English in 1800, became the richest ship-owner in France and a Baron of the French Empire.

The air of St.-Malo seems to have produced a fine crop of men devoted to the pen as well as to the sword. Chateaubriand was born here and is buried on the island of Le Grand Bé, his grave facing out to sea as he wished. At low water you can walk out to le Grand Bé, one of a string of islets surrounding the town, some only visible when the tide goes down. Anyone who has sailed into the harbour will be aware of the hundreds of dragons' teeth hazards that severely test navigation skills.

An excellent viewpoint for this offshore panorama is from the ramparts, and two walks right round the town are a must, with completely different aspects at low and high water. The walls are one of the few relics of the original town. The greatest battle of all in St.-Malo's colourful history was fought, sadly, within living memory, in 1944, when three-quarters of the town was destroyed, but subsequently skilfully rebuilt in the solid 18th century style. Its cathedral, St. Vincent's, has now been fully restored from 12th century nave to 18th century façade.

It's altogether a most agreeable place to stroll around, to shop and then to sit in one of the cafés in the square, resting cobble-tired feet and watching all the invariable activity. Lively all the year round, so a good off-season choice.

The beaches, sandy and rocky, are wonderful here just below the walls, at nearby Paramé and *via* a delightful ferry ride, at Dinard, so it's ideal for children too.

Just outside the walls is the vast yacht harbour, with some mighty impressive boats tied up, and the lock into the Rance. Many's the frustrated hour we've spent there shaking fists at the lock-keeper, who, green light or no, is knocking off early for lunch, condemning us to another unscheduled day locked in, when the plan was to be out to sea or exploring the river.

A trip up the Rance to Dinan by whatever means is a must. With highly attractive towns at either end of the voyage and the most gorgeous scenery in between, it's worth doing some homework on the timetables at the tourist office. It's a longish trip, very dependent on the tides; a car at the other end would be ideal.

If you have to be a prisoner, I can think of few more agreeable places but if there is no boat to sleep in, problems arise. Unfortunately, like that other picturesque favourite port of mine, Honfleur, (see *FE3*) it seems that the hotels have it too easy and take advantage. The **Hotel Elizabeth**, for example, highly rated by most guides, has tiny cramped rooms, some in a bleak annexe where luggage has to be humped up three floors, and a room here with minimal bathroom cost me a ridiculous 400f. The picturesque **Hôtel de la Porte St.-Pierre** is a disaster: *'this was the worst hotel we encountered for welcome, room and character'*. wrote one poor sufferer, and I would agree that they too are cashing in on too much publicity.

I would pick as the best of an indifferent bunch, recommended to me by a local friend:

Le Croiseur
(H)M–S
*2 pl. de la
Poissonerie
(99) 40.80.40*

In a very central position by the fish market, but relatively unknown and with friendly owners. The rooms are nothing special but perfectly adequate, at 90f or 200f for one with a shower. No baths.

I would recommend staying outside the walls and strolling into the town for dinner at one of the many restaurants: there is plenty of choice along the beach stretching all the way round La Grande Plage, a truly fabulous beach extending through Paramé to Rothéneuf. Since the prospect is so pleasing, I have picked out those with sea views. Nearest to the walled town is.

La Grotte aux Fées
(HR)S
*36 chaussée du
Sillon
(99) 56.83.30*

An old-fashioned hotel with just the road between it and the beach. All the rooms are clean and pleasant but some of them are particularly charming, like no. 19, all blue and white, twin beds, sea-view, for 200f. The cheapest is 88f. Friendly staff, and meals from 72–92f.

**Logis de
Brocéliande**
(H)M
*43 chaussée du ＼
Sillon
(99) 56.86.60
Closed 25/12–10/1*

A stylish little hotel with smart furnishings, a garden, and only ten bedrooms which means the personal touch from Mme Auffret. Absence of a restaurant gives you the chance to sample St.-Malo's many possibilities, even in high season. 255f a double with bath. Recommended.

Hôtel Surcouf
(H)M
*15 r. de la Plage
(99) 40.20.08*

The only hotel with terrace giving direct access to the beach. Small, well-equipped, efficient. The double rooms cost from 160–200f o.o.s. and from 206–215f in July and August. Bar but no restaurant.

Les Charmettes
(H)S
*64 bd. Hébert
(99) 56.07.31*

I set out to find a simple cheap hotel overlooking the sea —— no easy task in this area —— but I believe **Les Charmettes** would fill all but the most demanding bill. It is a nice, faded French family pension, with shaggy garden and parking at rear and the sea to fore. The rooms are fine, clean and wholesome; four of them have balconies overlooking the sea and at 90f for a double or 190f for a family room for four, I consider them excellent value. Patron René Cobert is friendly and helpful and the hotel is open year round.

Good honest value in this S bracket, wanting only a confirmatory report to merit an arrow.

► **Le Villefromoy**
(H)L
34 bd.
Chateaubriand
(99) 40.92.20.
Closed 15/1–31/1

I think this must be one of the nicest hotels I know. It stands one road back from the sea, but from my balcony a gap allowed a fabulous view of the water and coastline. A drink in the evening sunshine there completed the purring satisfaction at having discovered such a gem.

Jean-Guillaume Douët de la Villefromoy was an *antiquaire*, as was his father before him, and when he converted their 1860s house in 1984, he furnished it with beautiful pieces of polished furniture and objects d'art. But this is no museum. The rooms are light and bright, from the yellow of the staircase to the sky-blue of the salon; there is spaciousness along with the graciousness.

The bedrooms are all furnished with luxury but restraint (perhaps I appreciated the cool creams and whites all the more after a regime of the orange and black vinyl beloved by so many French hoteliers). The only hint of decadence was the mock marbling in the splendid bathrooms but even that was discreetly, beigely, inoffensive.

The hotel is really two houses joined by a clever glass passageway, where M. Douët de la Villefromoy greets his guests. The rooms in the older house, facing the sea, are obviously the best in this expensive area, and I didn't begrudge a franc of the 400f for mine, no. 3. Those facing the road (not a busy one) are equally comfortable and attractive but, without the view, they cost only 250f.

Breakfast came with a unique linen cover, drawstrung like a pudding cloth, over the hot croissant dish. Pity the jam and butter were plastic but really that was the only fault I could find with the whole experience.

La Villefromoy.

M. Douët de la Villefromoy is a friendly and attentive host, but like other members of the *Châteaux Independants* who have turned their lovely homes into lovely hotels, he does not set out to offer the kind of service that goes with a big staff. If you insist on having your bed turned down and pyjamas spread out, with a chocolate on your pillow, you will be disappointed here. But you'd be missing a beaut.

In fact I found it hard to leave, after an early morning walk along that fabulous beach, tide obligingly well out, heading towards the pleasing prospect of the turrets and towers of St.-Malo, with only a jogger and a little boy turning cartwheels to share the bay. Here's one I shall certainly return to, given half an excuse. Meanwhile a certain arrow.

The restaurant scene in St. Malo is rapidly improving. The **Duchesse Anne** used to be the only quality choice and two years ago when I suggested to a local that there were plenty of smaller restaurants to choose from he looked over his specs and said firmly 'but not of quality, Madame.' He was right then perhaps but several new welcome possibilities have since appeared.

To the left of the Porte St.-Vincent stretches a row of eateries, tables on pavement, displays of shellfish, agreeable bustle; we have eaten at most of them over the years, when a pleasant situation in the heart of this most colourful town took precedence over a gastronomic experience. You can hardly go wrong there with a plateful of *moules* or a dozen oysters and you don't need any quide's advice when you can see for yourself what looks good on which plate. Indisputably the aristocrat of this bunch, crowned with a Michelin star, is:

►La Duchesse Anne
(R)M–L
5 pl. Guy La Chambre
(99) 40.87.53
Closed Dec.; Jan.; Wed.

I hardly dared go back to the **Duchesse Anne**. It was our port in many a storm. From earliest sailing days, I remembered its familiar old-fashioned décor, comfortable *patronne,* delicious straightforward food, with great affection. But for many years now it has been *the* destination for English yachties, who telephone weeks ahead from London to book a table, and gain sublime courage in the face of all manner of marine adversity at the thought of the meal ahead. They sit there in their brass-buttoned blazers happily braying brave experiences and weather forecasts to their fellow mariners across the room, while crunching through their annual fix of lobster and oysters. Weekends are planned around the **Duchesse Anne**, Jersey millionaires hovercraft across for lunch, Rolls are parked outside. Surely by now this fame must have changed the place, they must have 'smartened' it up a bit, *noove cuis.* must have arrived, the prices must be sky-high?

But, miraculously, no. There were the remembered varnished walls, tiled floors, lace curtains, coat-rail in the middle of the two small rooms, buttercups and forget-me-nots on the tables. Best of all, it is still very, very French. Prudent locals book well ahead to defend themselves against the Brit take-over, as I realised to my cost when I tried to get a booking for the same day; I had to re-arrange an entire week's schedule to come back later for the first available space, but I'm very glad I did.

No set menu, everything cooked to order, but no long wait for the first course; the service, under Madame's all-seeing eye, is so efficient that if you don't deploy delaying tactics you could be out in an hour.

I had fresh asparagus — and I mean fresh — generous, with perfect hollandaise, then a superb sole stuffed with lobster. Desserts proved dull and it would be well worth accepting the invitation to order the speciality *Tarte Tatin* at the start of the meal. It arrived, before my envious eyes, on the next table, oozing caramel, surmounted with *crème fraîche*.

With coffee and half a bottle of modest wine (26f for a Sylvaner to 240f for Pommard), my bill came to 100f, which I considered a bargain.

Our favourite little restaurant used to be **l'Abordage** by the fish market, but it has changed hands recently and is now a disappointment. Far better make for:

Chez Gilles
(R)M
2 r. Pie qui boit
(99) 40.97.25
Closed Sun. p.m.;
Mon. p.m.; Tue.
p.m.; Wed. p.m.
Thur. o.o.s.

Bright, modern, efficient, full of locals, it offers an excellent three-course menu for 78f.

We chose *langoustines* with perfect home made mayonnaise, all in lavish quantity, and a good *terrine de poissons*, then *vol au vent* overflowing with scallops, *lotte* and prawns, excellent steaks and the house speciality — a *crème caramel* with coconut.

Le Chalut
(R)M–S
8 r. de la Corne de
Cerf
(99) 56.71.58
Closed Wed.

Determinedly nautical in theme, with lifebelts and nets on walls, a small lively restaurant in the centre of town. Excellent seafood and more — the 65f menu has some extremely interesting ideas and the home-made fruit tarts — redcurrant and raspberry when I was there — are way above the all-too-familiar sog. Popular, so book.

L'Astrolabe
(R)M
8 r. des Cordiers
(99) 40.36.82
Closed Tue.

Step down into this newish little restaurant, pleasantly rustic, in a quiet street, to sample the fine cooking of Daniel Le Heran, who trained with Paul Bocuse and at Lasserre. He and his nice young wife Patricia are working hard to make a success of this venture — an upmarket restaurant aimed at catching some of the **Duchesse Anne**'s overflow and now succeeding in its own right. Menus are 90f and 162f with some very interesting items. I have a feeling they may go up when the restaurant becomes more established, so go soon.

Les Écluses
(R)M
Gare Maritime
(99) 56.81.00

Superb position behind the locks in the Bassin Vauban; the huge plate glass windows make the most of the stunning view across the water to Dinard, facing due west into the evening sun. Very modern and glossy and not particularly cheap, but quite different from St.-Malo's other serious restaurants and already popular with discerning locals, who praise its fish above all other. Menus at 69f and 120f.

A pleasant place to drop in for *le five o'clock* tea with home-made cakes, light lunches, English breakfasts, is **Tea-Time**, 4 Grand'rue, open every day 11 a.m.–6.30 p.m. The best *pâtisserie* in town, though, is undoubtedly **Cheflet**, 10 rue Porcon (up Grand'rue, turn left), with delectable specialities like *Le Mâlo*, to bring home as presents, perhaps, or to eat in their teashop. Wonderful fruity ices and chocolates too, all made by the son of the family. Opposite is a good present shop, **Le Vaisseloire** for classy household desirables, but a real find is **Le Mazagran**, 9 Grand'rue, that has porcelain seconds at knockdown prices. Lots of expensive shops for model clothes and yachties gear but try **Dégriftés** in r. des Marine for bargains (*dégriffés* are model clothes with the labels removed.) And for cheeses it's the **Boutique des Fromages** in r. de l'Orme that has the best choice, in best condition.

Map 4B	**STE.-MARINE** (Finistère) 5.5 km W of Bénodet

Over the new bridge, seemingly a handshake away from Bénodet on the other side of the river Odet, is the nice little harbour of Ste.-Marine, with its complement of simple hotel, restaurant, bars, and an unusually good *crêperie,* **La Cremaillère**. It also has a Michelin-starred restaurant, the **Jeanne d'Arc**, which I fully intended to investigate, until locals warned me off: 'You don't want to go there — far too expensive.' So, what with all the choice of eating nearby and because it looked rather grim and unloved, sited surprisingly on the road out to the beach, I never did. Any reports therefore particularly welcome.

What I did investigate further was the stunning beach nearby, the Plage du Téven. Given a few palm trees and a grass skirt or two, this could well be a South Sea Islands poster. Miles of fine white sands round a gently curving, south-facing bay. A choice of outstanding walks here, along the beach towards the promontory of Île Tudy, or a totally contrasting scene round the headland towards the harbour. This gives a unique view of sea, estuary, bridge and river, with the picturesque Bénodet just across the water. Make a considerable detour if necessary for this one.

Map 1C	**ST.-MICHEL-EN-GRÈVE** (C. du N.) 18 km SW of Lannion

A most impressive bay, three miles long and backed by high cliffs. When the tide goes out, it does it with a vengeance for 1½ miles, so it's a long hike for a swim. The sand is so firm that it is used as a race track for the Lannion races.

Prominently overlooking the bay is:

Hotel de la Plage
(HR)S
(96) 36.74.43
Closed 3/1–1/4

A long established favourite family hotel, with simple rooms made special by their astounding view. Good value at 90f to 150f with bath. Full pension is not insisted on but is usually taken, because it offers such consistently good food.

Basic 'nosh' and lots of it is what the customers were evidently enjoying the night we ate there. Our three courses cost 55f, with house wine at 20f, but the most popular dish seemed to be their renowned *plâteau de fruits de mer* for 90f.

Hotel de la Plage

One suggestion: we felt decidedly cheated, having driven some way to enjoy the waterside situation on a beautiful summer evening, to find all the blinds down to keep out the sun! The cleverdicks were sitting outside on the super terrace, where they serve 'snacks', but as these seem to include everything from a bowl of soup to the loaded *plateau*, my advice for a fine night is to book a table there rather than in the distinctly fuggy dining room. The *patronne* and her staff are the essence of friendliness and will do all they can to accommodate the odd English taste for fresh air.

Map 4D   **ST.-NICHOLAS-DES-EAUX** (Morbihan) 16 km SW of Pontivy on the D1

A hamlet built on the hillside above the river Blavet, with old thatched cottages either side of a 16th-century church. The whole area is green and attractive and would make a peaceful inland stop.

Le Vieux Moulin
(HR)S
(97) 51.81.09
Closed Feb.; Mon.
o.o.s.
V.

A nice old converted farmhouse with guaranteed tranquillity, highly recommended by an English friend who visits Pontivy regularly and chooses always to stay here. Menus start at 53f and the 12 rooms cost from 83–165f.

Map 2H	**ST.-OUEN-LA-ROUERIE** (Î. et V.) 25 km S of Avranches on the D40

►**Le Château des Blosses**
(H)M
(99) 98.36.16
Closed 1/12–1/3

An enthusiastic reader first recommended **Le Château des Blosses** some years ago now, but because the book I was working on at the time concerned Normandy, I never followed up the idea. I should have done, because in fact the border passes through the grounds of the **Château**, and I have been missing a gem.

It is the home of M. and Mme Jacques Barbier and their numerous children, and they have furnished five of their bedrooms as very luxurious guest rooms. Each has its own modern bathroom, is spacious, light and elegantly furnished and to stay in such beautiful surroundings, peacefully situated just off the main road south is a treat indeed. Breakfast, featuring home-made conserves, farm butter, fresh eggs, a *petit déjeuner gourmand*, as M. Barbier puts it, is included in the price of 210–250f for two people. If you book ahead, Mme Barbier will cook a three-course dinner for 100f, which is very congenial way to sample French home cooking in an unusually upmarket French home.

If it's anything like so good as the home-made apéritif, recipe secret, that I sipped with the Barbiers recently, it's not to be missed. Otherwise there are plenty of alternative eateries in Pontorson, 15 km away.

The **Château** would make a good base for a weekend or longer stay, as well as a convenient overnight stop, with Combourg and Fougères within easy explorable distance, not to mention Mont St.-Michel, and I rate it very highly on all counts. Definitely different.

Map 5B	**ST.-PHILIBERT** (Finistère) 5 km S of Trégunc

A hamlet in the **Nevez** peninsula, a few km before the spectacular Pointe de Trevignon.

Le St.-Philibert
(R)S
(98) 50.02.79

A little village bistro, run by a pleasant youngish couple, husband cooking simple meals that offer excellent value. I asked him when he closed and the encouraging answer was '*Jamais*'. There is a pretty dining room and terrace and straightforward menus at 54f. *Sole meunière*, immaculately fresh, costs a very modest 45f.

Map 1B	**ST.-POL-DE-LÉON** (Finistère) 5 km S of Roscoff

'Capital of the Artichoke' is the town's title and it's not hard to see why. That delicious edible thistle sways proudly in many a field for miles around. In summer farmers' carts stagger under twice their width of pruned foliage, frustrating those motorists with a ferry to catch, while swarms of farm workers are to be seen planting out the fledgling plants for next year's crops. How odd that never once in the region were we offered that simple, wholesome, cheap vegetable as an *hors d'oeuvre*.

St.-Pol is the market centre for other vegs too of course,

sending early crops of cauliflowers and potatoes all over France and providing the onions and garlic strings for the Roscoff 'Onion Johnnies', those archetypal beret-ed Bretons-on-a-bicycle.

Don't miss the Tuesday market which fills the main square with colourful produce and overflows into the surrounding streets with household goods stalls and untrendy garments.

It's a lively likeable town — a refreshing change from tourist-orientation — whose unique spires dominate the flat countryside for kilometres around. We could certainly locate them from as far away as Trébeurden. They belong to two of the most impressive Breton Gothic buildings, the Kreisker chapel (Kreis-ker means lower town) and the former cathedral, their gracefulness attributable to Norman influences; that of the Kreisker chapel survived its originator, St.-Pierre in Caen, which was destroyed in the war (but now reconstructed). The pale stone of the 13–16th-century cathedral came for Caen and its layout is based on that of Coutances.

Make the visit doubly worthwhile by eating at:

Hôtel de France
(HR)S
29 r. des Minimes
(98) 69.00.14

A creeper-covered old building set in a garden in a quiet street between chapel and cathedral. A recent change of management has meant deletion from the Michelin and other guides, but certainly every local I spoke to placed this as No. 1 value in the district, dismissing the more obvious 16th-century charms of the **Pomme d'Api** as too touristy. I was glad I had booked a table, so overflowing it was with residents and locals alike.

The new owners are not anxious to publicise their rooms until they have been re-furbished. Meanwhile 100f buys a simple double room.

The *hors d'oeuvre* trolley is a big attraction, featuring on even the most modest menus. For 40f one could tackle a substantial platter of assorted *crudités*, fish, meat etc., go on to *darne de poisson* or *jambon gratiné* with port wine and cream sauce, and finish with cheese and dessert. We ate extremely well for 60f — *salade de langoustines tièdes*, sole and three more courses, and, for real blow-out, the 100f version, with gargantuan platters of seafood, would take some beating.

As the *cuvée blanc* costs only 22f this is all very good news, and only a certain lack of welcome and never-a-smile loses an arrow.

Map 1G   **ST.-SERVAN** (I. et V.) 3 km S of St.-Malo – *Mkt: Thurs, Fri*

Having always approached St.-Malo by sea before and being without land transport, I had no idea of the size of the town and was amazed and distressed at the amount of traffic to be negotiated on the approach roads. St.-Servan, which used to be called Aleth, is now virtually a suburb and a very noisy and fume-ridden main street it has. But take time to explore the little harbour and another altogether more agreeable impression emerges. It's a picturesque little horseshoe facing across the river, with lovely views of Dinan from the cliff path, the Corniche d'Aleth, flanked by the unique Solidor tower — three towers in one in fact, built in 1382 by Duc Jean IV de Bretagne, to keep an eye on the troublesome pirate city next door. Facing the port is:

L'Âtre
(R)S
(99) 81.68.39
Closed Tue. p.m.
o.o.s., Wed.

A genuine little local restaurant, with good fishy menus from 65f and lots of atmosphere.

Le Valmarin
(H)M–L
7 r. Jean-XXIII
(99) 81.94.76
Closed Feb. P.
AE, V.

In a quiet side street, near a small park. St.-Servan would not be my first choice for a holiday, but as a base so close to St.-Malo, the **Valmarin** has much to offer. It is a pleasant old grey house set in its own garden, with charming owners, M. and Mme Le Gal who have never run a hotel before and make you feel you are their guests not customers. Unlike some erstwhile private houses turned hotels, the **Valmarin** gleams with new paint, and the bathrooms work. The rooms are spacious, the ceilings high, the atmosphere delightfully calm. All this warrants, I feel, a price of 280–380f for a double room. Breakfast is the only meal, and a very good one too, served on a silver tray, with good china and linen, and real butter and jam.

An unusual hotel, full of character, but perhaps too pricey in this un-smart area to merit an arrow.

Le Valmarin.

Map 1G	**ST.-SULIAC** (I. et V.) 9 km S of St.-Malo

The peninsula that sticks out into the river Rance west of
Châteauneuf is rich in history and legend. It was a settlement in
prehistoric times but was named after a Welsh monk, who built
a monastery here in the 6th century. In the interesting church
high above the river is a strange granite head, perhaps St.
Suliac's. A very popular gutsy monk was he who rid the district
of a terrorising dragon.

The traditional Gargantua, many years prior to Rabelais'
character, lived in this area and you can see his tooth-menhir in
the village of Chablé. So much earth was needed to bury him
finally in his burial mound at Mont Garot that the Baie de la
Baguais was created. Or so they say.

Nowadays St.-Suliac is a delightful old village of granite
cottages sliding down a hill to the landing stage; not much here
except a cluster of houses, a few boats and:

La Grève 🚩🚩
(H)S(R)M
(99) 58.40.35

The whole upstairs of the house was being taken apart when I
was there and Mme Dore showed me the mess of plaster and
paintpots only reluctantly. It does take some imagination to
picture how the rooms will be, but one thing's certain — they
will be brand new and they will have gorgeous views of the
water. Ready for the '86 season with any luck.

Meanwhile there's a big terrace, a little bar patronised by the
locals and a very pretty *rustique* dining room where seafood
specialities appear on the 75f and 132 f menus. When the rooms
are ready, demi-pension will cost 140f per person.

Map 2B	**ST.-THÉGONNEC** (Finistère) 9 km SW of Morlaix

For an unforgettable, uniquely Breton experience no-one,
however uninterested in churches, should omit a visit to an
enclos paroissiale or parish close. To encounter, in a humble
grey granite village, as gateway to the parish church, a
monumental Renaissance triumphal arch, to enter the tiny
cemetery and find a colossal elaborately carved calvary, flanked
by a dignified decorated *ossuaire* or funeral chapel, to penetrate
the gloom of the church's porch and be taken aback with the
impact of light and colour — gold and red and blue and green
and white — is to gain a first-hand interpretation of a slice of
history.

Intense rivalry existed in these villages in the 17th century;
unprecedented prosperity based on international trade *via*
Morlaix, flax, canvas-making and agriculture, encouraged the
rich merchants and parish councils to vie with one another in
elaborate and expensive memorials. The competition between
two of the most noteworthy — Guimiliau and its neighbour
St.-Thégonnec — went on for two centuries. Village triumphs
were not confined to arches, each in turn superseded by yet
another costlier embellishment. Imagine the local goings-on!

The interior of St.-Thégonnec is disappointing but it wins
hands down on its calvary, the last word, the last calvary to be
built in the Léon region, in 1610. Its grinning, frowning,
blindfolded, bound, threatening, busy, posing, intensely

individual carved mannekins feature on many a postcard and guidebook cover. The funeral chapel came some 70 years later, and even if you have no wish to go inside to see the painted life-size figures representing the Entombment, spare a glance for the decoration on the façade — you'll see no finer Renaissance architecture in Brittany.

All this makes a visit to the otherwise unremarkable village a good idea, but St. Thégonnec has another jewel:

►**Auberge St.-Thegonnec**
(HR)S
pl de la Mairie
(98) 79.61.18
Closed Mon. p.m.;
Tue. o.o.s.
'S' Hotel of the Year

H

R

Hard to categorise the **Auberge**. 'S' signifies 'simple' not only in prices but in ambiance, and here the quality of the furnishings, the elegance of the *couverts*, and the service are far from simple. I came to the conclusion (partly because I very much wanted to make it my Hotel of the Year in this category!) that the essence of the hotel is simplicity and so it should qualify as the shining example in this bracket.

It is simple in its praiseworthy lack of pretentiousness (the fresh flowers on the tables are pinks not carnations), in its obvious desire to please (which in turn means good service), in its pleasure at a client's satisfaction (Marie-Thérèse Le Coz smiles and smiles), in its honesty ('We are a restaurant with only a few simple rooms') and above all in its approach to the food Alain Le Coz prepares.

I shall quote the 56f menu:

A mousse of chickens livers, raisin studded
A platter of assorted fish, smoked over beech wood
Fresh mackerel, home marinaded
Fresh local *crudités*.

A wing of skate, simply poached on a bed of finely chopped red pepper
A chunk of local cod on a *mousseline* of lime
A mixture of offal — calf liver, kidneys, sweetbreads — simply pan-fried in butter, lemon and chervil.
A generous rumpsteak, perfectly spiced with expensive red peppercorns.

A cheese-board in prime condition, or a choice of simple home-made desserts.

We chose fruit and had a cornucopia of peaches, nectarines, grapes, left on the table. A request for a slice of pineapple was willingly met by the waiter, skilfully paring and arranging a portion — no fuss, no bother, and they were busy.

Gros Plant sur Lie cost 31f, *Côtes du Rhone* 35f, but there is an extensive and impressive wine list and the 'simplicity' turns into luxury high up the menu scale at 90f, 120f, 180f and even an ambitious *menu dégustation at* 240f. All remarkable value.

The 7 rooms are truly simple, but immaculate, from 90–155f.

A very special place, which stands out as the Hotel of the Year in the 'S' category.

Map 4C	**SCAËR** (Finistère) 36 km E of Quimper

| **Hotel Brizeux**
(H)S
56 r. Jean-Jaurés
(98) 59.40.59
Closed 3/1–15/2;
Mon. o.o.s. | I include this little hotel not because I know it myself but because a friend likes it well enough to drive all the way from his home in Bénodet to eat here on the 55f menu. It lies on the hub of six yellow roads, so may well make a useful stopping place, with seventeen rooms from 80–170f. |

Map 2B	**SIZUN** (Finistère) 33 km SW of Morlaix

On the banks of the Elorn, with an outstanding 16th-century triumphal arch to its parish close, impressively floodlit on summer evenings.

There is a fairly basic restaurant, **Les Voyageurs**, near at hand but in a much more attractive setting is an excellent *crêperie*;

| **Milin Kerroch**
(98) 68.81.56
Closed Tue. o.o.s | In the Centre de Loisirs at the entrance to the village. It's all very agreeable to sit in the old converted watermill overlooking a lake and sample the variety of *crêpes* on offer. Lots of amusements for the juvenile. |

Map 2B	**TAULÉ** (Finistère) 7 km NW of Morlaix

| **Relais des Primeurs**
(HR)S
(98) 67.11.03
Closed Sept.; Fri.
p.m.; lunch o.o.s. | Turn off the *route express* towards the station of Taulé to find this little grey stone hotel, whose rooms at 80–107f and menus from 48f might well make an economical and agreeable alternative to the coastal hassle. Locals recommend the food as being reliably fresh and *copieuse*. |

Map 2H	**LA TEMPLERIE** (Î et V.) 11 km from Fougères, 174 km from Cherbourg

On the N12 east of Fougères:

| **Chez Gallover 'La Petite Auberge'**
(R)M
(99) 95.27.03
Closed 17/8–6/9;
Sun. p.m.; Tue.
p.m.; Wed. P.
V. | *'High-spot meal of our tour. We were lucky to get in, as we got the only two vacancies by going early (it opens at 8 p.m. and seats about 36). It was soon packed and rightly so. The patron takes the orders and cooks at one end of the restaurant. The three course meal at 65f was ample and excellent (a)* jambon de Bayonne *and artichoke hearts (b)* entrecôte grillée *and* côte de veau *(c) three sorbets and chocolate gâteau. I had the temerity to ask him for my* entrecôte *well-done, as I can't stand blood. He didn't flinch and produced the most tender well-done steak I've ever had. The three sorbets were superb — especially the passion-fruit. Everything was fresh and home made.' — Ken Bell.*

I hardly need check on a report like this, but I look forward to doing so in this case. |

Map 5D	**TOUL-BROCH** (Morbihan) 2 km E of Baden, 7 km SE of Vannes, 9 km SW of Auray, on the D101

Le Gavrinis
(HR)M
(97) 57.00.82

Modern bright Logis, approved of by readers for its wholesomeness and good food. We found it efficient, if a little clinical; certainly it's the kind of hotel a guidewriter could recommend without fear of retribution.

The *carte* is an ambitious one: *huitres frémies au sabayon de Riesling*, at 68f, *magret de canard aux kumkats*, but I think the cheaper menus are probably a better bet here. The 60f *Menu Er-Lannic* gets a red Michelin R, offering a *terrine aux foies de volaille*, a *matelote de poissons au cidre* and *pâtisserie*. Oysters don't appear until the 135f *Menu Gavrinis*.

Rooms are irreproachably clean and functional, at 65–200f.

If I sound a little unenthusiastic, it is probably partly because of the **Gavrinis'** position, on the road, in a dull patch of countryside. With such a gorgeous coastline nearby, it seems a shame not to stay within sight of the sea, but that depends where priorities lie.

Map 1C	**TRÉBEURDEN** (C. du N.) 9 km NE of Lannion, 72 km NE of St.-Brieuc – *Mkt: Tues*

If it weren't so stunningly beautiful, I would say it was scruffy; it's as though the owners of the lovely villas set in the shade of the pine trees, comfortable on their own terraces looking out at their private vistas of sea and rocks and sand and yachts and islands, have decided that their town should have no amenities to attract the hoi-polloi, that the straggly grass sprouting on the front, the broken wire fences, the hot dog stalls are no concern of theirs. But neither need they be to anyone else who has an eye for Trébeurden's extraordinary natural amenities.

Three gorgeous main beaches to choose from, according to wind direction, inclination to swim, to sunbathe, to clamber over rocks, for sun or shade. For children a veritable paradise, with little islands to reach at low water, causeways to explore, rock pools to delve in, hard sands to dig, fine sands to picnic upon.

It's a surprisingly big town, straggling in all directions, with no real heart, few shops, few restaurants. The new developments of modern flats have been tackled haphazardly, tucked in amongst the old villas at random, with considerable scrub in between. All sounding most unattractive and yet somehow managing unconcernedly to over-ride these lapses. Even in the 'bourg', seemingly several kilometres away from the beaches, a turn of the head to left or right will win a glimpse of water, so eccentrically indented is this coast. The viewing table upon the Pointe Bihit is a must for a unique panoramic view of all the ins and outs as far as Roscoff.

The Tuesday market is a good one, with not only the usual stalls selling mounds of glowing southern fruit and vegetables and strictly-boned fiercely-pink brassières (who buys them? where do they try them on?) but the eccentrics — the slabs of soap perfumed with natural oils of honeysuckle, olive, peach and vanilla, that perfume the hands all day, and the herbalist with Provençal patterned cotton bags full of mixtures guaranteed to cure all known ills from depression to *gaz*.

We always buy far more than we can possibly consume for the sheer pleasure of seeing the stallholder slice off a hunk of farm butter, sniff the Cavaillon melons, shave the Bayonne ham, settle the goat's cheeses on the ferns.

Trébeurden may not be perfect but I could never tire of the place, not least because of:

►Ti al-Lannec
(HR)L–M
(96) 23.57.26
Closed 22/3–12/11;
Rest. closed Mon.
lunch.
AE, V.
'L' Hotel of the
Year

Where do travel writers go for their hols? This travel writer has no doubt that she would look no further. The **Ti al-Lannec** is my favourite hotel, and thinking hard of all the other beautiful hotels in the world I have been privileged to visit, I can think of no other with such a glorious site.

In fact travel writers rarely get holidays. I suspect only commercial travellers can share with them the joy that spending more than one night in the same hotel brings. On the last tour it had been twelve hotels in fourteen days and so a whole week with toothbrush unpacked and creases hanging out was unheard-of luxury. But in July there was no help for it. Breton seaside hotels don't take kindly to one-night stands in high season and there can be no question of random last-minute bookings. So, sighing heavily, it had to be seven whole days and nights based on Trébeurden, picked after a good deal of homework. I knew nothing of the hotels along this coast before, since previous visits had been boat-based, but putting together all the clues, garnered from friends, readers, books, **Ti al-Lannec** started off a clear winner and stayed that way.

It stands high in the pine trees, a dignified granite house with a modern extension built on to the rear; encircling the plate-glassed dining room unfolds the sparkling watery panorama. A luxurious lounge next door shares the view and makes after-dinner fraternising easy. The whole hotel is furnished with perfect taste, antiques mingling with high quality modern, classy drapes and carpets. Not too large, so that a country-house atmosphere prevails, encouraged by deep armchairs, flowers, chat and the concern of M. et Mme Joanny and their efficient band of helpers.

I don't know how they pick them or train them, but I have never come across such friendly staff. The girls who bring breakfast and clean the rooms smile and chat and wish you the equivalent of Have a Nice Day; nothing is too much trouble.

The 'little touches' are manifest everywhere. I often amuse myself by considering how I would furnish the perfect hotel room, to make it as comfortable as home. Mme Joanny has put all my ideas into practice. (What do other hotels expect you to do with drip dry shirts and knickers? Drape 'em on the curtain pole?) **Ti al-Lannec** provides a drying rack in the bathroom, a full-length mirror, lots of deep towels, good soap, efficient lighting — basic enough you would think, but how rarely does one find them all?

And the breakfasts! How often have I railed against plastic butter and jam, not enough coffee served with cold sterilized milk? How often have the jammy croissant crumbs prickled in bed because there was no plate? At **Ti al-Lannec** breakfast for *two* comes on *two* trays, served on pink and white porcelain; the jam is a different home-made flavour every day, the honey runs from a practical little glass and silver jug (buy them in the market for good take-home presents), the butter and the coffee

ti al lannec

are copious, the croissant buttery-flaky, the hot brioche home-made.

The bedrooms and two suites are all different; all are charming but I wouldn't have swapped ours, no. 1. Its brown and white Laura-Ashley-ness was echoed in sepia photographs, white cambric bedspread on brass bedstead, white voile canopy draped above, nice antique furniture. Best of all, its French windows opened on to a little, almost-private, corner lawn, so we could lie in bed and admire our own personal view, or sit outside underneath a white umbrella in a white deck chair for a magical aperitif hour, facing west across the bay into the evening sun that made us reluctant to stir enough to change for dinner.

Dinner in that dining room is worth stirring for. We ate on the menu that changes every three weeks. *Pensionnaires* can stay that long and never have the same dinner twice. Their menu is a three-course no-choice but everyone I spoke to said that, where necessary, alternatives had been willingly and helpfully substituted. Lots of fish appears of course and the cooking I would call traditional with interesting variations.

All this is good — very good indeed — but the best thing of all about **Ti al-Lannec** is its owners. The Joannys, she with a hotel-keeping background, bought "the House on the Moor" with fingers crossed and since then have been constantly improving, never missing a pointer to perfection. They are ideal hosts — attentive, efficient, friendly and I am delighted that they should be my Hoteliers of the Year.

For 1986 rooms will cost from 320f to 415f, *demi pension* from 315–360f. per person. Menus at 135f, 175f and 240f.

The other luxury hotel in the town is the Relais et Château, Michelin-starred Manoir de Lan-Kerallec. With a clientèle exclusively rich American and a cuisine exclusively expensive *noove cuis.* clichés, we didn't like it half so much. Other more modest choices in the town:

Glann Ar Mor
(HR)S
12 r. de Kerariou
(96) 23.50.81
Open all year;
Rest. closed Wed.

Signposted from the bourg. Rare to find a simple hotel with cooking of this quality. Chef–patron M. Colas used to cook at Ste-Anne-La Palud's starred **La Plage** and has brought his considerable skills to menus starting here at 55f. All the rooms are plain but comfortable and at 78f a double are a snip — considerably better value than any elsewhere with a sea view, but **Glann Ar Mor** is only a few minutes drive from a variety of beaches. Young Mme Colas is a friendly and helpful hostess. Full pension is 139f.

I suspect a future arrow.

Ker-An-Nod
(HR)M
r. de Pors Termen
(96) 23.50.21
Closed Nov.–
Easter
H R

Mme Brigitte Penven has changed the policy of her nice old hotel, with the best situation in the town facing right on to the beach. She no longer takes *pensionnaires* but has transformed her old dining–room into Le Jardin, a charming fresh trellissed room, green and airy, looking out to sea, where light snacks can be taken at any hour from *'midi à minuit'*. Interesting salads and omelettes or just one dish like *langoustines mayonnaise* are easy on the pocket, but there is a good three-course daily menu too at 80f. No compulsion for residents to eat in, but they could do far worse.

The rooms are lovely, with smashing sea views from the more expensive ones — 230f for one of good size with modern bathroom, 190f for those at the back, with showers. A pleasant lounge makes possible bad weather more bearable.

Exceptional value in this generally expensive area for those who like to eat out sometimes, and another potential Trébeurden arrow.

Coup d'Roulis
(R)S
73 r. des Plages
(96) 23.52.30
Closed 30/9–
Whitsun

In the town, a nice little stone-built restaurant run by the family Evrard. Son Jacky is chef and prepares meals that nod towards modern cooking but are substantial enough to satisfy appetites whetted by a day on the beach.

For 55f we ate *crabe à la mayonnaise* and *raie aux câpres*; for 88f an *assiette de fruits de mer* and poached sole, deliciously stuffed with a *fondu* of leeks, and served with perfect *beurre blanc.* Then fresh strawberries and (indifferent) cheese-board.

Very good value we thought, but locals said even better was their speciality lobster. You choose your victim from their *vivier* and order it cooked the way you like best.

ÎLE GRANDE

A few kms north of Trébeurden, juts out the one-time island where Joseph Conrad spent his honeymoon, now a strange promontory edged with rocky coves, surrounded by islets. Easy to get disorientated with so much sea in so many directions. The little fishing port still provides many of the local restaurants with their catch and the island still benefits from the character of the many grey stone fishermens' cottages dotted about. Fishermen still live in some no doubt, but now there are more bathing drawers than nets draped from their windows; the farmers let out their land to campers and it is from holiday makers that most of the ready money comes.

This is DIY territory; with hotels yielding to food and souvenir shops, but it's still worth a visit for the never boring endless variations on the same watery theme. I could spend months walking, swimming, exploring and even then there would be yet another beach, yet another little harbour.

Map 1C

TRÉGASTEL (C. du N.) 8 km W of Perros Guirec

The coast along here is dominated by the power of its smooth pink granite rocks, crumpled into hints of all manner of strange beasties — the Witch, the Puffin, the Pile of Pancakes, the Corkscrew and King Gradlon's Crown, near the Grève Blanche. To add to the fairytale cornucopia, on a small island beyond the Baie de Ste.-Anne there is an extraordinary pastiche of the mediaeval castle, Costaëres. The only hope of working out the convulations is to climb up to the *table d'orientation* for a view all along the coast.

Inland, a little away from the beaches, in verdant calm:

Hôtel Bellevue
(HR)M
20 r. des Calculots
(96) 23.88.18
Closed 30/9–8/5

An upmarket family hotel, particularly popular for its unusually good food. Nice garden, well-furnished comfortable rooms from 195–265f. Only lunch is served to non-residents (90f) and demi-pension is from 240–298f per person. Recommended.

Map 1D

TRÉGUIER (C. du N.) 30 km N of Guingamp

A smashing little town, high above the confluence of two rivers which together form the river Tréguier — Breton for "three corners".

St.-Yves, a local lad, is the patron saint of barristers, many of whom, stately in gowns and wigs, attend his annual fête here on May 19.

The picturesque little town, all nice old houses and cobbled streets, centres on St. Tugdual's cathedral, with its exquisite nave, surely the most beautiful Gothic building in Brittany. The difficult unpliable local granite has somehow been worked here to achieve the lightness and delicacy which I sadly miss from the Norman Caen stone architecture. Look at the marvellous tracery of the 15th-century cloisters to see what I mean.

Not much down by the water, except a marina from whence cometh all those blazers and Docksiders reading the *Daily Telegraph* in the cafés in the square. They, poor things, having only marine transport, can't drive out to the best restaurant two km away:

►Kastell Dinech
(HR)M
rte. de Lannion
(96) 92.49.39
Closed 15/9–28/9;
1/1–1/3; Tue. p.m.;
Wed.

Signposted right off the Lannion road. A real old Breton farmhouse that has miraculously retained its character while becoming a deservedly popular hotel and restaurant. The honeysuckle still rambles untamed over the grey stone walls, there are dried flowers in pottery jugs, straw hats pinned on the wall; the dining room is long and low and raftered, brightened with coral tablecloths and country flowers, and the bedrooms

Hotel Kastell Dinec'h.

have been decorated with unsophisticated Laura Ashley prints, a shining example of how 'inexpensive' does not have to mean orange vinyl and brown lino. Those bedrooms in the main house are largest and prettiest but we weren't grumbling about ours in the converted barn wing, simple but bright with yellow paint, good bathroom, for 190f.

The three arms of the farmhouse enclose a garden and a terrace with lots of reclining chairs and tables which lead to regular meeting-ups over drinks and the comparing of the day's discoveries; the clientèle has a strong English complement.

Menus at 58f and 70f are miracles. Mme Paumels says she would dearly love to put the prices up a little but is barred by the Government from doing so. Unlike other disgruntled restaurateurs however, she has not resorted to short cuts. The food is as good and varied as ever. On the cheaper menu of 56f we ate a *feuilleté* of *moules* with home-made puff pastry enclosing generous mussels and *petits légumes*, with a *sauce au beurre blanc* which, if I were nitpicking, (which I am not at this price) I might say was a leetle thin, then sea trout, then hot apple pie. On the 70f menu were nuggets of lobster, *sole à l'oseille*, Brie with a walnut salad and fresh apricot charlotte. Amazing.

Arrowed for charm and excellent value food.

Le Petit Savoyard
(R)S
17 r. le Peltier
(96) 92.43.04
Open every day

Near the town centre, well signposted from all directions, a nice warm little bistro, old stone walls, unfussy.

M. and Mme Lutard specialise in dishes from their native Savoie, like *fondues* and *raclettes*, good on a chill off-season night when everything else around dies, but there is always plenty of seafood on their good value menus — 48.50f for four courses or 80f if you want oysters, *langoustines*, crab.

POINTE DU CHÂTEAU

Don't fail to take a memorable drive out along the river from Tréguier for 10 km to this most extraordinary sight on this extraordinary coast. The atmosphere of the bay is distinctly eerie, with dozens of strange menhir-type rocks rearing sheer out of the water, like the backgrounds of early Florentine paintings, two-dimensional. The atmosphere silences even the children, who stop in their tracks and gaze wide-eyed at the spectacle; perhaps the spirits of the shipwrecked still haunt. Twice I've seen it, both times at low water, both in calm weather. In a storm it must be terrifying.

The first time we picnicked on the turf high above, with a much-travelled friend who said he'd never in all the world seen anything like it; this summer we drove out after dinner to see if the rosily setting sun might soften the menace that perhaps we had imagined. Not at all. The fierce colours made the scene even more awe-inspiring. See if you don't agree.

Map 4b

TRÉGUNC (Finistère) 9 km W of Pont Aven

A fairly uninteresting village, but well situated for coastal excursions.

Le Menhir
(HR)M
17 r. de
Concarneau
(98) 97.62.35
Closed 31/12–15/3;
Mon. o.o.s.

A little Logis on the main road but with a pleasant dining-room looking over the rear garden, as do most of the rooms.

M. Kerangel's cooking has brought him lavish praise from Gault-Millau, who admire his *nouvelle cuisine* presentations — *mousseline de St.-Pierre au coulis de poivrons rouge* and *aiguillettes de carnard au cidre* — heady stuff for a little village inn. I too admire his enterprise and the freshness of his ingredients, but it did just occur to me that perhaps the summit of his talent has already been reached; certainly the menu prices have shot up to 110f (apart from a very basic 59f version). The rooms are fine at 160f with bath and *demi-pension*, obligatory in season, is 195–370f.

L'Auberge les
Grandes Roches
(HR)M
(98) 97.62.97
Closed 15/11–10/3;
Mon. o.o.s.

Signposted from the church down the V3. Aptly named indeed; the menhir shaped rocks in the front garden are gigantic.

It's a sophisticated/rustic kind of building, well-tended, efficient, quiet, with modern rooms at 145–196f. A safe bet if you can get in — it's a popular conference hotel, which perhaps makes it a bit impersonal.

Map 2H

TREMBLAY (I. et V.) 42 km N of Rennes on the N776

Turn right (west) in the village and follow the clearly marked signs to:

Roc Land
(HR)M
(99) 98.20.46
Closed 1/2–10/2; 1/
7–15/7; 15/10–31/
10; Sat; Mon.
o.o.s.

Spic, modern, *soignèe*, calm, pine-encircled; a Logis de France. Swings in the *parc*, elegant dining room. Altogether a safe and useful overnight stop on the main road south. Rooms 155f, menus start at 65f.

Map 2E

TRÉMUSON (C. du N.) 8 km W of St.-Brieuc on the N12

Le Buchon
(R)M
(96) 94.85.84
Closed Mon. p.m.;
Tue.

If you don't want to get involved in the St.-Brieuc traffic hassle, this could be a useful stop, situated as it is on the *Nationale* just outside the town, with easy parking. It's a smart little restaurant, specialising in fish, with good menus at 65f and 80f.

Map 1D

TRÉVOU-TRÉGUIGNEC (C. du N.) 12 km E of Perros Guirec

Yet another wide sandy bay, high above which stands:

Ker Bugalic
(HR)M
(96) 23.71.15
Closed 30/9–1/4

Creeper-covered old Breton house making the best of the view; nice gardens and earning a red R in Michelin; unusually good menus at 60f, no compulsion to eat in. Friendly trouble-taking management. Eighteen rooms, all full when I tried to look, at 140–200f. Good vibes.

Bellevue
(HR)M
(96) 23.71.44
Closed 30/9–Easter

An eccentrically gabled older hotel with a character *patronne*, who proudly and embarrasingly insisted on showing me every one of the bedrooms, occupied or not; some had balconies and stunning views. Peaceful garden. I can't vouch personally for the food, but the dining-room is certainly very pleasant and great baskets of expensive cherries scattered about promised better than the usual pension dessert. Menus start at 50f and rooms are 100–160f.

Map 6D

LA TRINITÉ-SUR-MER (Morbihan) 4.5 km NW of Carnac

A famous yachting centre in a gorgeous position at the mouth of the Crach river. Pontoons are lined with hundreds of boats, from the family sailer to the ocean racer, and its very pleasant to stroll alongside being nosy. When a big race is on you will see lots of famous names here and the town hums but it's a very short season (the French aren't natural frostbite sailors like our inured Solent hardies) and even on a fine June Sunday there was little activity, with the bars along the front depressingly empty. There are some beautiful sheltered bays for a day's excursion but I found the town too artificial for a longer stay and failed to find a hotel that might make it worth while.

The restaurants disappoint too. Following Gault-Millau's rave report I had high hopes of **Les Hortensias**, a ravishingly pretty little restaurant, all hydrangea pinks and blues, but the food didn't live up to the décor — chi-chi expensive.

Surprisingly no little fishy restaurants along by the harbour either, so what *do* the yachties do?

Perhaps they make for a recommendation of Dr Glyn Daniel's: 'our favourite pub':

Le Rouzic
(HR)M
(97) 55.72.06
Closed 15/11–15/
12; Rest. closed
Sun. p.m.; Mon.
o.o.s.
AE, EC, V.

A prominent rather solemn building on the prom, which I must confess I thought unpromising. However, I know Dr Daniel's judgment to be sound in the case of *FE4*, so I am sure it is worth another look. Rooms are 115–212f and menus start at 71f.

Map 5E

LE TOUR DU PARC (Morbihan) 119 km from Rennes, off the Muzillac–Port Navalo road, the D20

The Presqu'île du Rhuys is remarkable for its micro–climate — so mild that the flora is the same as the South of France. There are several little holiday villages on the south coast, with good sandy beaches, but none of particular charm that I could find. One unusual possibility, however, is:

La Croix du Sud
(HR)M
(97) 26.40.26
Rest. closed Sun.
p.m.; Mon.

Mme Caron calls her modern complex a hotel motel, which might well sound daunting. In fact there are eight 'bungalows' in the grounds of a normal hotel, which I think might be an atractive proposition for families who like being self-contained without isolation. For two people the cost is 192f and meals can be taken in the (rather over-plush) restaurant, or not. There is a club atmosphere, with a swimming pool which is free and tennis court which is not, with a choice of beaches nearby. Rooms in the main hotel are from 89f to 218f and menus start at 113f. Very upmarket camping.

Map 1E	**VAL ANDRÉ** (C. du N.) 16 km N of Lamballe

A sizeable town, with a sheltered beach of fine sand. It's all very pleasant to sit by the west-facing harbour and watch the fishing boats busy about. Just here is:

La Cotriade
(R)M–L
(96) 72.20.26
Closed mid-Dec.–
mid-Jan.; 31/5–18/
6; Mon. p.m.; Tue.

A seemingly unassuming little restaurant with plastic tables outside for itinerant drinkers, giving little hint that it boasts a Michelin star for its predominately fishy cooking. If the 95f menu happens to suit your tastebuds, you've got a bargain. For me it was *salade tiède de St.-Jacques* (could have been oysters hot or cold or *plâteau de fruits de mer*), followed by a no-choice *feuilleté de barbue, crème d'oseille*. This was very good news indeed; the bad is that the menu does not change for several days at a time with no notice given what and when, and the next one up is 170f; *à la carte* is even more pricey, with starters and main courses costing 95-ish apiece, and lobster a heady 230f.

So best to study the menu before commitment and then rub hands and congratulate yourself.

Map 5E	**VANNES** (Morbihan) 107 km SW of Rennes
Mkt: Wed, Sat	You have only to look at a map to guess at Vannes' perfect setting. At the head of the Gulf of Morbihan this is a good place to check up on the various alternatives offered by the *vedettes vertes* to see the gulf. I am told the gastronomic tour is well worth the money. See Morbihan (p. 89).

The canalised waterway drives into the heart of the town. The approach along the quays lined with masts and rigging and old grey houses is already full of charm, leading directly to the main square full of café tables facing into the sun and ideally placed for getting bearings and deciding on routes.

The obvious one is to pass through the 16th-century St. Vincent's Gate into the shade and calm of the mediaeval town. Or comparative calm, because although there are fewer cars here, there are many more tourists — some say too many. Personally I like the liveliness of the place, particularly after a spell beach-combing, and have wandered round some of the ancient cobbled streets, shaded by gabled houses nearly meeting overhead, almost alone, except in high summer.

Everyone takes his camera up to the House of Vannes to photograph the carved rubicund peasants, 'Vannes and his Wife', projecting like figureheads from the eaves. Then on to the photogenic pl. Henri IV, lined with 18th-century gabled houses, and then to gape, not knowing what to say, at the cathedral St.-Pierre, an incongruous hotchpotch of ideas from the 15th to the 19th centuries.

Then down to the Postern Gate and ramparts, particularly

impressive in summer, when floodlighting throws the ancient towers into dramatic relief. The moat has been filled with flower gardens. Look down upon it from the narrow bridge and don't miss the old wash-houses built 300 years ago and looking like a film set for that period.

Unfortunately there are no hotels in the colourful old section of the town nor along by the water; once outside the ramparts the character degenerates immediately into noisy industrialisation, and I would choose to stay more peacefully somewhere right away and come in for occasional stimulus and a good meal at:

► **Le Lys**
(R)M
51 r. Mar.-Leclerc
(97) 47.29.30
AE, DC, V.
Closed 4/–24/3;
Sun. p.m.; Mon.
o.o.s.
New Management

A cuisine of a refinement and sophistication somewhat unexpected in this noisy thoroughfare. The décor is red plush, black lacquer, probably more suitable for an intimate o.o.s. evening than a mid-summer lunch, but the young chef, Fernand Corfmat, has a light touch. That is not to say that he does not know when best to blend traditional with *nouvelle*; for all his youth he is far too experienced a hand to follow only one route to dishes that are as interesting as they are professional. Strictly seasonal as all good menus should be, based on the best suppliers of fish (*salade tiède de rouget*, perfumed with *vinaigre de framboise*), of meat and game (*saucisson de lapereau cuit à la vapeur* and *blanquette d'agneau à la menthe fraiche*), and fruit (superb sorbets). The wine list is a good one and the welcome from the elegant Mme Corfmat cheering.

This is the time, while the Corfmats are still new and endeavouring to build up their clientèle, to sample such superlative cooking. I can't imagine that a menu like this for 60f (or 78f or 120f) can easily be bettered and I can't imagine that they can stay at this price much longer. Meanwhile an arrow.

Marée Bleue
(R)S
8 pl. Bir-Hakeim
(97) 47.21.23
Closed 17/12–7/1;
Sun. p.m. o.o.s.

This no-nonsense, strictly functional, eating place in a noisy ugly street just outside the old walls offers the best value for kilometres around. At lunchtime it is packed with office workers, eating their way through a remarkable four courser for 60f, which includes expensive items like *langoustines*, oysters, *gigot*. Service is brisk, wine is cheap, it's a Vannes institution.

La Benjamine
(R)M
9 r. des Halles
(97) 54.08.34
Closed Sun. p.m.;
Mon.

This is the name that kept cropping up all over Brittany whenever I asked someone where to eat in Vannes. It's a pretty, modern restaurant in the heart of the mediaeval quarter. Modern and traditional cuisines are combined on menus very reasonably priced considering the chic-ness of the place – a *terrine de légumes* for starters, followed by straightforward *rognons de veau moutardés* on a 54f menu.

Map 3H

VITRÉ (I. et V.) 37 km E of Rennes, 30 km S of Fougères

No doubt about the mediaeval origins of this hilltop town, fortressed against its Norman neighbours — it is probably the best preserved and intact in Brittany, from towering 15th-century castle, to ramparts, to old streets a-tangle with dignified top-heavy houses.

Impressive from any approach, have cameras ready arriving from Fougères, on the hill looking down, or from the west from the top of the Tertres Noirs, for a fine panorama of castle, town and Vilaine valley.

Petit Billot
(HR)M
5 pl. Mar-Leclerc
(99) 75.02.10
Closed 15/12–15/1;
Fri. p.m.; Sat.
o.o.s.

Central, with bedrooms that vary considerably in price according to size and position. Those in the new wing, with bathroom, are a good-value 175f; in the older part they start as low as 70f. The food is excellent, well-meriting a red Michelin R for the 59f menu. Recommended by several readers.

Map 1C

LE YAUDET (C. du N.) 5 km W of Lannion on the D88

At the head of a little bay of altogether different character from the beaches all around. Picnic on the grassy headland by the little chapel and take in the view; chances are that even in high season nothing more brash than the chug of a fishing boat or the lyricism of a lark will disturb the calm. Down far below is a perfect horseshoe bay, rocks, sand at low water, surmounted with conifers, rare in these parts. Wonderful walks. The coast road to Locquémeau is a must. Back in the village:

Les Genêts d'Or
(HR)S
(96) 35.24.17
Closed 15/11–15/
12; 15/1–15/2; Sun.
p.m.; Mon. o.o.s.

A pretty little hotel, used by locals as well as summer visitors, which I would choose in preference to any of the Lannion alternatives. 14 simple rooms at 70–110f and menus from 50f.

Wine Hints from Jancis Robinson

HOW TO READ A WINE LIST

Wine lists in France, just like their counterparts in British restaurants, can be confusing – and sometimes even terrifying, with the only affordable bottles hidden below a stack of great names at even greater prices. There are certain ground rules in their layout, however.

The most basic of wines made in France are called *vins de table*, and may well be listed under this heading, to differentiate them from wines with some sort of geographical designation, either *Appellation Contrôlée* (AC) or, slightly more lowly, *Vins de Qualité Supérieur* (VDQS). The 'house wine' in many French restaurants is of the simpler *vin de table* sort and may be described as Vin de la Maison, or Vin du Patron meaning 'our wine'. There are many branded table wines too, the sort that carry a brand name, and these should be listed under a special heading, *Vins de Marque*. There is also a newish breed of rather superior *vin de table* which is worth looking out for, and which may be listed under the heading *Vins de Table*, or the region where it was made, or under the general heading *Vins de Pays*. These are superior quality *vins de table* which are good enough to tag their provenance onto their name.

All other wines will usually be grouped under the heading of the region where they were made and, usually, split according to red wines (*rouges*) and whites (*blancs*). The following are the main wine regions of France, in the order in which they *usually* appear on a smart wine list (though there is, exasperatingly, no standard convention):

Champagne

Almost all champagne is dry, white and sparkling, and only the wines of the Champagne region in northern France may call their wines champagne. Other sparkling wines are Vins Mousseux, though they may boast on their label that they were made by the rigorous *méthode champenoise*.

Bordeaux

France's biggest and best-known region for top-quality dryish reds, wines that we call claret. Most of such wines are called Château This or Château That, which will vary from about 60 francs a bottle to the earth and then some. 1982, 1981, 1979 and 1976 are vintages worth drinking now. Bordeaux's great white wines are sweet (*doux*) dessert wines from Sauternes, though there are now some good value dry (*sec*) wines too.

Bourgogne

We call this small, highly-priced region Brugundy. Its dry whites such as Montrachet are the greatest in the world; its reds can be lovely scented, smooth liquids, though there are some highly-priced disappointments.

1985, 1983 and (especially) 1978 were good years for reds, but good wines are produced with reassuring frequency.

Beaujolais/Mâconnais

This is the region just south of Burgundy proper that can offer some less expensive versions of Burgundy's white wines from the vineyards round Mâcon and some easy-drinking, gulpable reds from the vineyards of the Beaujolais area. Drink all these wines young, though some 1983 Beaujolais is still delicious.

Rhône

Mainly red wines and generally very good value. The whites can be quirky and heavy, but there has been a run of extremely good vintages of the meaty or spicy reds.

Loire

France's other great river is best-known, rather neatly, for its white wines – all with lots of acidity and great with food. Most Loire wines are designed for early consumption, though old Vouvray can be a bargain.

Alsace

France's most overlooked wine region, perhaps because it is almost in Germany. Fragrant, dry whites named after the Germanic grape varieties from which they are made. (This practice, varietal naming, is still uncommon in France though it is gaining ground.)

Since *French Entrée* territory is so far from France's vine land, the visitor is offered a much more catholic selection of (French) wines than in wine regions further south. The French take chauvinism seriously and on a local scale. Remember that most dry white wines do not improve with age, so don't begrudge being asked to drink a very young vintage. Merely feel grateful that you can enjoy the wine while it's young and fresh. As for matching specific wines with food, I subscribe to the view that you should start by deciding what colour and weight you feel like drinking rather than following the choice dictated by the 'white with fish and red with meat' rule. If you want white with a rich meat dish, it makes sense to choose a full-bodied one such as white burgundy, while light-bodied, fairly tart reds like Beaujolais and Bourgueil make better fish partners than a rich Rhône would.

COMMON WINE NAMES – AN ALPHABETICAL GUIDE

The following are the words most likely to be encountered on labels and wine lists, with brief notes to help you towards the clues they give to what's inside the bottle. Especially good vintages are listed. If no vintage is listed, choose the youngest vintage available.

Alsace – Wine region, see above. 1985, 1983.

Anjou – Loire source of lots of medium rosé and a bit of safe, unexciting dry white.

Appellation Contrôlée – France's top 20 per cent of wine, named after the area where it is made.

Barsac – Sweet white bordeaux. Part of Sauternes so all Barsac is Sauternes but not all Sauternes is Barsac. 1983, 1979, 1976.

Beaujolais – Light, juicy reds. 1983, 1978.

Beaune – Southern town in the Burgundy heartland. Any wine carrying this name alone will be expensive. 1985, 1983, 1979, 1978.

Blanc de Blancs – Sounds fancy but means very little. Literally, a white wine made of white grapes, unusual in a champagne but obvious in a still white.

Bordeaux – Wine region, see above. 1985, 1983, 1982, 1981 1979, 1978, 1976, 1975 for reds.

Bourgogne – 'Burgundy', a wine region, see above.

Bourgueil (Pronounce 'Boor-gurr-yeh') – Light red from the middle Loire.

Chablis – A much traduced name. True chablis (and the only sort of chablis you're likely to encounter in France) is steely-dry white burgundy from a village of the same name in the far north of the Burgundy region. 1985, 1983, 1981.

Champagne – Wine region, see above.

Châteauneuf-du-Pape – Full-bodied spicy red from the southern Rhône. 1985, 1983, 1981, 1979, 1978.

Chenin (Blanc) – The white grape of the Middle Loire, medium dry usually.

Corbières – Straightforward southern red.

Côte(s) de – 'Côte(s) de X' is usually better than a wine named simply 'X', as it means it comes from the (superior) hillsides above the lower ground of the X vineyards.

Coteaux de – Similar to 'Côte(s) de'.

Coteaux d'Ancenis – North Loire VDQS varietal whites. All dry except for Malvoisie.

Coteaux du Languedoc – Lightish southern red.

Coteaux du Layon – Small Middle Loire area producing some excellent but many unexciting medium dry whites.

Coteaux du Tricastin – Lightish version of Côtes-du-Rhône.

Côtes de Provence – Appellation for the dry white, herby red and, principally, dry pink wines of Provence in south-east France.

Côtes-du-Rhône – This big appellation with some new-style dry whites but mainly lightish spicy reds like Châteauneuf is usually good value.

Crozes-Hermitage – Convenient, earlier-maturing but still quite concentrated version of (almost always red) Hermitage. 1985, 1983, 1982, 1978.

Cru – Means 'growth' literally, *Grand cru* means 'great growth' and really rather good. *Cru classé* means that the growth has been officially classified as up to some definite scratch, and most of the world's best clarets are *crus classés*.

Doux – Sweet.

Entre-Deux Mers – Dry, and rarely exciting, white from Bordeaux.

Fleurie – Single-village beaujolais; superior. 1983, 1981, 1978.

Gaillac – Inexpensive white and sometimes red from south-west France.

Graves – Red and usually-dry white from a good-value area of Bordeaux.

Gros Plant Nantais – Very dry, austere white. Muscadet without the fruit.

Gewürztraminer – Perfumed grape grown in Alsace to produce France's most easily-recognisable white wine.

Hautes-Côtes de Beaune or *Nuits* – Affordable red and white burgundy from the slopes, high in altitude but not, for once, necessarily quality.

Hermitage – Long lived tannic red from the northern Rhône. 1985, 1983, 1982, 1978, 1976.

Juliénas – Single-village beaujolais; superior. 1983, 1981, 1978.

Loire – Wine region, see above.

Mâcon – Southern end of Burgundy, source of good-value whites and some unexciting reds.

Margaux – Médoc village producing scented clarets.

méthode champenoise – The Champagne region's way of putting bubbles into wine and usually the sign of a good one.

Meursault – Very respectable burgundy, almost all white. 1985, 1983, 1982, 1981, 1978.

Minervois – Better-than-average southern red.

mis(e) bouteilles au château – Bottled at the Château (as opposed to in some merchant's cellars) and usually a sign of quality.

Moelleux – Medium sweet.

Monbazillac – Good-value country cousin to Sauternes.

Montrachet – Very great white burgundy. 1985, 1983, 1982, 1981, 1978.

Moulin-à-Vent – Single-village beaujolais which, unusually, can be kept. 1983, 1981, 1978, 1976.

Mousseux – Sparkling.

Mouton-Cadet – Not a special property, but a commercial blend of claret.

Muscadet – Lean, dry white from the mouth of the Loire. Very tart.

Muscat – The grape whose wines, unusually, taste and smell grapey. Dry in Alsace; very sweet and strong from places like Rivesaltes, Frontignan and Beaumes de Venise.

Nuits-St-Georges – Burgundy's second wine town. Bottles carrying this name are often expensive. 1983, 1980, 1978, 1976.

Pauillac – Bordeaux's most famous village, containing three of the five top châteaux. Very aristocratic claret. 1983, 1982, 1979, 1978, 1976, 1975.

Pomerol – Soft, fruity claret. Similar to St Emilion. 1983, 1982, 1981, 1979, 1978, 1975.

Pommard – Soft, fruity red burgundy. 1983, 1979, 1978.

Pouilly-Fuissé – Famous appellation in the Mâcon region. Dry, white and sometimes overpriced.

Pouilly-Fumé – Much tarter than Pouilly-Fuissé, made from the Sauvignon grape (see below) in Loire.

Premières Côtes de Bordeaux – Inexpensive red and sweet white bordeaux.

Primeur – Wine designed to be drunk within months of the vintage e.g. from November till Easter. Beaujolais Nouveau is a 'Primeur'.

Puligny-Montrachet – Steely white burgundy and often very good. 1985, 1983, 1982, 1981, 1978.

Riesling – Germany's famous grape produces great dry wine in Alsace.

Ste-Croix-du-Mont – Inexpensive sweet white bordeaux.

St Emilion – Soft, early-maturing claret from many little properties, most of which seem to be allowed to call themselves *crus classés*. 1983, 1982, 1981, 1978, 1976, 1975.

St Estèphe – Sometimes rather hard but noble claret. 1982, 1979, 1978, 1976, 1975.

St Julien – Another Médoc village housing many great châteaux. 1982, 1979, 1978, 1976, 1975.

Sancerre – Twin village to the Pouilly of Pouilly Fumé, and producing very similar wines.

Santenay – Light red burgundy. 1985, 1983, 1980, 1978.

Saumur – Town in the middle Loire giving its name to wines of all colours, degrees of sweetness and some very good sparkling wine too.

Sauvignon – Grape producing dry whites with lots of 'bite'.

Savigny-lés-Beaune – Village just outside Beaune responsible for some good-value 'proper' red burgundy. 1980, 1978.

Sec – Dry.

Sylvaner – Alsace's 'everyday' light, dry white. Often the best wine you can buy by the glass in a French bar.

Touraine – An area in the middle Loire producing inexpensive Sauvignon and other wines.

VDQS – *Vin Délimité de Qualité Supérieure* (see above) – between AC and Vins de Pays.

Vin de Pays – Quality level at the top end of table wine. Many good-value inexpensive reds and some whites stating their region of origin on the label.

Vin de Pays des Marches de Bretagne – The only wine with an obviously Breton name. Light, tartish, usually white.

Vin de Table – The most basic sort of wine made in France. Very few excitements in this category. The blends with the name of a Burgundy merchant on the label are usually the most expensive.

Volnay – Soft red burgundy. Wine onomatopoeia? 1985, 1983, 1979, 1978.

WHAT TO BRING BACK

Provided you forgo any other liquor, and provided you make all the purchases in an ordinary (i.e. non-duty-free) shop, you may bring back eight litres of wine to Britain without paying any duty.

Eight of the litre bottles so common in French supermarkets make exactly this amount of course. And eleven 75cl and twelve 70cl bottles make so little more than eight litres that no Customs official is likely to complain. The label will state a bottle's capacity.

Excise duty that would be charged by British Customs officials is currently 84p on a 75cl bottle and 78p on a 70cl bottle (plus 15% VAT of purchase price abroad), and it is largely this that you are saving by importing your own wine. The extra cost of transporting a bottle from Bordeaux to London as opposed to Paris is negligible. Duty is the same on any bottle, however, regardless of the value of the wine. This means that savings are at their most dramatic – and most worth the effort – for the least expensive wines. You can buy seven litres of *vin de table* in France for around 30f, when the same amount of equivalent quality wine in Britain would cost almost as many pounds.

The corollary of all this is that you should bring back seven litres of the most ordinary wine you find you enjoy drinking, if your tastes and pocket are modest. Connoisseurs on the other hand should confine themselves to bringing back the odd bottle too obscure or rare to be found in this country. Many good mature wines are cheaper here than there – though this of course is dependent on the franc/sterling ratio.

Glossary of cooking terms and dishes

(It would take another book to list comprehensively French cooking terms and dishes, but here are the ones most likely to be encountered)

Aigre-doux	bittersweet
Aiguillette	thin slice (aiguille – needle)
Aile	wing
Aioli	garlic mayonnaise
Allemande (à l')	German style, i.e.: with sausages and sauerkraut
Amuses-gueule	appetisers
Anglaise (à l')	plain boiled. Crème Anglaise – egg and cream sauce
Andouille	large uncooked sausage, served cold after boiling
Andouillettes	ditto but made from smaller intestines, usually served hot after grilling
Anis	aniseed
Argenteuil	with asparagus
Assiette Anglaise	plate of cold meats
Baba au Rhum	yeast based sponge macerated in rum
Baguette	long thin loaf
Ballotine	boned, stuffed and rolled meat or poultry, usually cold
Béarnaise	sauce made from egg yolks, butter, tarragon, wine, shallots
Beurre Blanc	sauce from Nantes, with butter, reduction of shallot-flavoured vinegar or wine
Béchamel	white sauce flavoured with infusion of herbs
Beignets	fritters
Bercy	sauce with white wine and shallots
Beurre noir	browned butter
Bigarade	with oranges
Billy By	mussel soup
Bisque	creamy shellfish soup
Blanquette	stew with thick white creamy sauce, usually veal
Boeuf à la mode	braised beef
Bombe	ice cream mould

Bonne femme	with root vegetables
Bordelais	Bordeaux-style, with red or white wine, marrow bone fat
Bouchée	mouthful, i.e. vol au vent
Boudin	sausage, white or black
Bourride	thick fish soup
Braisé	braised
Brandade (de morue)	dried salt cod pounded into a mousse
Broche	spit
Brochette	skewer
Brouillade	stew, using oil
Brouillé	scrambled
Brulé	burnt, i.e. crême brulée
Campagne	country style
Cannelle	cinnamon
Carbonade	braised in beer
Cardinal	red-coloured sauce, i.e. with lobster or in pâtisserie with redcurrant
Charcuterie	cold pork-butcher's meats
Charlotte	mould, as dessert lined with spongefingers, as savoury lined with vegetable
Chasseur	with mushrooms, shallots, wine
Chausson	pastry turnover
Chemise	covering, i.e. pastry
Chiffonade	thinly-cut, i.e. lettuce
Choron	tomato Béarnaise
Choucroute	Alsation stew with sauerkraut and sausages
Civet	stew
Clafoutis	batter dessert, usually with cherries
Clamart	with peas
Cocotte	covered casserole
Compôte	cooked fruit
Concassé	i.e. tomatoes concassées – skinned, chopped, juice extracted

Confit	preserved
Confiture	jam
Consommé	clear soup
Cou	neck
Coulis	juice, puree (of vegetables or fruit)
Cassolette or cassoulette	small pan
Cassoulet	rich stew with goose, pork and haricot beans
Cervelas	pork garlic sausage
Cervelles	brains
Chantilly	whipped sweetened cream
Cocque (à la)	i.e. oeufs – boiled eggs
Court-bouillon	aromatic liquor for cooking meat, fish, vegetables
Couscous	N. African dish with millet, chicken, vegetable variations
Crapaudine	involving fowl, particularly pigeon, trussed
Crécy	with carrots
Crême Pâtissière	thick custard filling
Crêpe	pancake
Crépinette	little flat sausage, encased in caul
Croque Monsieur	toasted cheese and ham sandwich
Croustade	pastry or baked bread shell
Croûte	pastry crust
Croûton	cube of fried or toasted bread
Cru	raw
Crudités	raw vegetables
Demi-glâce	basic brown sauce
Doria	with cucumber
Emincé	thinly sliced
Etuvé	stewed, i.e. vegetables in butter
Entremets	sweets
Farci	stuffed
Fines herbes	parsley, thyme, bayleaf
Feuillété	leaves of flaky pastry
Flamande	Flemish style, with beer
Flambé	flamed in spirit
Flamiche	flan
Florentine	with spinach
Flute	thinnest bread loaf
Foie gras	goose liver
Fondu	melted

Fond (d'artichaut)	heart (of artichoke)
Forestière	with mushrooms, bacon and potatoes
Four (au)	baked in the oven
Fourré	stuffed, usually sweets
Fricandeau	veal, usually topside
Frais, fraiche	fresh and cool
Frangipane	almond creme patisserie
Fricadelle	Swedish meat ball
Fricassé	(usually of veal) in creamy sauce
Frit	fried
Frites	chips
Friture	assorted small fish, fried in batter
Froid	cold
Fumé	smoked
Galantine	loaf-shaped chopped meat, fish or vegetable, set in natural jelly
Gallette	Breton pancake, flat cake
Garbure	thick country soup
Garni	garnished, usually with vegetables
Gaufre	waffle
Gelée	aspic
Gésier	gizzard
Gibier	game
Gigôt	leg
Glacé	iced
Gougère	choux pastry, large base
Goujons	fried strips, usually of fish
Graine	seed
Gratin	baked dish of vegetables cooked in cream and eggs
Gratinée	browned under grill
Grêcque (à la)	cold vegetables served in oil
Grenouilles	frogs; cuisees de grenouille – frogs' legs
Grillé	grilled
Gros sel	coarse salt
Hachis	minced or chopped
Haricot	slow cooked stew
Hochepot	hotpot
Hollandaise	sauce with egg, butter, lemon
Hongroise	Hungarian, i.e. spiced with paprika
Hors d'oeuvre	assorted starters
Huile	oil

Île flottante	floating island – soft meringue on egg custard sauce
Indienne	Indian, i.e. with hot spices
Jambon	ham
Jardinière	from the garden, i.e. with vegetables
Jarret	shin, i.e. jarret de veau
Julienne	matchstick vegetables
Jus	natural juice
Lait	milk
Langue	tongue
Lard	bacon
Longe	loin
Macedoine	diced fruits or vegetables
Madeleine	small sponge cake
Magret	breast (of duck)
Maïs	sweetcorn
Maître d'hôtel	sauce with butter, lemon, parsley
Marchand de vin	sauce with red wine, shallot
Marengo	sauce with tomatoes, olive oil, white wine
Marinière	seamens' style, i.e. moules marinière (mussels in white wine)
Marmite	deep casserole
Matelote	fish stew, i.e. of eel
Medaillon	round slice
Mélange	mixture
Meunière	sauce with butter, lemon
Miel	honey
Mille feuille	flaky pastry, lit. 1,000 leaves
Mirepoix	cubed carrot, onion etc. used for sauces
Moëlle	beef marrow
Mornay	cheese sauce
Mouclade	mussel stew
Mousseline	Hollandaise sauce, lightened with egg whites
Moutarde	mustard
Nage (à la)	poachedin flavoured liquor (fish)
Nature	plain
Navarin (d'agneau)	stew of lamb with spring vegetables
Noisette	nut-brown, burned butter

Noix de veau	nut of veal (leg)
Normande	Normandy style, with cream, apple, cider, Calvados
Nouilles	noodles
Os	bone
Paillettes	straws (of pastry)
Panaché	mixed
Panade	flour crust
Papillote (en)	cooked in paper case
Parmentier	with potatoes
Pâté	paste, of meat or fish
Pâte	pastry
Pâte brisée	rich short crust pastry
Pâtisserie	pastries
Paupiettes	paper thin slice
Pavé	thick slice
Paysan	country style
Perigueux	with truffles
Persillade	chopped parsley and garlic topping
Petits fours	tiny cakes, sweetmeats
Petit pain	bread roll
Piperade	peppers, onions, tomatoes in scrambled egg
Poché	poached
Poëlé	fried
Poitrine	breast
Poivre	pepper
Pommade	paste
Potage	thick soup
Pot-au-four	broth with meat and vegetables
Potée	country soup with cabbage
Pralines	caramelised almonds
Primeurs	young veg
Printanièr(e)	garnished with early vegetables
Profiterole	choux pastry balls
Provencale	with garlic, tomatoes, olive oil, peppers
Purée	mashed and sieved
Quenelle	pounded fish or meat, bound with egg, poached
Queue	tail
Quiche	pastry flan, i.e. quiche Lorraine – egg, bacon, cream
Râble	saddle, i.e. rable de lièvre
Ragout	stew

Ramequin	little pot
Rapé	grated
Ratatouille	provencale stew of onions garlic, peppers, tomatoes
Ravigote	highly seasoned white sauce
Rémoulade	mayonnaise with gherkins capers, herbs and shallot
Rillettes	potted shredded meat, usually fat pork or goose
Riz	rice
Robert	sauce with mustard, vinegar, onion
Roquefort	ewe's milk blue cheese
Rossini	garnished with foie gras and truffle
Rôti	roast
Rouelle	nugget
Rouille	hot garlicky sauce for soupe de poisson
Roulade	roll
Roux	sauce base – flour and butter
Sabayon	sweet fluffy sauce, with eggs and wine
Safran	saffron
Sagou	sago
St.-Germain	with peas
Salade niçoise	with tunny, anchovies, tomatoes, beans, black olives
Salé	salted
Salmis	dish of game or fowl, with red wine
Sang	blood
Santé	lit. healthy, i.e. with spinach and potato
Salpicon	meat, fowl, vegetables, chopped fine, bound with sauce and used as fillings
Saucisse	fresh sausage
Saucisson	dried sausage
Sauté	cooked in fat in open pan
Sauvage	wild
Savarin	ring of yeast sponge, soaked in syrup and liquor
Sel	salt
Selle	saddle
Selon	according to, i.e. selon grosseur (according to size)

Smitane	with sour cream, white wine, onion
Soissons	with dried white beans
Sorbet	water ice
Soubise	with creamed onions
Soufflé	puffed, i.e. mixed with egg white and baked
Sucre	sugar (Sucré – sugared)
Suprême	fillet of poultry breast or fish
Tartare	raw minced beef, flavoured with onion etc. and bound with raw egg
Tartare (sauce)	mayonnaise with capers, herbs, onions
Tarte Tatin	upside down apple pie
Terrine	pottery dish/baked minced, chopped meat, veg., chicken, fish or fruit
Thé	tea
Tiède	luke warm
Timbale	steamed mould
Tisane	infusion
Tourte	pie
Tranche	thick slice
Truffes	truffles
Tuile	tile, i.e. thin biscuit
Vacherin	meringue confection
Vallée d'Auge	with cream, apple, Calvados
Vapeur (au)	steamed
Velouté	white sauce, bouillon-flavoured
Véronique	with grapes
Vert(e)	green, i.e. sauce verte with herbs
Vessie	pigs bladder
Vichyssoise	chilled creamy leek and potato soup
Vierge	prime olive oil
Vinaigre	vinegar (lit. bitter wine)
Vinaigrette	wine vinegar and oil dressing
Volaille	poultry
Vol-au-vent	puff pastry case
Xérès	sherry
Yaourt	yoghurt

FISH – Les Poissons, SHELLFISH – Les Coquillages

Anchois	anchovy	*Langouste*	crawfish
Anguille	eel	*Langoustine*	Dublin Bay prawn
Araignée de mer	spider crab	*Lieu*	ling
Bar	sea bass	*Limand*	lemon sole
Barbue	brill	*Lotte de mer*	monkfish
Baudroie	monkfish, anglerfish	*Loup de mer*	sea bass
Belon	oyster – flat shelled	*Maquereau*	mackerel
Bigorneau	winkle	*Merlan*	whiting
Blanchaille	whitebait	*Morue*	salt cod
Brochet	pike	*Moule*	mussel
Cabillaud	cod	*Mulet*	grey mullet
Calamar	squid	*Ombre*	grayling
Carrelet	plaice	*Oursin*	sea urchin
Chapon de mer	scorpion fish	*Palourde*	clam
Claire	oyster	*Petoncle*	small scallop
Coquille St.Jacques	scallop	*Plie*	plaice
		Portugaise	oyster
Crabe	crab	*Poulpe*	octopus
Crevette grise	shrimp	*Praire*	oyster
Crevette rose	prawn	*Raie*	skate
Daurade	sea bream	*Rascasse*	scorpion-fish
Écrevisse	crayfish	*Rouget*	red mullet
Éperlan	smelt	*St. Pierre*	John Dory
Espadon	swordfish	*Saumon*	Salmon
Etrille	baby crab	*Saumonette*	rock salmon
Favouille	spider crab	*Seiche*	squid
Flétan	halibut	*Sole*	sole
Fruits de mer	seafood	*Soupion*	inkfish
Grondin	red gurnet	*Thon*	tunny
Hareng	herring	*Tortue*	turtle
Homard	lobster	*Tourteau*	large crab
Huitre	oyster	*Truite*	trout
Laitance	soft herring roe	*Turbot*	turbot
Lamproie	lamprey	*Turbotin*	chicken turbot

FRUITS – Les fruits, VEGETABLES – Les legumes, NUTS – Les noix
HERBS – Les herbes, SPICES – Les epices

Ail	garlic	*Basilic*	basil
Algue	seaweed	*Betterave*	beetroot
Amande	almond	*Blette*	Swiss chard
Ananas	pineapple	*Brugnon*	nectarine
Aneth	dill	*Cassis*	blackcurrant
Abricot	apricot	*Céléri*	celery
Arachide	peanut	*Céléri-rave*	celeriac
Artichaut	globe artichoke	*Cêpe*	edible fungus
Asperge	asparagus	*Cerfeuil*	chervil
Avocat	avocado	*Cérise*	cherry
Banane	banana	*Champignon*	mushroom

Chanterelle	edible fungus	Morille	dark brown crinkly
Châtaigne	chestnut		edible fungus
Chicorée	endive	Mûre	blackberry
Chou	cabbage	Muscade	nutmeg
Choufleur	cauliflower	Myrtille	bilberry, blueberry
Choux de Bruxelles	Brussels sprout	Navet	turnip
Ciboulette	chive	Noisette	hazelnut
Citron	lemmon	Oignon	onion
Citron vert	lime	Oseille	sorrel
Coing	quince	Palmier	palm
Concombre	cucumber	Pamplemousse	grapefruit
Coriandre	coriander	Panais	parsnip
Cornichon	gherkin	Passe-Pierre	seaweed
Courge	pumpkin	Pastèque	water melon
Courgette	courgette	Pêche	peach
Cresson	watercress	Persil	parsley
Échalotte	shallot	Petit pois	pea
Endive	chicory	Piment doux	sweet pepper
Épinard	spinach	Pissenlit	dandelion
Escarole	salad leaves	Pistache	pistachio
Estragon	tarragon	Pleurote	edible fungi
Fenouil	fennel	Poire	pear
Féve	broad bean	Poireau	leek
Flageolet	dried bean	Poivre	pepper
Fraise	strawberry	Poivron	green, red and yellow
Framboise	raspberry		peppers
Genièvre	juniper	Pomme	apple
Gingembre	ginger	Pomme-de-terre	potato
Girofle	clove	Prune	plum
Girolle	edible fungus	Pruneau	prune
Granade	pomegranate	Quetsch	small dark plum
Griotte	bitter red cherry	Radis	radish
Groseille	gooseberry	Raifort	horseradish
Groseille noire	blackcurrant	Raisin	grape
Groseille rouge	redcurrant	Reine Claude	greengage
Haricot	dried white bean	Romarin	rosemary
Haricot vert	French bean	Safron	saffron
Laitue	lettuce	Salisifis	salsify
Mandarine	tangerine, mandarin	Thym	thyme
Mangetout	sugar pea	Tilleul	lime blossom
Marron	chestnut	Tomate	tomato
Menthe	mint	Topinambour	Jerusalem artichoke
Mirabelle	tiny gold plum	Truffe	truffle

MEAT – Les Viandes

Le Boeuf	Beef	Faux Filet	sirloin steak
Charolais	is the best	Filet	fillet
Chateaubriand	double fillet steak		
Contrefilet	sirloin	L'Agneau	Lamb
Entrecôte	rib steak	Pré-Salé	is the best
		Carré	neck cutlets

Côte	chump chop	Les Abats	Offal
Epaule	shoulder	Foie	liver
Gigot	leg	Foie gras	goose liver
Le Porc	Pork	Cervelles	brains
Jambon	ham	Langue	tongue
Jambon cru	raw smoked ham	Ris	sweetbreads
Porcelet	suckling pig	Rognons	kidneys
Le Veau	Veal	Tripes	tripe
Escalope	thin slice cut from fillet		

POULTRY – Volaille, GAME – Gibier

Abatis	giblets	Lièvre	hare
Bécasse	woodcock	Oie	goose
Bécassine	snipe	Perdreau	partridge
Caille	quail	Pigeon	pigeon
Canard	duck	Pintade	guineafowl
Caneton	duckling	Pluvier	plover
Chapon	capon	Poularde	chicken (boiling)
Chevreuil	roe deer	Poulet	chicken (roasting)
Dinde	young hen turkey	Poussin	spring chicken
Dindon	turkey	Sanglier	wild boar
Dindonneau	young turkey	Sarcelle	teal
Faisan	pheasant	Venaison	venison
Grive	thrush		

Readers' recommendations

F – Finistère; C. du N. – Côtes du Nord; M – Morbihan; I. et V. – Ille et Vilaine; L-A – Loire Atlantique

Place	Establishment	Recommended by
Aberwrach (F)	Café du Port (R)S	Gillian Rumble
Bénodet (F)	Gwel Kaër (H)M	Dr. & Mrs. G. Robson
	Hôtel de la Poste (HR)S	Dr. & Mrs. G. Robson
	La Cornouaille (R)M	Bill & Beryl Jackson
Bourg des Comptes (Nr. Guichen, I. et V.)	Relais de la Place (R)M	Dr. & Mrs. G. Robson
Binic (C. du N.)	Hôtel Le Galion (HR)M	Dr. W. Tait
Camaret-sur-Mer (F)	Hôtel Styrvesen (R)S	Gillian Rumble
Crozon (F)	Pergola (R)S	Bill & Beryl Jackson
Concarneau (F)	Jockey (H)S	
	L'Escale (R)S	
Le Conquet (F)	Hôtel Pointe-St.-Barbe (H)M	John Gilmour
Camoël (M)	La Vilaine (R)M	John Richards
Dinan (C. du N.)	Le St. Louis (R)S	Donald & Hazel Macaulay
Dinard (C. du N.)	La Prieuré (R)M	Dr. & Mrs. G. Robson
Douarnenez (F)	Hôtel le Bretagne (R)M	Audrey Croon
Le Frêt (F)	Hostellerie de la Mer (H)M	John Gilmour
Guérande (L-A)	Auberge de la Flambée (R)S	M. Selfe
Hédé (I. et V.)	Le Festival (R)S	M. Selfe
Herbignac (Nr. La Baule, L-A)	Pepinières de la Coët Caret (Chambre d'Hôte)	
Huelgoat (F)	Crêperie de l'Argoat (R)S	Sylvia Bellini
Jugon-les-Lacs (C. du N.)	Hostellerie de l'Ecu (R)M	Bill & Beryl Jackson
	Hôtel de la Grande Fontaine (H)S	Bill & Beryl Jackson
Josselin (M)	La Sarrazine (R)S	Julie Wilton
Landivisiau (F)	Du Leon (R)S	Jill Thomas
Lesneven (F)	Hôtel Breiz Izel (H)M	John Gilmour

Malestroit (I. et V.)	L'Aigle d'Or (R)M	M. Selfe
Matignon (Nr. St. Cast, C. du N.)	Hôtel de la Poste (HR)S	Mrs. C. Ager
Moëlan-sur-Mer (F)	Manoir de Kertalg (H)L	P. Stoughton
Nantes (L-A)	Le Rimbaud (R)S	Selina & John Wesley
Plancoët (C. du. N.)	Crêperie Relais de la Poste (R)S	Bill & Beryl Jackson
Paimpol (C. du N.)	Pré Vert (R)S	
Plouéscat (F)	Baie du Kernic (R)S	Jill Thomas
	Aub. du Kersabiec (R)S	Jill Thomas
Ploudier (F)	Rest. de la Butte (R)S	Jill Thomas
Pont-Aven (F)	Hôtel des Mimosas (HR)M	
Plomelin (F)	Château de Keramblez (HR)L	
Plouguerneau (F)	Les Aberiädes (HR)M	David Buddle
Quimper (F)	Rest. St. François (R)S	Bill & Beryl Jackson
Roscoff (F)	Chez Janie (HR)S	
	Les Chardons Bleu (R)M	
	Les Tamaris (H)M	M. Butterfield
	Hôtel Bellevue (HR)S	Kay & Richard Johnson
Rosporden (F)	Hôtel d'Arvor (R)S	Bill & Beryl Jackson
St. Guenole (F)	La Mer (HR)M	
St. Lymphard (L-A)	Auberge de Kerhinet (Chambre d'Hôte)	
	Aub. De Kerhinel (R)S	Dick Read-Wilson
St. Guelven (C. du N.)	Hostellerie de L'Abbaye de Bon Repos (HR)M	Dick Read-Wilson
St. Brieuc (C. du N.)	Champs de Mars (HR)M	John Langriere
St. Quay-Portrieux (C. du N.)	Gerbot d'Avoine (HR)M	R. Stallard
Ste Anne-La-Palud (F)	Mme Gassac (Chambre d'Hôte)	Bill & Beryl Jackson
Tréguier (C. du N.)	Le St. Bernard (R)S	Gillian Rumble
Tréboul (F)	Ty Mad (HR)M	Audrey Croon
	Au Chasse Marée (R)M	Audrey Croon
	Hôtel Moderne (R)M	Audrey Croon

Readers' new recommendations

F – Finistère; C. du N. – Côtes du Nord; M – Morbihan; I. et V. – Ille et Vilaine;
L-A – Loire Atlantique

Place	Establishment	Recommended by
Arradon (M)	Hotel Le Guippe (HR)S	Matt Huber
Benodet (F)	La Cigale (?)S	R. & D. Gardener
	Le Beau Rivage (H)S	
Beg Meil (F)	Hotel de la Plage (HR)M	P. Rodney
Betton (I. et V.)	La Flambée (R)	Diana Whitehill
Bubry (M)	Coët Diquel (HR)M	Mrs. D. Hodgkin
Concarneau (F)	La Gallandière (R)S	J. R. Lloyd
Le Croisic (L-A)	Le Brick (R)S	Dorothy Hanson
Crozen (F)	Chez Jo (R)S	C. A. Charles
Dahouët (C. du N.)	Hotel du Pont (HR)S	Dinah Scott
Elven (M)	Lion d'Or (HR)S	Michael Sharrock
Fouesnant (F)	L'Auberge du Bon Cidre	H. and I. Ward
Hédé (I. et V.)	Le Festival (R)S	M. Selfe
Lampaul-Guimiliau (F)	L'Enclos (HR)M	E. A. Machin
Lannouarneau (F)	Mme Le Goff (Ch. d'h)	Michael Ashton.
Larmor Baden (M)	Le Parc Fétan (HR)S	Don Slater
Louargat (C. du N.)	Manoir du Cleuzio (HR)M	
Lézardrieux (C. du N.)	Le Relais du Port (HR)S	Dinah Scott
Locquirec (F)	La Bourriche (F)M	M. and B. Collyer
Malestroit (M)	Le Canolier (R)S	Diana Whitehead
	La Croix d'Or (R)M	Mr. & Mrs. P. Jackson
Paimpol (C du N)	Le Bellevue (HR)S	Ian and Sheila Macrae
Pont Aven (F)	Le Chatel (Ch d")	
Pont l'Abbé (R)	L'Enclos de Rosveigne (R)M–L	
Pontivy (M)	Hotel du Porhöer (HR)M	Cdr. B. H. Wainwright
Port Navalo (M)	Modern Bar (R)S	Matt Huber
Ploërmel (M)	Le Démodé (R)S	
Roscoff (F)	Hotel Bellevue (HR)M	K. & R. Johnson
	Le Temps de Vivre (R)M	Michael Pitel
	Les Korrigans (R)S	C. Rutter-Fletcher
St Cast-le-Guildo (C. du N.)	Hotel Chrisflo (HR)M	R. Whiting
Ste Anne d'Auray (M)	Le Moderne (HR)M	Mr. & Mrs. P. Jackson
	La Belle Epoque (R)S	
St. Quay-Portrieux (C. du N.)	Ker Moor (HR)M	
Telgruc-sur-Mer (F)	Aub du Gerdann (R)M–L	M. Pitel
Vannes (M)	Le Pressoir, St Avé	Michael Sharrock
	L'Image de Ste Anne (HR)M	

Index